I0428658

Field Guide

to the

Wild World of Religion

2011 Edition

Pamela S. Dewey

Originally published 2005

Contents edited and updated for this 2011 Edition

Field Guide to the Wild World of Religion Website

The companion website to this *Field Guide* book is at:

www.isitso.org/guide

The website has a continually-growing collection of profiles of a variety of individuals and groups which have been or are currently influential in the Wild World of Religion.

About the Author

Pam Dewey holds a BA in Education, magna cum laude, from Michigan State University, with graduate work emphasizing education, sociology, and psychology. Her popular *Field Guide* website provides information, documentation, and commentary on many religious teachers and groups.

ISBN-13:
978-1467910491

Foreword

The American religious scene in 1955 was a very tame and predictable world. It matched the tame, predictable world of women's clothing, where most women going out shopping wore a dress with coordinating gloves, hat, and shoes. And it matched the tame, predictable world of children's toys, where almost every young girl yearned for a baby doll that said Ma-Ma, and almost every boy needed a coonskin cap. Choices of fashions, toys, preachers, and churches were limited and domesticated.

Fifty years later, the tame, predictable world of 1950s fashions and toys is long gone. Women go shopping in everything from sweatshirts and jeans to tube tops and short shorts. And both boys and girls want the latest Sponge Bob Square Pants video game. The same kind of transformation has gone on in the world of religion. It is no longer tame and predictable either.

Welcome to the Wild World of Religion of the 21st Century. Explore its habitats, identify some of the inhabitants, and learn about their characteristics and customs in this Field Guide.

Contents

Chapter 1

The Tame World of Religion

Drive through the side streets near the downtown section of any small American town or mid-sized city near noon on any Sunday morning, and you'll notice a recurring phenomenon. Some of the intersections will boast two, three, or even four different large church buildings, one on each corner. One may be an imposing Roman Catholic Church with high, arched stained glass windows and a big statue of its "patron saint" out front. The other three will be different flavors of what are often referred to as "mainline Protestant" denominations: possibly Methodist, Lutheran, Christian Reformed, Baptist, Congregational, Episcopal, or Presbyterian. All will look like they could hold several hundred people in their sanctuaries for the worship service.

But when the bells on the City Hall clock tower toll the noon hour, the group of people pouring out of the doors of each of these churches may well not be the crashing wave one might expect at all, but a mere trickle.

What is going on here? Is the population of the U.S. becoming mostly disinterested in religion? Wasn't it different back when these church buildings were much newer?

Back to the Fifties

Indeed it was different, in one way. There would have been a time when most of these buildings would have been filled close to capacity. If you visited those same neighborhoods in 1955, you might well have found the sidewalks crammed to overflowing with families dressed in their Sunday best coming out of each of the churches. And in addition to the big churches on the main street corners, out at the edge of town you would have found one or two much smaller, much humbler little buildings. They, too, might have been filled close to capacity with worshippers. A hand-painted sign on the side of the buildings would announce that here was a "Pentecostal" or "Holiness" church. What they lacked in size, they would make up for in the enthusiasm and volume of their singing and shouting.

But the reality wasn't exactly that there was much more deep "interest in religion" by the average American back in the Fifties. It was that attending church was much more of a *cultural expectation* in those days. A family planning a move to a new town would look for three things as soon as they settled on the purchase of their home—how close were the schools their children would attend, where was a convenient bank nearby, and what churches were nearby. Their choices would have been few and simple for

1

all these. For the Fifties were, in many ways, a much simpler time in history.

Simpler times, Limited Choices

If you were a teenage boy in 1957, your choices at the barbershop would have been very simple. If your dad was recently in the Armed Services, chances were pretty good he would insist the barber give you a very close-cropped "crew cut." If it was sheared straight across the top, it would be called a "flat top." The other cut acceptable to most parents would have been only slightly longer on top, parted on one side, and combed neatly over, perhaps with a dab of Brylcreem to keep it looking neat all day. It was the sort of haircut that nice, clean-cut young singer/actor Pat Boone would wear.

For the adventurous young man wanting to be different, there was one other choice—if he could get past his parents' protests. He could let the hair grow **much** longer on top so that it would tousle down over his forehead, and **much** longer on the sides so he could slick them back with a comb to meet in the back of his head (giving a distinct resemblance to the back end of a duck ... thus the term "D.A."). He might well have used not just a dab of Brylcreem to finish the look, but a whole gob of something even gooier. (Thus the label that some put on such young men ... "Greasers.") And, if he could grow them, long sideburns would finish the look. It was the sort of haircut that scandalous young singer/actor Elvis Presley would wear.

If you wanted to watch TV in the evening, your choices were likewise simple and few. Your TV would likely have had only one rotating channel selection dial, which went from 2-12. And that didn't even mean you actually had a choice any time in the evening to watch 11 different programs. Your actual choices at any given time were only three. For there were only three networks—NBC, ABC, and CBS.

If you were a sports fan, there might be a few times during the week when one of these networks would be showing a sporting event. If you were a science fiction fan, your choices might have been even slimmer, with only one or two sci-fi shows available. If you liked national and world news, you would have to wait for the one hour in the evening when each of the networks ran their regular newscasts. And, no matter what your desire for programming, in most areas you'd have to just go on to bed at midnight. Most TV stations closed down transmission at that time, returning to the air with programming early the next morning.

If you were born after the 1950s, you may be surprised to learn that there really were national televangelists back in those days. However, like everything else, your choices of these were also simple and few. There were three to pick from. For the Roman Catholic perspective, you could watch

2

the weekly program of Bishop Fulton J. Sheen. To hear a basic Mainline Protestant version of the Gospel, you could tune in to the occasional televised Billy Graham crusade. And, if you were more adventurous, you could catch the weekly show of "healing evangelist" Oral Roberts, televised from one of his crusades in his huge travelling tent. If you were enthusiastic about Roberts' show, there's a good chance you were one of those who attended one of the little churches on the edge of your hometown.

Back to the Future

How does the picture of the simplicity of choices in the 1950s line up with the reality of the 21st century? The adventurous grandson of that young man with the Elvis haircut of the Fifties has a lot more possibilities with which to startle his parents. Even if you live in a small rural town, chances are these days that you'll barely blink an eye at the outlandish hairstyle of the bag-boy at the local Wal-Mart—whether it is a purple Mohawk, a pony-tail down to his waist, a spiky neon orange mop that looks like he just got out of bed and didn't comb his hair, or perhaps even a totally bald skin-head look.

The average American turns the TV on these days and chooses not from three options, but 53 or 103 or more. Cable and satellite TV now make those paltry choices of the 1950s seem pathetic. The sci-fi fan can find a channel that will feed his obsession 24 hours a day, seven days a week. The news hound can likewise feed his addiction around the clock, either with continuous hourly updates of the latest news, or continuous commentary on current events by professional pundits. Whether you want sitcoms, nature shows, sports, comedy, or the latest adventures of Sponge Bob Square Pants, the sky is the limit.

And this also applies to the world of TV religion. In 2000 AD, you could still choose a Roman Catholic evangelist—but now he … was a she. Mother Angelica, a roly-poly, unendingly cheerful little nun created her own 24-hour-a-day cable network in 1984 that featured teaching, preaching, worship, and entertainment with a Roman Catholic twist. Although (as of 201) she has been retired as a result of a series of strokes in 2001, you can still see re-runs of her *Mother Angelica Live* talk show on her EWTN (Eternal World Television Network.)

The mainline Protestants still have a presence, represented by Baptist Charles Stanley, Presbyterian D. James Kennedy, and, until the past few years, even an aging Billy Graham. Oral Roberts was still doing a little preaching on occasion up until a short time before his death in 2009, although his son Richard had been the primary voice for the Oral Roberts Evangelistic Association for quite some time.

But, just as with the exploding presence of specialized networks and their almost unlimited programming choices, the world of televangelism has exploded since the advent of cable and satellite programming. And most of the explosion has not included that Old-Time Mainline Religion of the 1950s.

The quiet before the storm

If you reached adulthood in the 1950s, and got married and had a family of your own, chances are very good that you and your family would be found attending the church denomination of your childhood when Sunday morning came around. Whether that church was St. Catherine's Roman Catholic Church, Central United Methodist, or the First Baptist Church of Anytown, it was probably a pretty tame, predictable place. The differences of doctrine among the Protestant Churches in your town would have been distinct enough to the dedicated members of each of the denominations. But they would probably not be as clear to outsiders as the differences in superficial matters such as the style of music or sermon presentation in each of the denominational churches.

It wasn't unheard of for people to "change churches" in the 1950s. But seldom would some family leave one congregation and go to another in the same town over a matter of doctrinal considerations. The typical reason for a move would be "in-house politics" at their old congregation—a dispute over who was in charge, or who would make decisions about expenditures. In fact, it wouldn't be all that uncommon for there to be a "First Baptist Church" and a "Second Baptist Church" in the same small town. But it would not be because the First Baptist congregation outgrew its building and started a sister congregation. It would be because a disgruntled faction of members and deacons and elders from First Baptist stomped out and started their own new church so that they could do things their own way.

This is not to say that, in the 1950s and on into the 1960s, there were not a few "unusual" religious groups working around the fringes of American society to make converts. The "Moonies" (followers of the Reverend Sun Myung Moon) were one such group that occasionally made the news, standing on street corners and handing out flowers. The "Children of God" (followers of "Mo" Berg, who used sexual favors by women members to lure new converts) were even more notorious for a time. There was even a flurry of activity to combat the recruiting tactics of such groups. Some frightened parents whose teens had run off to join a commune of such people hired "deprogrammers" to kidnap their own children and try to talk some sense into them.

But these groups were all squarely on the outside of the mainstream of society, and easily recognized as strange and unconventional. There were also a few slightly more respectable alternatives to the mainline Protestant Churches that were fairly small in the 1950s, but beginning to grow in numbers and influence. These would include the Mormons, the Seventh

Day Adventists, and the Jehovah's Witnesses (JWs). In most towns their presence was barely noticed, even if they had a small permanent building in which they met. They did engage in evangelistic efforts, but most people were more bemused than troubled when approached, for instance, by JWs going door to door to pass out their *Watchtower Magazine*.

The Advent of the Wild World of Religion

And then something happened to change this placid scene. Perhaps it was the unrest and uncertainty in society, with the Cold War giving way to a hot war in Vietnam. Perhaps it was a rising resistance to the traditions of the past in general. Perhaps it was an appetite for novelty in religion that matched the cravings for novelty in the secular parts of society. Perhaps it was even, in part, due to the advent of Cable TV. Perhaps it was all of these things, and more, coming together to convince both youths and many adults that the old answers of the Old Time Religions of America just weren't adequate to the challenges of the second half of the 20th century.

As the public began craving new answers to old questions, a whole new breed of religious leaders began to arise, offering assorted spiritual flavors to appeal to every type of spiritual palate. Many of the ideas and answers they offered weren't really totally new. They were often just re-packaged, warmed-over strange ideas that had been tried in the past and found wanting. Clothing styles today often go through cycles of reincarnation of the styles of decades past. And it is becoming more and more common for producers to film remakes of hits of long ago (such as *King Kong*). In the same way, religious novelties of an earlier time can look brand new if they can be repackaged and promoted by just the right persuasive spokesperson.

Besides, the average American in the 1970s and later had grown up in that tame religious world described earlier. Most would never have been exposed to the more obscure and controversial ideas that had been part of the fringes of religion for a century before. Once these ideas began entering the mainstream of American society via television, shortwave radio stations, and popular religious books written by entertaining authors, few individuals looking for spiritual enlightenment recognized that many of these teachings were not fresh spiritual meat, but rather warmed-over leftovers.

The Wild World on the Airwaves

There is no quicker way to get an overview of the extent of the change in American religion than to turn on a 24-hour religious cable network and just watch the passing parade for a few hours. Since few people without an intense interest in religious matters already would have any interest in spending that much time on the topic, the average American is blissfully unaware of the astonishing variety of religious activity that is promoted over the airwaves these days.

This is one reason for this *Field Guide* book—to give the uninitiated a brief overview of this increasingly wild world, without the necessity for them to do all of their own research. Just who **is** that strange man on at 1 AM on the Public Access channel, promoting the idea that the Devil himself had sex with Eve in the garden, and was the actual father of Cain, while Adam was the father of Abel? Is that other fellow on his own prophecy show at 8 PM really an expert in what the Bible says about world events? Should I trust his dogmatic statements that bad times are coming very soon, and if I send money to support his efforts at spreading his teachings, God will snatch me away in the near future up to heaven, while all Hell breaks out here on Earth?

Has that man who seems to keep knocking people over by waving his suit jacket at them (a bit like a football player in a men's locker room snapping a wet towel at other players!) really been an instrument of God to heal thousands upon thousands of people of ailments, even those as serious as cancer and AIDS? Is there documented proof of his claims? Did that man on another video actually discover, as he claimed, the **real** Noah's ark, and the graves of Noah and his wife? Did he really talk to angels in person in a cave under the Temple Mount in Israel, where they were guarding the Ark of the Covenant? And did he, as his promoters claimed so convincingly, actually see and touch the **real** Ten Commandment stones that were inside that ark ... not the imitations touched by Charlton Heston in the movie?

All of these ideas and claims and many, many more are believed **not** just by small pockets of wild-eyed people on the fringes of society today, but by masses of people squarely in the mainstream of American life. You will meet some of the powerful persuaders of the Wild World in these pages, and get glimpses of how their efforts affect not just the minds and intellectual beliefs of their followers, but some of the most mundane aspects of their daily lives.

In the 1950s, most individuals who actively practiced some type of religious faith had relationships with church leaders in their own hometown. They asked for advice from the pastor of their own local church, they trusted him to teach them about God in his weekly sermons and Wednesday night Bible Study classes. If they watched televised preachers such as Billy Graham, it was just as a supplement to their own local church life.

But in the 21st century, increasing numbers of people look to a man—or a woman—on their television screen as their "pastor" or "mentor." They don't study their Bible with a live teacher in a classroom, but with a voice on a tape or CD or DVD in the convenience of their own home. When making deeply personal decisions regarding such private matters as marriage, jobs, and finances, many people who consider themselves Christians may not look for common sense advice from friends, relatives, or local spiritual advisors. They may make such decisions based, instead, on the advice—or even dogmatic orders—on recordings or in written literature from their chosen long-distance spiritual leader. Is that leader a spiritual giant—or a charlatan? Is he or she a humble servant of God—or a strutting, carnal dictator? Many naïve people have never thought to even question whether the individuals in whom they place their long-distance trust are deserving of that trust. For those brave enough to face the possibility of disillusionment, the information in this *Field Guide* may prove invaluable.

Field guides to natural wildlife are helpful to the person who wants to learn more about the friendly and not-so-friendly—and, in some cases, downright dangerous—creatures out there in the natural wild world. Such books, along with a sturdy flashlight, will allow someone to stay alert and safe in that wild world, even when darkness is closing around them. This *Field Guide* is intended to provide both data and a source of light, so that the reader may safely explore the contemporary Wild World of Religion. True apostles of Jesus Christ, true prophets of God, and true teachers inspired by God should surely have no fear at all of having light shone on their teachings and works. Such light will only make truly spiritual works shine brighter. It is those who are self-appointed apostles, prophets, and teachers who may have reason to fear light shining on their teachings and activities.

Chapter 2

Habitats of the Wild World

The scene is a courtroom somewhere in the heartland of the USA. The presiding judge for the trial is adjusting his robes so he can sit down comfortably; the prosecuting attorney is at his table checking his notes. Across the room, the defendant has taken his place at the table next to his attorney. And it is now time for the jury of the defendant's peers to file in and take their positions in the jury box.

There comes the housewife, followed by the retired postal clerk, the auto mechanic, the high school teacher, and the bookkeeper. And next to file by to find their seats are the telephone operator, the Burger King assistant manager, the dental hygienist and the … officer from the Starship Enterprise. She's in full uniform with insignia, communicator, and phaser gun.

No, this scene is not based on fiction. It is based on an incident at the Whitewater Trial in 1996. Although the occupations mentioned above were not necessarily those of the Whitewater jurors, the presence of the Star Ship Enterprise juror is fact.

Well, it's not exactly fact. The alternate juror in question was actually a 31-year-old file clerk from Arkansas named Barbara Adams. But she was, indeed, dressed in the full regalia of an officer from the crew of the fictional television show *Star Trek*. And she wasn't just pulling a prank for the day … she wore the uniform throughout her stint on the jury. (She was excused from her position fairly early in the trial for talking to a television reporter.) When she went back to her file clerk job, she continued to wear it for special occasions, as she had for a long time.

Ms. Adams is a devout *Trekkie*—one of those fans of the *Star Trek* show whose interest in the show goes far beyond just a hobby. This is not merely a person who has collected videotapes, DVDs, action figures, posters, and other memorabilia. This is a person who has immersed herself in a total subculture of people who dedicate most of their free waking moments, outside of work and eating, to a focus on the alternate reality of the *Star Trek* universe.

Those who inhabit only the normal reality of American life may be totally unaware that such a subculture exists, unless they have seen the amusing and amazing documentary video by director Roger Nygard titled *Trekkies*. The 1999 video takes the viewer on a safari exploring the world of Trekkies. It covers the regional and national conventions, where they dress up as their favorite characters and rub shoulders with others who share their obsession. It follows them as they buy and swap collectibles—from small action figures costing a few dollars, to authentic props from the *Star*

Trek movies and TV series, which fetch prices in the thousands of dollars. And it explores the private lives back home of some of the most devoted of the breed.

In her home town, Ms. Adams is an active member of one of the *Star Trek* clubs that meet regularly throughout the country. These are not just casual social clubs where fans swap stories and collectibles. Many model themselves after more traditional fraternal organizations. The members take their crew positions and titles very seriously, and engage in charity works in the same way the Knights of Columbus or the Masons do.

Although most Trekkies probably don't even own a full uniform, like Ms. Adams wore at the Whitewater trial, she is not unique. The *Trekkies* video featured Dr. Denis Bourguignon and the whole staff at his Orlando dental office, who dressed as *Star Trek* crewmembers, and conducted the business of cleaning and fixing teeth in an environment totally dominated by the *Star Trek* theme. The walls were covered with *Star Trek* posters, starship models hung from the ceiling, and memorabilia filled the shelves on the walls. New prospective employees did not have a choice regarding whether or not to become a part of the theme—willingness to wear the Enterprise uniform was a prerequisite to employment.

The video noted that there were even serious classes at the time that one could take in order to learn to speak the fictional language of the enemies of the Enterprise, the Klingons.

Other Alternate Realities

Most Americans do not realize that this Trekkie subculture exists, even though it is inhabited by many thousands of their countrymen. And the world of the Trekkies is not the only such subculture in America that is a virtual society, within the larger society, to which most Americans are oblivious. There are likely thousands of such subcultures built on shared interests.

Families who have one or more children who are competitive dancers (tap, ballet, jazz, and more) make up another such subculture. Parents and siblings of these children are often required to build their whole schedule outside of work and school around the needs of the latest scheduled competition of the dancers in the family. The family's finances may even be in jeopardy from the incredible expense involved in outfitting their children with costumes for their competitions, paying for travel expenses and accommodations necessary to compete on the national level, investing in years of private dance lessons, and much more. They are so immersed in the competitive dance subculture that all of their friends and acquaintances may be limited to people they meet at the practices and competitions. The world of competitive dance is their reality, their culture, their own society.

The same can be said for any number of competitive subcultures, from figure skating to gymnastics to modeling, both for adults and children. The average American never thinks about those groups of people whose primary concerns revolve around upcoming beauty pageants or Olympic tryouts. They may even assume that most people spend their time outside of work, school, and sleep the same way they and their neighbors do: watching TV, reading the latest best-seller on the NY Times booklist, hosting back-yard barbecues, going to sporting events and concerts, working on a common hobby like coin collecting or scrap-booking, and so on.

Occasionally, there are TV documentaries that give a glimpse into American subcultures such as youth beauty and talent pageants. And this may raise the consciousness of many Americans about that particular subculture. They can comprehend how some families might be driven, by aspirations for their children, to become part of such a subculture for a few years. But there is another set of American subcultures that seldom get any time in the national media. If the average American ever got a glimpse inside these cultures, they might find some of the stories as amusing and amazing as the story of the Trekkies. A closer inspection might even leave them puzzled and troubled at times.

American Spiritual Subcultures

Most of those directly involved in the Trekkie subculture realize that the whole subculture is based on fiction. They are serious about their participation, but serious because they are having fun. The occasional emotionally or mentally disturbed individual might become obsessed with the Trek world to the point where they couldn't distinguish fiction from reality. Even so, such people are in an extreme minority.

But there is a set of subcultures, ranging in size from a few dozen people to hundreds of thousands, in which the individuals are just as devoted and intense as are Trekkies or beauty pageant moms. Yet they do not believe that their subculture is based on either fiction or short-term, temporary individual or family aspirations.   The people in these subcultures are just as immersed in their unique interests as any Trekkie is in the trivia of *Star Trek*. Many of them spend most of their time outside work, school, and sleep involved in the activities of their subculture, to the exclusion of many of the standard interests and hobbies of most Americans. These are the spiritual subcultures within a number of modern American religious movements.

This reference is not to people in general who embrace a particular religious belief system, or belong to any of the thousands of denominational or independent church congregations in America. Whether one is a Baptist, a Catholic, a Methodist, or an independent Pentecostal, it

10

is not unusual at all to be an active part of one's community of faith. Nor is it unusual for one's closest friends to be those who share similar religious beliefs. And diligent attendance at weekly worship services, Bible studies, and church social activities is a normal part of the lives of many Americans. Regular personal, individual Bible study and prayer are also a normal part of the lives of many. Thus the knowledge that their neighbors might attend a different church denomination or have a different circle of regular church friends than themselves is not puzzling or troubling to most people.

What many, if not most, Americans are not aware of are the growing number of spiritual subcultures based almost entirely on the personality and powers of persuasion of one man or one very limited group of men. Inside some of these subcultures, leaders exert an unusual level of influence over the daily lives of their supporters, to the point of almost micromanaging their lives. This can include legislating everything from what clothes to wear to what positions followers may use during sexual intimacy with their spouses.

The next chapter will explore ways in which such subcultures are created by aspiring gurus in the Brave New World of 21st Century American religious movements.

Chapter 3

A Shocking Future Arrives

If you were a man in his 30s living in a small town in 1962, and were drawn to pornography, it wouldn't have been all that easy to feed your addiction. There would likely have been no place locally where you could find movies or live action. You would have had to travel as discreetly as possible, making excuses to friends and family, to some nearby city. And once there, you would have had to go to some really sleazy neighborhood to find a triple-X rated movie theater, a neighborhood that you would normally have been afraid to travel in after dark. If you lived near enough to a larger city, you might even have had an opportunity to go to a real burlesque house, where women performed live. But finances and time (and believable excuses) would likely have limited your opportunities to make this trek.

Another possibility would have been to answer a cryptic ad in the back of a "men's magazine" that promised celluloid pleasures—likely, cheap 8 millimeter black and white films of amateur ladies in various states of undress, doing mundane things like making a peanut butter and jelly sandwich. They would come in a brown paper wrapper with no return address, and you'd hope that your wife or kids (or parents, if you still lived at home) wouldn't get to the package before you.

Maybe, if you had just the right sophisticated friend from a bigger city, you might persuade him to order an actual "dirty French movie" for you. But then you'd have to figure out how to explain to your wife why you needed to rent a 16mm projector for a poker night with the guys.

Imagine such a man time-travelling to the 21st century. If he didn't think it was blasphemous to say so, he'd likely think he was in Paradise! The video rental shop on the corner in almost any small town will offer him a large collection of full-color videos of full-length movies, full of less-than-scantily-clad young women, doing much more than making lunch. He can play such videos on the same DVD player on which his kids watch cartoons, as long as he waits long enough until everyone in the house is fast asleep, and uses headphones to make sure no one hears what he's listening to in the family room. If he travels for his job and stays in motels, it will be even easier to just watch the Playboy Channel on the cable TV in his room, or order the latest X-rated film on Pay-Per-View. Even more conveniently—he can just download the most grotesque, raw porn from the Internet directly onto the hard drive of his own laptop computer, and view it anywhere, including at his office during work hours if he is daring enough.

What does this have to do with the Wild World of Religion of the 21st century?

Where were you in '62?

A book titled *Faiths, Cults and Sects in America* (later titled *God is a Millionaire* when it came out in paperback) hit the shelves of America's bookstores in 1962. Authored by *Newsweek* reporter Richard Mathison, it promised to reveal "the strange beliefs, the swindles, the bizarre teachings and frequently erotic rituals into which millions of Americans pour their faith and money." His book labeled some groups, such as Mormons, Jehovah's Witnesses, Seventh Day Adventists, and Unitarians, as "established cults." Others were farther out on the fringe, such as the flying saucer cults popular at the time, Voodoo cults, and groups centered around some Hindu yogi. Mathison noted:

> The National Council of Churches has announced that two thirds of the people in the U.S.—about 104 million in 268 recognized religious bodies—follow some creed or faith with reasonable persistence. Of these a fraction, an estimated six to seven million, belong to the cults and sects which include a wide variety of beliefs, but have in common a recognizable deviation from "normal" Protestantism or Catholicism. Some fundamentalists are assured the world will end any day and have a phrase in the Old Testament to prove it. Others are willing to test the solidity of their faith against the bite of a rattlesnake. Still others seek by ecstatic excitement the immediate, transforming religious experience that will give them a glimpse of True Reality. (p. 13)

All of this is still true. In the 21st Century there are many groups which "deviate from the norm," many that embrace odd distinctives such as snake-handling or the prediction of imminent Armageddon. What is different now?

What is different is the numbers and distribution of the adherents of these groups of people. Yes, men may have been just as likely to be tempted by porn back in 1962 as in 2005. But the purveyors of porn in 1962 had very limited distribution channels for their wares. Likewise, many folks were susceptible to being attracted to unusual religious claims in 1962. But the purveyors of such claims didn't have such easy access to potential converts as they do today. Most were limited by the technology of the time to placing an ad in the back of magazines such as *Capper's Farmer*, sending out literature via the U.S. mail, and/or broadcasting for a half hour every night, or maybe even only once a week, on an obscure radio station. And these outlets were expensive for the individual just getting started in a ministry. Some relied for developing a following almost exclusively on word of mouth, such as in circles of bored California Society Matrons who were fascinated by the latest claims regarding the most fashionable Hindu yogis who allegedly were in contact with Ascended Masters. While such fellows and their promoters might get followers quickly in the Los Angeles suburbs, their effect on mid-America would be almost non-existent.

It wasn't easy, prior to the 1970s, to attract a wide following of people for any new religious venture. And even those limited numbers attracted to a new religious novelty were limited in how easily they could feed their new interest. Their opportunities might consist of a booklet or two or newsletter a month sent out by their new teacher of choice, and a catalog of articles one could request. Most groups, even those that could afford to buy radio or TV time, or to produce a glossy monthly magazine to send out to supporters, grew slowly. Sunday morning slots on network stations were expensive or non-existent. Such slots on local channels were perhaps more available, but they reached only a limited audience.

It's a new world out there now.

Brave New High-Tech World

It started slowly, with the invention of the personal audio tape player, which became widely available in the 1970s. Suddenly, just like the top-40 songs played on the radio, religious messages on the radio were no longer ephemeral, fading away by the next day after broadcast. They could be recorded straight from the airwaves by combination radio/tape recorders, and listened to over and over by hungry Bible students. Those who made such broadcasts could, for the first time, record an unlimited number of extra copies and make them available by mail to those hungry Bible students to listen to over and over. And those students could share the recordings with friends, thereby increasing the audience far beyond those who happened to tune in to late night radio.

This was followed by the personal video recorder in the 1980s. Now viewers were able to use their new recorders to capture forever the TV shows of their favorite teacher or preacher, to play over and over again. And those teachers and preachers could make video presentations available by mail to their supporters, frequently to be played to groups for "home Bible studies."

Then came cable TV, which greatly increased the number of outlets for would-be preachers and teachers. No longer were they consigned to the Sunday morning church hour on the three networks, or the wee hours of the night on obscure local stations. They first had access to national cable channels such as TBS out of Atlanta and WGN out of Chicago. And, ultimately, they started getting their own "dedicated" religious networks such as Pat Robertson's CBN and Jan and Paul Crouch's TBN. By the 1990s, many cable lineups included several 24/7 religious channels—including, eventually, Mother Angelica's EWTN Roman Catholic channel.

Add into the mix the explosion of shortwave radio, which provides wide coverage for dirt-cheap prices. The audience for shortwave stations might originally have been primarily limited to long-haul truckers who were kept awake late at night on the Interstates by everything from the bizarre antics of the purveyors of UFO encounters and various conspiracy theories, to the latest would-be end-time prophet. But the appeal has long since jumped to housewives doing dishes, businessmen commuting long distance to work everyday, and more. Thus many smaller ministries now choose to buy time on a shoestring on various shortwave channels, or even set up their own broadcast towers and blanket the airwaves with their own brand of theological novelties around the clock.

At the same time as the rise of these new media outlets came the development and proliferation of the desktop personal computer (PC). Prior to the 1970s, only the government and big corporations could afford to own the huge computers of the time. Even just maintaining a mailing list and generating mailing labels was a major production, and expensive. A ministry might rent time on a central computer somewhere in the city to handle these jobs. But with the advent of the PC, even the smallest ministry acquired the ability not only to maintain their own lists, but also to churn out "personalized" letters to supporters. The name of the potential donor, and personal information about him/her, could be sprinkled throughout the letter to make it appear as though the televangelist was taking a personal interest in the individual. "I was just kneeling by my bed, John, and God showed me a vision of you in your home there in Brown City, and put it on my heart to pray for the needs of you and your family." A scanned graphic image of the televangelist's signature could be added to the end of the letter, and printed in a different color ink, and it would appear that the man had personally signed this intimate correspondence! Although most people are sophisticated enough about computers now to realize this ruse, in the early days it was easy to fool the average donor. In fact, to this day many naïve supporters still believe that their favorite televangelist really does take a personal interest in them, and that such letters are crafted one by one.

Do-it-yourself Church

In the 1950s, some local churches broadcast their worship services live on local TV and radio, with the clear note that the service was being provided for "shut-ins" such as the infirm elderly, the sick, and the severely handicapped. It never occurred to most people that such a second-hand experience should take the place of "real church" for those able to make it to the live event. Nor did most think that it could take the place of actual relationships and conversations with real people that would be available through the activities of a local church. Even Billy Graham, who regularly

15

had televised crusades and regional personal appearances, never implied in any way that his activities were a substitute for the local church. In fact, his appearances were always sponsored by a group of area churches. If someone "came forward" at one of his revivals in a conversion experience, he immediately encouraged them to become affiliated with, and attend regularly, a local church in their area.

But, starting in the 1970s, with a new breed of televangelists and all the new technology available, it suddenly dawned on many people that they didn't need to "get religion" from a church on the corner or a pastor who lived in their own town at all. They could get weekly sermons, regular Bible studies, and religious music right in the privacy and convenience of their own home. In fact, the sermons were often more polished and more consistently inspiring, the Bible studies more in-depth … or at least more entertaining, and the music presented with more professionalism, than any local church could provide.

They could even "interact" with their chosen religious leader by sending letters to his ministry headquarters, and by receiving those "personalized" letters from him.

Perhaps even more importantly, they could have a selection of theological novelties from which to choose that was far greater than was available from the few local churches in their own town.

Thus arose a phenomenon that has utterly exploded in the 21st century—the Do-It-Yourself Church. One of the primary power sources fueling this phenomenon is that other central fact of life in the 21st century—the Internet and its World Wide Web.

Chapter 4

Oh, What a Tangled World Wide Web

Online Religion

Fifty years ago it was a major effort for an aspiring new guru to find prospective followers. Now he can grab them as they surf by on their way to check the latest forecast on Weather.com! With the right web-design software and just a bit of programming savvy, a single individual can have a religious website that is as elaborate and impressive as that of a major church denomination. And he can be as formal or as folksy as he chooses, setting the tenor of his ministry. No one need know it is just one man and his PC in a small apartment in a small town. He can craft a persona to present to the public that has nothing to do with his real world. He can even go online himself to get a variety of degrees and credentials from questionable, unaccredited cyber colleges and other institutions, and string BA, MA, and ThD after his name on his home page—next to the digitally touched-up picture of himself and his lovely wife. Few potential supporters will bother to look up the details of the source of his academic credentials.

When his ministry grows, his website can grow with it. What was first just a few pictures and articles can grow to include daily sermons in streaming audio or video. He can post whole books outlining his own theology online to read, daily news reports of the progress of the ministry and its projects, and forums on which supporters can share their enthusiasm for what they are learning from their chosen guru with others of like mind. At the bottom of every page of the site can be the link to click to immediately make a credit card donation to the ministry.

Fifty years ago, the average preacher had to get on the sawdust trail, preaching in tent revivals across the land, if he wanted to get a wide audience to pay attention to him. Now a preacher can gather supporters while sitting at his own desk, and enter the living room of every one of them who has a computer every day—even multiple times a day. And he can create the illusion of a personal relationship with each one.

The Internet: The Good, the Bad, and the Ugly

There is no way to turn the clock back, of course. The appeal of the Web is so wide now that it's hard to find groups or businesses that **don't** have a webpage, from small town Little League teams to village tanning parlors. Virtually anyone who **wants** to make use of the Internet **can** make use of the Internet. Even homeless people around the country can have their own virtual home in Cyberspace! They can obtain an email address from one of the free email services such as Yahoo. They can check their email and surf the Web at free Internet connections at their local library. Indeed, right from that library connection, they can even create their own "home" on the net—a homepage on one of the many free website hosts on the Web.

And the good, the bad, and the ugly in the Wild World of Religion will be right around the cybercorner from them ... and from all the rest of us. The greedy charlatans, the mentally-unbalanced megalomaniacs, the self-appointed apostles and prophets of new "end times prophecy" sects, and the self-proclaimed miracle healers—all can all set up their wares on the same Internet cyberstreet as the sincere, legitimate ministry outreaches to the poor, the biblically-sound Bible teachers, and the truly God-inspired motivational preachers. It has never been more important for the "consumer" to be aware of how to sort out the claims of all of these groups and individuals that are competing for their attention as well as their money.

Therefore, it is certainly convenient that the medium that allows the charlatan to sell his wares is the same medium that can best equip the public to investigate his claims. For millennia, religious con-artists have relied on the fact that most people have very short memories. A prophetic guru could dogmatically set a date for the Second Coming of Christ, and when the date came and passed, he need only wait a few years—maybe only a few months—for people to forget what he had predicted. Before long, new people would come along who were totally unaware of his record of prophetic failure. Then he could hang out his prophetic shingle once again, set a new date, and gather around himself a new set of starry-eyed disciples.

Or the pious head of a small religious group could be exposed as a philanderer who was secretly attempting to seduce the wives of a number of his followers. If he could escape town before being caught and tarred and feathered—or worse—by the husbands, he could travel to another state and set up a new ministry again, gathering a new following of the gullible.

The rise of the Internet has really put a cramp in the style of such men. Computers don't forget in the way people do. And distance means nothing when communication between Alaska and Florida is instant. A person who posts a prophetic proclamation on the Worldwide Web needs to understand that others can capture and store it on their computers. Therefore, even if he removes it from his own website when it becomes obvious it has not come to pass in time, the record still exists. And the man whose ministry is the subject of a carefully-documented investigative report by the local newspaper in his own town, revealing him to be misusing ministry funds and deceiving his supporters, needs to realize he can't "move away" from his record and start fresh. That local newspaper likely

18

has a website with archives of their articles. Any web-searcher using Google to look up the minister's name will have access to the record stored in those archives.

For the ministry with integrity this is no threat, of course. The records on the Internet of good deeds are just as permanent as the records of evil deeds.

The Web has also put a damper on another type of religious gimmick. Many religious groups have historically relied on being able to very carefully ration out information about their beliefs to prospective members over an extended period of time. They may have doctrines and practices which seem so ridiculous on the face that they know they ought to reserve revelation of those until the new member is firmly committed to the group. Thus the door-to-door evangelists for the group, or their radio preachers or magazine authors, will focus on putting the most benign, most appealing façade possible on the organization. For centuries, this has worked. Such groups were able to keep their most esoteric beliefs, and the inner workings of their system, hidden from prying eyes. Actual entry to group meetings is often by invitation only, and only offered after a careful screening process to assure that the prospective member is ready for the "deeper" truths.

But the Web has thrown open the doors to these hidden sanctuaries, and has made information about the secret doctrines and practices of such groups available instantly to all who are looking for more information than they can squeeze out of the evangelists at their door. Disillusioned former members often put up websites outlining "the rest of the story" that most have only discovered in the past after it was too late to turn back.

Of course, just because such information is posted on the Web doesn't necessarily make it The Gospel Truth either. Sometimes, former members of groups have unreasonable grudges and personal agendas that color their commentaries. What is most useful from such sources in the long run may well be the fact that most do not limit the information on their websites to personal opinion, but provide solid documentation. They will post scanned copies of original documents, excerpts from recorded messages in the form of sound clips or transcripts, reports from public news sources, and more. Thus readers are able to reconstruct some of the reasons for the opinions shared on the website and come to their own conclusions.

Religious Research on the Worldwide Web

There are a wide variety of websites on the Internet that critically evaluate the teachings and activities of certain religious teachers and groups. They are sometimes referred to as *cult-watch* sites. These sites represent a wide variety of perspectives on religious movements.

Secular *Cult-Watch* Websites

To the average secular—perhaps atheist or agnostic—observer, the bickering among Christian teachers and groups over doctrines, methods, and styles of authority may seem silly. Not wishing to get into any debate over these "in-house" differences, their concern about religious *cults* is limited in most cases to those they believe may be actually physically dangerous to themselves or others. A group which is alleged to be involved in physical or sexual abuse of children, or to be in danger of mass suicide within the group, or whose teachings—such as perhaps racial hatred—may possibly lead to physical harm to outsiders, is viewed with alarm. When such groups are profiled on **secular *cult-watch* sites,** the emphasis is usually on sharing documentation of those factors of the group's activities that give evidence of such potential danger.

Religious *Cult-Watch* Websites

Many Internet websites that specialize in profiling and documenting the teachings and activities of various religious groups and teachers are created by those who have a particular religious doctrinal stance they wish to defend. They may define any group that deviates from the very narrow doctrinal "orthodoxy" to which they subscribe as a *cult*. Thus, the doctrinal teachings of such groups may receive a very thorough profiling on most **religious *cult-watch* websites**.

Ex-Member *Cult-Watch* Websites

Once an individual or a group of individuals manage to extricate themselves from involvement in a religious group that they are convinced held them in some sort of spiritual bondage, they may feel called to warn others to avoid the group. They may desire to reach out to those who are still in the group, and attempt to help them also "see the light." In most cases, their primary focus is not so much on the error of the doctrines of the group that they left, but the methods used by the leadership of the group to keep them deceived. Thus, the material on most **ex-member *cult watch* websites** may emphasize historical documentation on the abuses of power exercised by the founder and/or later leaders of the groups, and incidents of deception used to mislead members.

Christian Apologetics *Cult-Watch* Websites

Apologetics: "A branch of theology devoted to the defense of the divine origin and authority of Christianity." (*Merriam Webster Online Dictionary*)

While many religious *cult-watch* sites, as mentioned above, define a cult as any group which deviates from their own narrow doctrinal perspective, some Christian Apologetics sites take a broader view. While allowing for wide doctrinal variance across denominational lines, they start with the assumption that there is a minimum standard of "historical orthodoxy" to which a teacher or group needs to adhere in order to be accepted as authentically Christian. Any group which deviates from this standard may be considered a *cult*. Thus, much of the material on such **Christian Apologetics *cult-watch* websites** is devoted to comparing the doctrines of questionable teachers and groups to their particular broad definition of historical orthodoxy.

"Spiritual Abuse" *Cult-Watch* Websites

> "Spiritual abuse is the misuse of a position of power, leadership, or influence to further the selfish interests of someone other than the individual who needs help. Sometimes abuse arises out of a doctrinal position. At other times it occurs because of legitimate personal needs of a leader that are being met by illegitimate means. Spiritually abusive religious systems are sometimes described as legalistic, mind controlling, religiously addictive, and authoritarian. The most distinctive characteristic of a spiritually abusive religious system, or leader, is the over-emphasis on authority. Because a group claims to have been established by God Himself the leaders in this system claim the right to command their followers." (www.watchman.org/profile/abusepro.htm)

An increasing number of websites, as well as books available in Christian and secular book stores, have brought to the attention of the public the reality that abuse within some religious groups is not limited to just physical matters. When a leader or group uses claimed "authority from God" to harm the mental, spiritual, and emotional wellbeing of participants, the result is spiritual abuse. This can be just as dangerous and debilitating as physical abuse. Thus, much of the content on **spiritual abuse *cult-watch* websites** may be devoted to documentation of those factors in the teachings and methods of the groups and teachers under consideration which may contribute to the potential for spiritual abuse.

Another Perspective

All of these types of websites have merit. The reader will likely find sites from each variety helpful. Even if one does not agree with the website authors' ultimate subjective evaluation of the teachers and groups that they profile, most include accurate documentation from which one can glean useful information.

The *Field Guide* website and this *Field Guide* book take a *different* point of view from all of the above. As the author, I am concerned about:

- ✓ **Any** religious organization, any leaders of such religious organizations, and any religious teachers that in any way insert themselves, their system, or their teachings between the individual believer and that believer's immediate access to God—and to the simple truths of the scriptures.
- ✓ **Any** religious teaching which subverts the basics of simple faith in the teachings of Jesus as seen in the Sermon on the Mount—and turns *faith* and *salvation* and the *daily Christian walk* into a complex, convoluted process, through twisting of scripture, or through requiring or encouraging extra-biblical and unbiblical gimmicks and standards.
- ✓ **Any** teacher or religious group that distorts the simple truths of scripture to use for an illegitimate or evil purpose—whether it be to validate their own warped views such as rabid racism, to justify oppression of one group of people over another, to excuse their own sinful actions, or any other reason.
- ✓ **Any** teacher or religious group that would, subtly or openly, strip from the individual believer his right and ability to think and act for himself under the guidance of the Holy Spirit.

See the **Web Resources and Books for Further Research** chapter for recommendations of a variety of resources to aid in evaluating the potential for spiritual harm of various groups.

A Closer Look

The technological and social factors that have led to so many changes in modern America have given rise to several troubling trends in the Wild World of Religion. The next chapter will take a closer look at some of these.

Chapter 5

Troubling Trends

The technological and cultural changes of the past several decades have transformed the face of the religious landscape of the USA in many ways that may not be obvious to those who have not studied the topic. The content of this *Field Guide* brings into focus, as through binoculars, various inhabitants of the increasingly Wild World of Religion. The purpose for this is two-fold:

1. To provide a **reference work** that gives an overview and documentation on a collection of ideas, individuals, and groups representative of a variety of significant modern American religious movements.

2. To share some of the concerns of the author about some disturbing trends which now affect large numbers of people. It is impossible to cover every individual, group, and movement that has had an impact on people. Those included in this volume are a sample of some of the most influential people and fastest-growing groups.

Trend One: Religious Homogenization

An individual in the 1950s who had no religious background, and who wanted to find out first-hand about Christianity, would have had to do a lot of footwork, visiting the various churches in his community. If he chose, on subsequent Sundays, to visit a Roman Catholic Church, followed by a Lutheran, a Congregational, a Baptist, and a Pentecostal, he would come away with a feeling of diversity. There would be a diversity of style, from ceremonial, to formal, to informal. Each setting would have a unique vocabulary that would include different buzzwords, from "extreme unction" to being "filled with the Holy Ghost." There would be a varying emphasis in the content of the sermons. Some preachers would sound more like college lecturers, some would sound like inspirational motivational speakers, and some would thunder in harsh exhortations and threats. There would be a diversity of musical styles from ancient to modern, and from magnificent classical pipe organ performances to piano-playing that might sound at home in a honky-tonk bar. If the visitor was listening carefully, he would note a variety of doctrines being espoused, doctrines which were so divisive that they would be praised in one group and condemned in the next.

Those who were part of each of these diverse congregations would know what to expect when visiting the churches of their own denomination in other cities. They would feel right at home, as that is the point of the term "denomination": A group that has its own style, practices, policies, and unique doctrinal emphases that differentiate it from most other groups.

Those denominations and those diversities still exist in the 21st century. But what has changed is the "popular" face of religion: what the non-religious public views as Christianity today. For the world of cable and satellite television now offers to that public a homogenized version of Christianity that little resembles the reality out in the towns and cities.

Citizens of countries in Europe, Asia, Africa, and South America may have a distorted understanding of what American Society is like because their only exposure to it is through American television programs— some of them current, some maybe decades old. Just imagine if all you knew about the U.S. was what you saw on the *Beverly Hillbillies, Columbo, Three's Company, Friends, Law & Order*, and ... *MTV!* The average lifestyle of a person in a small town in the U.S. Midwest would be totally outside this warped picture.

The same is now true for the landscape of American religion. Those not involved in any particular denomination or local church may have no exposure to Christianity other than what they see on TV. And what they now see on TV has come a long way from the Sunday morning church hour of the 1950s, when the local Methodist church would air its church service, live, for shut-ins.

The face that Christianity presents to the public now, 24 hours a day on Cable TV, is primarily orchestrated by one small group of people—those affiliated with the Charismatic Trinity Broadcasting Network (TBN). There is also a Roman Catholic network, EWTN, but it is so focused on Catholic doctrines and practices that it does not have an appeal to the general public. TBN, on the other hand, often features famous faces from outside the field of religion, and many programs full of attractive, contemporary music, that can catch the eye and ear of a channel surfer. More recently, they have begun featuring talk shows on a variety of topics, including health and family relationships.

Although there are other, smaller, religious cable networks around the country, TBN is a relative giant in the field. "Across America and around the world TBN is carried by TV stations and cable systems to millions of homes. As a matter of fact, TBN is featured on over 5,000 television stations, 33 satellites, the Internet and thousands of cable systems around the world. And the number continues to grow!" (tbn.org website promotional information)

So what brand of theology will one absorb from watching a week's worth of programs on TBN?

It is a nebulous, homogenized theology that exists nowhere out in the real world, for it has no solid foundation at all. TBN founder and host Paul Crouch may sit and interview a guest preacher on a certain topic during one hour. Those on the television studio set with them may nod their heads, agreeing enthusiastically with everything the guest says. The next day, on the same show, a different preacher can expound on a perspective that is diametrically opposite the position of the man from the day before on a certain biblical topic or doctrine—and again, those present will nod their heads and agree enthusiastically with everything the man says!

How can this be? It can be, because there is no **systematic** set of beliefs that is represented on TBN, other than a general Charismatic emphasis. Evidently, no one on the TBN staff has the job of carefully examining all the teachings of the various speakers who appear on the network to see if they can be harmonized in any sensible way. It is obvious to outside observers that many of them cannot. However, since those involved seem to have never taken the time to attempt the harmonization, the loose ends are left loose.

Paul Crouch has made it abundantly clear why this is so—he is opposed to any suggestion that doctrine should be critically evaluated and examined by Christians. Note the following quotes from one of his monologues on the topic:

"That old rotten Sanhedrin crowd, twice dead, plucked up by the roots ... they're damned and on their way to hell and I don't think there's any redemption for them ... the hypocrites, the heresy hunters that want to find a little mote of illegal doctrine in some Christian's eyes ... when they've got a whole forest in their own lives. ..."

"I say, 'To hell with you! Get out of my life! Get out of the way! Quit blockin' God's bridges! I'm tired of this! ... This is my spirit. Oh, hallelujah!' ..."

"Have you ever seen the old movie, Patton? ... He's my hero; he's my hero. Old nail-chewin', tobacco-chewin', cussin' Patton—but he read the Bible every day. I have a feelin' we'll see old General George in heaven. ... "

"There's a wonderful scene in Patton ... they're tryin' to get the Third Army across the bridge in France and there's an old, dumb jackass—donkey—right there on the bridge and it's blockin' the whole convoy of troops ... General George roars up, pulls that ivory- handled revolver out ... and he shoots the donkey. ...

"There's a spiritual application here. ... I want to say to all you scribes, pharisees, heresy-hunters, all of you that are around pickin' little bits of doctrinal error out of everybody's eyes and dividin' the Body of Christ ... get out of God's way, stop blockin' God's bridges, or

25

God's goin' to shoot you if I don't ... let Him sort out all this doctrinal doodoo!"

"I don't care about your doctrines as long as you name the name of Jesus, as long as you believe He died dead [sic] and was buried but came out of the tomb on Sunday morning and ascended to the Father ... I don't care about anything else! Let's join hands ... to get this gospel preached in all the world. "

"The rest of this stuff is what Paul the Apostle calls dung—human excrement! It's not worth anything! Get rid of it ... and get on with winning the lost. "

"I refuse to argue any longer with any of you out there! Don't even call me if you want to argue doctrine, if you want to straighten somebody out ... Get out of my life! I don't even want to talk to you ... I don't want to see your ugly face!" (As quoted in *Foundation Magazine*, March-April 1991, from a transcript of Crouch's *Praise the Lord* show.)

Trend Two: Increasingly bold claims of the miraculous

The average person unfamiliar with the varieties of religious beliefs of Protestantism would not be aware that the people they see on TBN are **not** representative of the fundamental beliefs of most of the denominations in the United States. They are almost all part of what is termed the Charismatic Movement. And most would be identified, even by denominations that consider themselves Charismatic (such as the Assemblies of God), as being on the extreme fringe of the movement. A "mainstream" Charismatic believes that miraculous incidents, including instant healings and deliverance from demons, did not end in the first century after the death of the Apostles, but continue to this day. And he believes that the "gift of tongues"—the ability to speak in an "unknown language" in prayer or in a church service—is also for today.

Those on the outer fringes of Charismatic belief, however, not only believe these things are possible, they insist that astounding healings—on the order of curing AIDS, and sight returning to one born blind, and quadriplegic polio victims walking again—are, or should be, everyday occurrences. They insist that "power encounters" with the supernatural demonic forces of the Devil do occur in public crusades attended by hundreds of thousands around the world, accompanied by astonishing signs and wonders. And they are convinced that uncontrollable laughter, violent shaking, or the uncontrollable urge to make animal-like sounds (such as roaring like a lion or crowing like a rooster) among large numbers of people at a religious gathering is evidence of the presence of the Holy Spirit in great power.

Some of these unusual activities are actually shown on certain programs on TBN, such as the broadcasts from the public appearances of healing evangelist Benny Hinn. But many viewers seem unaware that **all** the regulars on TBN shows are either involved with or supportive of this brand of what some have dubbed "Hyper-Charismania."

The problem with these claims of the miraculous is that they are bold—but in most cases utterly unsubstantiated. For instance, a number of researchers over the last few decades have attempted to contact various Charismatic ministries and get medical documentation regarding healings that were claimed to have happened at crusades. Just because someone **tells** Benny Hinn on a stage in Atlanta, Georgia, that he believes that he has been healed of cancer doesn't make it so. It is undeniable that no astonishing, inexplicable, instantaneous healings, such as a withered arm on a crippled child being "made whole," have **ever** been caught on film. And none of the researchers have been provided with clear medical documentation for the grandiose claims of the miraculous. This does not mean, of course, that God doesn't heal. It merely means that the incredible level of hype surrounding certain ministries, which attempts to validate that God is blessing the ministry because of the astonishing miracles claimed, is open to hard questioning.

In all too many cases, Charismatic preachers don't establish their teachings clearly on scripture. Instead, they build them around **experience**, the kind of subjective experiences described above. A Roman Catholic and a Methodist used to believe that their theological differences were so serious that they were unable to view each other as "brothers in the faith." But if Christian brotherhood is not based on biblical truth, but on contemporary experience of what is believed to be a manifestation of the miraculous, then the barriers between denominations disappear. And you have one homogenized group of people. If speaking in tongues, or rolling on the floor of a church service convulsed with "Holy Laughter," is evidence of someone being "saved" or "filled with the Holy Ghost," then all who manifest these things must agree that "doctrine isn't important." And if doctrine isn't important, why waste much time trying to teach doctrinal concepts from the Bible? This seems to be the approach of many of the teachers on the Trinity Broadcasting Network.

Trend Three: Greed and Gullibility

So what do the TBN preachers talk about? Watch long enough and it will become obvious. There is precious little about "suffering for righteousness' sake," or "turning the other cheek," or giving generously to the poor. What there is a lot of is—the promise of health, wealth, and prosperity. Viewers are bombarded with a constant message that God's greatest wish for them is not an intimate walk with Jesus, and the growth within of the fruit of the Holy Spirit (love, joy, peace, longsuffering, goodness, meekness, and temperance). No, His greatest wish is that they always be healthy and wealthy. And if they aren't, there is something wrong. In fact, what is likely wrong is that they haven't "sown good seed" so that God can send them a harvest of health and prosperity. How does one sow such seed? Why, by sending it to the one who is teaching you about health and prosperity! (That certainly guarantees **the teacher's** chances of prosperity, anyway!)

And thus this troubling trend of greed and gullibility grows. The preacher becomes a wealthy superstar. And his listeners, believing his spiel that he got that way by "sowing seed," want to become like him. So they sow their seed to him. Which makes him a wealthier superstar. And makes them … poorer but no wiser. Numerous investigative reports on some of these superstar televangelists in recent years have documented for the public the incredibly lavish lifestyles they live, and the frequently deceptive methods they use to get there. Sometimes such reports affect donations to the ministries of such televangelists for a time. But the human ability to believe illusions has insured that almost every one of them has been able to rebound, and get gullible viewers to go right back to sending in money to support the lavish lifestyle of the televangelist. (Details on some of these shameful shenanigans can be seen in the **Who's Who Digest** chapter.) Religious hucksters have been around since the first century, of course. But they used to exist around the fringes of society, preying on a limited few. Now they are peddling their wares in a setting accessible to the majority of living rooms in America, 24 hours a day.

Trend Four: The Walmart-izing of the local church scene

In the 1970s and earlier, most American towns and cities had a variety of churches, and each one of them filled a unique niche in the community. Even the largest seldom had congregations over 500 or so. If a church got much bigger than that, it would be common for it to spawn a sister congregation on the other side of town. This is much like the business sector of towns during the same time period. A wide variety of local businesses would fill the needs of local shoppers, from grocery stores to pharmacies, hardware stores, clothing stores, toy stores, and more. If a town was large enough, it might even support a grocery store on each end of town, catering to the needs of the surrounding neighborhoods.

And then came Walmart (and similar discount stores). Now shoppers could find almost all of their wants under one roof, from lettuce to ladders, from aspirin to Barbie Dolls. The wholesale buying power of such chain stores allowed them to sell all of these things more inexpensively than could the local shops. Thus began the decline of local businesses in many towns. Even those that managed to survive have seldom grown larger. They appeal mostly to either old-timers who like doing business with familiar faces, or people who like the convenience of not having to drive to the outskirts of town to get to the mega-store.

This same trend has developed in the Wild World of Religion. As mentioned earlier, the big, thriving churches of the 1950s would be in the center of the town, and the tiny independent Pentecostal churches would be on the outskirts. Those big church buildings are still in place in most towns, but they are no longer thriving. Their congregations are dwindling, as fewer and fewer of the latest generations of Americans have been attracted to "that old-time religion." And the independent Pentecostal churches are still on the outskirts of town—but they are no longer in those tiny buildings. Of course, most prefer the label "Charismatic" now, rather than Pentecostal. The Charismatic movement is one of the fastest growing religious "brands," in both America and the world. (See the **Pentecostal and Charismatic: What's the Difference?** chapter for an explanation of the two terms.) Many towns now boast huge Charismatic mega-church complexes on the outskirts of town. The sanctuaries of some of these churches can hold many thousands, and some of them even fill those sanctuaries two or more times on a Sunday with different crowds. In the hallways outside many of these huge sanctuaries, one can find almost a "mall" of facilities. There may be everything from cappuccino shops and bookstores, to conference rooms for AA meetings, single parent clubs, and senior citizen gatherings. Farther down the hallway will be the gym for the "Praisercise" classes, and Youth Ministry rooms that feature videogame machines, pool tables, and a stage for the visiting contemporary Christian music bands that play for special events.

Little wonder that many of the families who have drifted away from the stagnating "old" churches, which seem to have so little to offer other than a church service on Sunday morning and Wednesday evening, have ended up checking out the Walmarts of Religion. The music for the mega-church worship service is often very professional, inspirational, and contemporary. The enthusiasm of the audience is infectious, and the dynamic personality of the Pastor very appealing to many. The one thing which visitors may find missing, if they know to look for it, however, is the same thing missing from many Charismatic TV shows—solid biblical teaching. The sermons in many such churches seem to be a steady diet of "health and prosperity" teaching and little else.

Trend Five: One-Doctrine Wonders

Hal Lindsey's *Late Great Planet Earth* book became an instant best seller in the early 1970s. In the intervening thirty years it has been read by millions, including Baptists, Methodists, Pentecostals ... and even, reportedly, by the late Pope John Paul II! Most people are fascinated by speculation regarding when and how the world will end. The supermarket tabloids regularly feature sensationalist headlines about the latest interpretation of the nebulous prophecies of Nostradamus. However, for most readers, the fascination with prophecy about the "End Times" is a passing interest at most, and a hobby at best.

This is not so with those in the religious subculture of the End Times Prophecy Movement. Just as the most dedicated Trekkies make their obsession with *Star Trek* the central focus of their life, a large number of Christians spend every spare moment reading, hearing, discussing, speculating, and worrying about how current world events and conditions might line up with the prophecies of the Bible. The most radical among them may even make serious life choices based on the conclusions they reach. They may decide to build a fortified, armed hideaway designed to help them survive "the Tribulation." They may invest all their financial reserves in gold and silver coins, and move to a Caribbean Island to escape what they believe to be the coming collapse of American society. They may cancel plans for a college education, marriage, or having children because they are convinced The End is imminent. More than one has even tried to help speed the Second Coming of Christ along by plotting to destroy the Muslim Dome of the Rock in Jerusalem, so that a Jewish temple can be built on the location—a pre-requisite, they believe, to Jesus' return.

Most of these people likely have some sort of basic theological beliefs about other aspects of life. They may have accepted Jesus Christ as their Savior, and believe that the Bible is their guide to life. But, at some point in their spiritual quest, they have shifted almost all of their focus away from the Sermon on the Mount and the other basics of the Faith, and toward an all-consuming emphasis on prophecy. They devour all the latest books on the topic, watch endless prophecy programs on the Christian cable TV stations, and travel around the country to prophecy conferences, where alleged "prophecy experts" swap their latest speculations.

These people have embraced a One-doctrine Wonder which gives the primary meaning to their life, a doctrine that insists that we are living in the very Last Days of man's dominion over the Earth, and that it is vital to prepare immediately for The End.

But they are not alone in their obsession with such a One-doctrine focus to life. There are other individual doctrines around which whole religious subcultures have formed. Another such doctrine is the one that insists that miracles, particularly miracles of healing, were not just limited to the first century AD, but are available today. Those deeply involved in the Healing Ministries Movement devour all the latest books on how you can "claim your healing." They travel around the country to attend the latest "miracle crusade" by Benny Hinn or Morris Cerullo. They attend workshops on "how to heal." And they watch the endless parade of healing crusade television specials on TBN and other Christian networks. Such specials show huge stadiums in South America, Africa, and elsewhere, filled with tens—or even hundreds—of thousands of people. The crowds have gathered in hopes of receiving or witnessing a healing in the presence of Reinhard Bonnke, Claudio Friedzon, and others like them.

Still others focus much of their energy, time, and resources in promotion of the Hebrew Roots movement. The central tenet of this subculture is that, in order to fully understand salvation through Jesus Christ, you must explore and embrace the "Hebrew Roots" of Jesus; in other words, study the customs and beliefs of first century Judaism. Those deeply involved in this movement devour all the latest books and tapes of their chosen Hebrew Roots teachers, attend conferences and conventions that feature "Hebraic" music, pageantry, and dancing, and perhaps adopt such customs as wearing prayer shawls trimmed with blue and white tassels.

Another One-doctrine Wonder that has attracted a huge following in the past two decades is what has been termed "Word Faith" theology. This is the primary theological foundation of most of the programs on the Trinity Broadcasting Network, promoted by such popular televangelists as Kenneth Copeland, Kenneth Hagin, Rod Parsley, and Joyce Meyer. Its central feature is the belief that Christians have "power" in their own words to claim unlimited health and prosperity for themselves and others. Sometimes flippantly referred to by outsiders as the "Name it and Claim it" doctrine, this notion insists that God has promised unconditionally to give believers whatsoever they desire, if they will only claim it in total faith.

In Word Faith circles, other topics are at times addressed, such as family relationships, basic salvation messages, and prophecy. However, the lion's share of books, evangelistic tracts, TV programs, DVDs, conferences, and weekly sermons are focused on teaching people how to claim their health and prosperity.

The End Times Prophecy, Healing Ministries, Hebrew Roots, and Word Faith movements are only the tip of the iceberg of religious subcultures in America at the beginning of the 21st Century. But because they are four of the most influential and fastest-growing at this time, this *Field Guide* includes a more extensive overview of each of them.

Trend Six: One-man Wonders

Paralleling the One-doctrine Wonders is the emergence of a significant number of "One-man Wonders." These are individuals (primarily men, but a few women are in the category) who have attained a status of guru among their followers. Each one, within his/her own circle of supporters, is viewed as, at the very least, the most significant teacher on Earth today. And he or she may be viewed, at most, as a unique end-time apostle or prophet, one who has "restored truths lost since the first century."

This sort of religious figure has been with us since the first century. But, other than a few notable exceptions such as Joseph Smith, founder of the Mormon religion, and Ellen G. White, alleged "prophetess" of the Seventh Day Adventist movement, such gurus have had a very limited impact in the past. It is the 21st century's explosion of communication capabilities that has allowed modern religious figures to quickly gather a following over wide areas far from their home base. And it is this very long distance factor that allows followers to maintain illusions about their hero that might well be easily shattered if they were in personal contact with him. Most communication between teacher and student in this situation flows only one way, through a barrage of newsletters, recordings, radio and TV programs, financial support solicitations, and more. The student can try to communicate in the opposite direction, but any letters or phone calls from supporters will likely be answered by some low-level functionary in the guru's ministry.

In the past, such teachers as Billy Graham and Hal Lindsey have had a wide contingent of admirers who really enjoyed their books or broadcasts. However, those admirers usually had a local church to which they belonged, a local pastor whom they consulted for their problems, and a local group of like-minded believers with whom they enjoyed regular face-to-face fellowship. Their interest in Graham or Lindsey or others like them was a "side" interest, just as would be a hobby such as stamp collecting.

But the One-man Wonders of the 21st century are more than a side interest of their followers; each one is the spiritual center around which his followers live their lives. Some such men are relatively benign in their influence, although supporting them may be a major financial drain on their most dedicated followers. They are perhaps even unaware that some of their followers are focused so narrowly on their ministry. It is those who have delusions of grandeur of their own that are the cause of the greatest concern regarding this troubling trend. For such men and women can begin to believe so strongly in their own importance, and be so convinced that they have an intimate pipeline to God, that they begin imposing their own idiosyncratic teachings about every minute part of life on their followers. This can include the mundane—what sex positions are permissible for married couples, how long is too long for men's hair, how short is too short for women's hair, etc. It can also include the spiritual—the authority to declare who has the Holy Spirit and who doesn't, to cut off from fellowship those who do not bow to the teacher's every command, to give authoritative interpretation on the most obscure and debatable passages of the Bible. Those who are obsessed with one teacher in this way often find themselves associating or affiliating only with others who share their obsession. They frequently withdraw from fellowship with whatever local congregation they have been a part of, in order to gather with those of like mind to listen to CDs or DVDs of their new teacher together—weekly, or even daily.

Those groups that form around such teachers are susceptible to the next troubling trend.

Trend Seven: Spiritual Abuse and Deception in the Name of God

Although the six troubling trends listed above each have certain aspects which may be unbalanced and unbiblical, the most serious troubling trend goes far beyond that. In every generation since the first century AD beginnings of the Christian faith, there have been religious teachers and preachers who have gathered around themselves a following through the use of deceptive and abusive tactics. However, it is only the development of the technology of the late twentieth century that has allowed this phenomenon to reach epidemic proportions. A hundred years ago, the influence of most such individuals would have been limited, by time and finances, to one town or one county. Now they can extend their tentacles around the whole world instantly through television, short wave radio, and the Internet. Men with serious character flaws that would have been painfully obvious up close in the past can now fool their followers into believing that they are spiritual giants. They can conduct international ministries through the electronic media, which keeps them isolated from face-to-face interaction with most of their supporters.

Thus a rapidly growing number of teachers and groups can be found attracting and retaining supporters through deception, coercion, and scripture twisting. Many of these use mental, emotional, and spiritual abuse. Some even use physical abuse. These groups range from small home fellowships to multi-congregational denominations with thousands, tens of thousands, or even more members. Some, such as the Jehovah's Witnesses, have been around a long time, but are now able to grow more quickly and affect more people than ever before. Some started just last year, last month, or last week, and are able to grow quickly and affect significant numbers of people in a very short time.

Most people are absolutely sure that they could never become attracted to a "cult" or be deceived by a false teacher. They assume that only emotionally disturbed or very naïve and ignorant people could possibly fall for strange beliefs and weird practices at the edges of Christianity. But close examination of some of these very abusive and deceptive groups indicate that just common, average people by the **millions** are indeed capable of being misled down some very dark paths.

The following chapters offer some guidelines on how to evaluate your involvement, or the involvement of friends and family members, in religious groups. You may be surprised to find that religious deception might be closer to home than you have thought.

Chapter 6

The True Believer Revisited: Characteristics of Potentially Harmful Religious Groups

Personal from the author

Some time in the late 1960s, my husband George and I both read the popular book by Eric Hoffer, *The True Believer*. Hoffer had done an extensive study on the methods used by mass movements to make and keep converts. His book shared his conclusion that most of them, both secular and religious, use many of the same tactics.

George and I were both amazed at the wealth of insight and wisdom flowing from the pen of this self-taught former longshoreman. He made it clear just what in the psyche of the potential Communist Party Member, or the potential religious cult member, led them to get involved, and stay involved, with groups which most thinking folks would see right away were dangerous or outlandish at worst, and unreasonable and controlling at best. He seemed able to spot much of the foolishness out there in the marketplace of ideas, and label it for what it was. Except, of course, for the one marketplace idea near and dear to our own hearts. Although the religious group we had become involved with as young university students sure seemed to have many of the questionable characteristics that he brought out in the book, we figured that we were the exception that proved the rule.

Time went by. In 1974, I returned to Michigan State University to do some graduate work in the fields of education, social science, and psychology. In my "Social Psychology of Social Movements" class I met Hoffer's writings once again. They were joined by another classic in the field of Social Psychology, *When Prophecy Fails*. This book explored the history of groups that had predicted/prophesied "the End" to come in their own time in history, and how the members responded when the prophecy failed. (For details on the conclusions in that book, see the **When Prophecy Fails** chapter of this **Field Guide**.) I shared the book's information with George. Once again we were both amazed how closely the facts in the book lined up with our real-world experiences with the group we belonged to. Indeed, a date had been set by the leader of our group related to the events of the End Times, and that date had come and gone with no fulfillment. And the reactions of most in the group, including

35

us, had been exactly what the book said they would be. So did we apply the rest of the author's evaluation and commentary to our own experiences?

Of course not. Because, you see, the groups covered in the book were all false movements and churches. We, on the other hand, were absolutely sure that we were members of the "Only True Church of God on Earth Today." Once again, we were, in our own minds, the exception that proves the rule!

Proving the Exception

It was many years after the incidents described above before we were able fully to face our own folly ... and realize we had merely avoided making some hard, painful judgments. (For more details on our personal spiritual journey, see the *Afterword* chapter of this *Field Guide*.)

We realize now that there really are some solid signs that a religious group or teacher is attracting and keeping followers through humanly coercive methods, rather than through biblical methods blessed by God, and through the supernatural power of the Holy Spirit. If a few, some, many, or all of the factors below seem to apply to a group you are involved with, or considering involvement with, you can save yourself a lot of grief by facing reality and taking steps to get free **now**. If you choose, as we did, to remain in irrational denial, you may find some day that you wasted much of your life in bondage to mere men rather than in true service to God.

Signs of trouble

Does the group or leader:

✓ Demand the **exclusive** loyalty of followers?
✓ Condemn any serious questioning of the integrity of the leadership, even if followers have access to strong evidence of irregularities in matters of finance, morals, or ethics?
✓ Condemn any serious questioning of the policies or tactics of the leadership, even when such policies or tactics have been clearly shown to lead to emotional, mental, spiritual, or perhaps even physical suffering of followers?
✓ Forbid anyone with even minor questions or concerns about the leadership from expressing them to others in the group?
✓ Insist any questioning of the leadership is tantamount to questioning God, and is an affront to Him personally?
✓ Twist scriptures regarding authority, particularly in the Old Testament (e.g., "the rebellion of Korah"), to make it appear that

36

there is a direct correlation to contemporary circumstances, and that God's wrath will be felt once again by those who reject authority within the group?

✓ Make grandiose claims to such biblical roles as prophet or apostle, with nothing more than self-aggrandizement to establish the validity of such claims?

✓ Make grandiose, unsubstantiated claims to have "restored truths lost to the world for 1900 years"?

✓ Insist that the average person is unable to understand the Bible through independent study, but instead should rely entirely on the interpretations and explanations of the leader or group?

✓ Make extremely excessive demands on the time and financial resources of followers, to the point of physical or financial exhaustion?

✓ Insist or strongly imply that there is a direct correlation between financial contributions to the group and God's blessings and protection on the donor?

✓ Threaten that God will withhold blessings from—or perhaps even inflict His wrath upon—those who resist the leader's or group's demand for sacrificial giving beyond even the "prescribed" amount (such as the tithe)?

✓ Forbid or strongly discourage followers from reading or listening to material produced by any outside source?

✓ Encourage or demand that followers seriously reduce, or cut off entirely, relationships with family members outside the group?

✓ Discourage or forbid the development of relationships with friends who are not part of the group?

✓ Make decisions to expel members through a secret process not open to the observation of the average member?

✓ Encourage or demand that followers cut off all contact with former group members, even though such ex-members have not been found guilty of, or even publicly charged with, any flagrant violation of biblical standards of morality or ethics?

Few groups display **all** the characteristics above. If someone suddenly realized that the group they were involved with **did** have all of these characteristics, I would recommend that they run, not walk, to the nearest exit, and never look back!

But even if one recognized only two or three of these problem areas in a group, that should raise some very bright red flags. Quite frequently, new followers do not realize that many more of these conditions may exist within a group than are obvious on the surface. Only as they become more deeply involved than just getting some literature, or visiting group meetings a few times, will the "rest of the story" become clear. The time to look for danger signals is before one has invested so much time, effort, emotions, and resources into involvement that it becomes almost impossible to disengage without significant trauma. The truth of the Bible will remain the truth, and remain accessible to you, even if you find you must withdraw from support of the person or group that first pointed out that truth to you. There are no scriptures that put you into bondage to a human group or a human leader, no matter how persuasively some group or teacher may have tried to convince you that there are.

But what if it is not you who are involved with such a group or teacher? What if your concern is for a loved one who appears mesmerized by a situation which seems spiritually dangerous to you? The following chapter will offer some insight and guidance for those who find themselves in those circumstances.

Chapter 7

Prescription for Intervention

Suggestions for dealing with friends or family members who are, or are on their way to becoming, affiliated with what you believe to be a potentially harmful religious group

Those who have family or friends involved with groups which have some of the characteristics described in the previous chapter are often very concerned about their loved one's welfare. Such involvement usually puts a great strain on the relationship, as the new convert becomes more and more involved in the activities of the group and pulls further and further away from fellowship with any "unbelievers," including family and former close friends. The temptation is great to try to pry them loose. But **please note the following observations** before attempting such a project.

1. **Arguing doctrine** with a dedicated convert is usually a losing battle. By the time they are seriously committed to their newfound leader or group, they usually have pat answers for almost any biblical issue you can bring up. In addition, the organization's "reasoning" methods may be so convoluted that normal logic doesn't apply.

2. One of the doctrines that many such unhealthy groups inculcate very early in any convert is absolute, unquestioning loyalty to the organizational leadership, unquestioning agreement with its teachings, and unquestioning obedience to its policies. This makes it even more difficult to discuss any biblical matter. **The new convert will defer to the leadership** whenever they are confused about a Bible passage.

3. Many, many members of a wide variety of potentially harmful groups, including even such large groups as the Jehovah's Witnesses, have left—or been kicked out of—such groups in recent decades. In most cases, these people did not start down the path to exiting the group because of doctrinal questions, but rather because **they began to have doubts about some of the horrible fruit of some of the policies** of the group.

4. A few years ago, it was very difficult for a doubting group member to get any support from others, as there is often a system of spying within such organizations. Any doubts expressed, even to a close personal friend in the congregation, would usually be reported to the local leadership, and could

result in suspension or expulsion. Because the dedicated convert believes that the organization has the only path to salvation, the idea of disfellowshipment can be terrifying. Thus, even if they were beginning to have serious doubts about some matters, most members put them out of their minds, out of fear of retribution. With the advent of the Internet, this situation has changed somewhat. There are, around the world, a wide variety of **groups of former members of such potentially unhealthy religious groups specifically dedicated to helping people get free** from their former organizations. They have websites and anonymous discussion forums, where "doubters" can go to get accurate information and help in sorting through their questions.

5. It is helpful for family and friends to know at least a bit about the history, doctrines, and policies of the group with which their loved one is involved. This way they can know what they are up against if they wish to intervene in any way with their loved one's choice to be involved with the group. The only effective, practical method I have seen for having any chance of affecting the dedication of someone involved in such organizations is to **very gently nurture any areas of even slight doubt** that the convert may express. This must be done not by addressing them head-on, but by carefully and casually encouraging the person to talk about them.

6. **Keeping the lines of communication open** with a friend or relative who has begun studying with a troubling group or who has joined the group is difficult. The policies of many such groups encourage estrangement from family and non-group friends, and immersing oneself in an endless round of meetings and Bible studies, and perhaps even door-to-door or street witnessing. The really dedicated convert can spend almost all free time involved in these activities. Therefore it is **vital** to see that every opportunity for interaction with the convert is as **positive, supportive, and loving as possible**. Mocking their beliefs, arguing about doctrine, or complaining about the fact that they have little time for friends and family any more, will only lead them to conclude that they are being "persecuted for righteousness' sake."

7. **Love** is, in the end, **the only answer** for this situation. Love the person unconditionally. Express that love openly. Don't be drawn into hostile discussions that go nowhere, and that only end up convincing them, in their own mind, that you don't love God—and you don't love them.

Useful documentation

Use the books and weblinks listed in this book, including those in the *Web Resources and Books* chapter, and add your own efforts to search for more information about the group or leader about which you have concerns. An easy way to do this on the Web is to make use of one of the large Internet websearch engines. My favorite is:

www.google.com

If you find useful information on the Web, collect it and print it out—but not to give to your loved one right away. Keep it on hand for future use, if they begin to evidence doubts about their involvement. Even then, don't bury them in an avalanche of material, but dole it out in bits and pieces related to the specific questions they may begin to develop. If they become seriously disillusioned at some point, only then might it be helpful to offer them your complete collection of information.

And be sure to check the *Field Guide to the Wild World of Religion* companion website:

www.isitso.org/guide.

It has much more extensive information, documentation, and commentary on a number of troubling religious groups than could be included in this brief book.

Chapter 8

On Safari in the Wild World

In the tame world of religion of the 1950s, the path to becoming a preacher was very simple for the young man with aspirations to add "Reverend" to his name. He chose a denomination and headed for their *seminary*, a specialized college where he would be trained in the theological foundation of the denomination, and taught various skills, from public speaking to counseling. If he was successful in his studies and approved by the denomination's leadership, he would be "ordained" and given credentials that qualified him to be hired as a pastor by any of the denomination's congregations. He might choose instead to become a missionary or a travelling evangelist, but he would still accomplish those goals under the auspices of his chosen denomination.

Seminaries still churn out would-be pastors in the 21st century. But they are no longer the only path to the pastorate. In recent decades, the "self-made minister" is becoming a more and more common phenomenon. These men and women do their own independent study of the Bible, and may create their own idiosyncratic theology. They pick up speaking and writing skills by the seat of their pants. And then they declare themselves ready to spread their own brand of the Gospel, and gather their own disciples and supporters. It is may be surprising to many to learn that one does not need any specific education to be recognized by the government of many states as a "clergyman," with the authority to officiate at weddings, start a church congregation, collect offerings, and more. In Michigan, for instance, the would-be minister, if questioned about his credentials, only has to show evidence that a group (of any size) of people accept him as their spiritual leader. And then he will be afforded all the same rights and privileges as the pastor of the 500-member Methodist congregation who attended seminary for six years and has a Master of Divinity degree.

Most large church denominations still insist that the clergymen that serve their congregations have a seminary education, whether in a denominational seminary or one that serves multiple denominations. But the fastest-growing movements in the Wild World of Religion these days are often characterized by leaders and congregations with no denominational affiliations. These independent religious groups and their pastors invent and reinvent themselves as they develop. They may form loose alliances with other independent groups, with which they share the same emphases on certain topics. Most of the time, they are accountable to no central authority of any kind. This can, in some cases, be viewed as a positive situation. It can provide an environment in which a preacher can promote his own version of the Gospel without fear that someone will censor his efforts, causing him to have to "water down" his message. But, on the negative side, it can provide an environment in which an unscrupulous leader can deceive and abuse his followers without fear that some greater authority will step in and intervene.

The variety of religious groups and movements in the United States to choose from these days is wide indeed. It would fill a whole book to just name them all. And it would take several encyclopedia-sized sets of books to provide even minimal descriptions of their teachings and activities. But there are four such movements that have been very influential in changing the landscape of the Wild World of Religion in the past few decades. The next four chapters will take the reader on safari to get a closer look at these four movements. Although some individual leaders who are involved in the development and promotion of these movements are affiliated with historical church denominations, a large number of them are, indeed, independent entrepreneurs, accountable to no one but themselves.

End Times Prophecy Movement

Men and women have been predicting the imminent return of Jesus since His departure from Earth in the first century. The approach of the year 1000 AD saw a flurry of wild prophetic speculations regarding this event. The mid-1800s was also a period that saw the rise of a number of Millennial groups that believed their job was to warn people to "Repent for the End is Nigh!" But the advent of the specter of nuclear war since the 1950s has fueled an explosion in the number of ministries that have, as their primary emphasis, the promotion of the prophetic speculations of their founders. The financial success of the *Left Behind* series of books and movies is evidence of the fascination of the masses, including those with no church affiliation, with the possibility that we are, indeed, living in the End Times.

Word Faith Movement

Throughout much of the history of Christianity, living modestly and frugally, and patiently enduring suffering, have often been considered signs of true spirituality. Only the relative affluence of late 20th century America could have spawned a movement that literally insists that it is God's intention for every believer to be perpetually healthy and wealthy. The opulent TV studio sets populated by Word Faith evangelists, sometimes looking more like the gaudy décor of a brothel in the Old West than a modern living room, seem to give hope to those watching. If only they can appropriate the same formulas of faith used by these endlessly cheerful performers, they too can drive a Rolls and wear a Rolex!

Healing Ministries Movement

If one were to believe all the claims of some of the preachers in the Healing Ministries Movement, it would be puzzling why there are any hospitals left. There'd be no need for them. All that would be necessary would be for the Healing Evangelist to come hold Miracle Healing Explosions in hospital parking lots across the land, and have the staffs wheel out all the patients for an encounter with the "Man with God's Anointing." Unfortunately, years of investigation by sincere researchers have been unable to substantiate the grandiose claims of astonishing miracles of healing that have created huge followings for many of these preachers.

Hebrew Roots Movement

Jesus Christ of Nazareth was born into a Jewish family. His disciples were all Jewish, as were almost all the people he preached to throughout his ministry years. In order to understand some of the circumstances described in both the Old and New Testaments, and some of the analogies and metaphors used by Jesus, it would obviously be helpful to know what Jewish society was like in New Testament times, as well as what Israelite society was like in Old Testament times. Those involved in the Hebrew Roots Movement are convinced that teaching about the "Hebrew Roots of Jesus" (sometimes called the "Jewish Roots of Jesus") has been sadly lacking in most churches. So, all across America, former Protestant ministers are giving themselves the title "Rabbi" instead of "Reverend," and starting "Messianic Assemblies." Their gatherings may feature "Hebraic" music, blowing ram's horn shofars, wearing prayer shawls, learning Hebrew, studying the teachings of the historical rabbis such as those in the Talmud, and more. Although this movement had very little influence outside limited circles a decade ago, it has taken off in popularity in recent years. Hebrew Roots teachings are showing up in all sorts of strange settings—including in programs on the Trinity Broadcasting Network. Some Charismatics are even referring to the Hebrew Roots Movement as the "Fourth Wave" of restoration of the Full Gospel.

The *Who's Who Digest* chapter includes many names of men and women who are involved in one or the other of these movements. In fact, it is becoming more and more common for individuals to be involved in more than one. For indeed, the teachers and preachers who are leaders in these movements have begun cross-pollinating, yielding many strange new hybrid breeds of religious diversity in the Wild World of Religion.

Chapter 9

End Times Prophecy Movement

The Claims

A growing number of ministries, groups, and individual teachers are dedicated to promoting the message that we are living in the last generation before the Return of Christ. They have widely divergent teachings concerning the details of just how current world conditions and events fit into the biblical scenario of "the End Times." But they all agree that "prophecy is being fulfilled daily," and that it is extremely important for Christians to be able to understand "the times in which they live." They believe it is so important that they are convinced that sharing their own version of prophetic speculation ought to be an integral part of the preaching of the Gospel.

Although most denominations, religious groups, and Bible teachers have a specific point of view about some of the debatable issues of Bible prophecy, most give a fairly low priority to coverage of this topic in the bigger scheme of their belief system. Those groups, teachers, and ministries that are a part of the general End Times Prophecy Movement, on the other hand, place issues of Bible prophecy squarely in the middle of the reason for the existence of their group or their ministry. Although they may address other issues of biblical doctrine and Christian living principles, such topics are in the minority in their teaching recordings, magazine articles, television and radio programs, personal appearances at seminars and conventions, and on their websites. It is not usually their teaching of the Bible in general that attracts new prospective supporters, but rather their prophetic speculation schemes. And although their listeners and supporters may adopt their perspective on a variety of other doctrinal matters, it is the prophecy teaching that establishes the credibility of such teachers in the minds of their followers.

The Allure

We live in a world full of turmoil. Especially since the events of 9/11/01, many people have much less of a sense of basic security than they have ever experienced before. More and more are fearful, not just of specific problems such as terrorist acts or wars, but of "the unknown" in general. The attacks on the World Trade Center and the Pentagon made it clear that there are forces in the world that could conspire to unleash the "totally unexpected" in a way never before experienced in the U.S..

Into this swirling uncertainty step teachers who claim to have The Keys to unlocking a future that is certain. They claim to be able to *unveil* the future so that their followers can have the assurance of knowing what's next in the unfolding of history. Even though not one of them agrees totally with any other one of them regarding the details of these keys or the process of this unveiling, that makes little difference to those who are attracted to each one. For few people ever bother to **compare** the teachings of a wide variety of these teachers and groups. It is typical for an individual Bible student to be attracted to just **one** source of prophetic teaching, and to invest all of his/her energy into absorbing every bit of minutia put out by that one source.

They are usually not disappointed. Most End Times Prophecy ministries put out an endless stream of "amazing information"—at least once a month in a newsletter, perhaps once a week if they have a regular television show, and even more frequently if they have a website. This adds to their allure for those who wish to be constantly reassured with new evidence that their chosen prophecy guru is able to open the secrets of the Bible in regard to the times in which we live. In addition, the fact that they are kept in the know by their guru may give them a sense that they are among an elite group that has the special favor of God. Many such teachers feed this sense by affirming that their ministry is so important to the "Plan of God" for the world that supporters of that ministry are, indeed, part of what might be termed a *Spiritual Special Forces* brigade.

Concerns

The primary purpose of prophecy in the Bible, even *predictive* prophecy, is to clarify to specific people what God plans to do **to** them or **for** them—based upon their own actions. The focus is not on the **event** that may come, but on the **hearts** of the people involved. Nations whose leadership and citizenry are involved in blatant disobedience toward God are warned to repent to avert His anger. Nations that are discouraged because they are under chastisement from God are encouraged with promises of a bright future **if** they will turn and obey. It is also clear that many of these promises of good and evil are based on universal principles—**any** nation which will undertake to serve God can count on His eventual blessings; **any** which turn their back on Him can count on His eventual intervention to discipline them.

In this context, study of Bible prophecy is a useful tool to encourage the individual Christian, or groups of Christians, to consider carefully the fruit of obedience and disobedience to God.

But this is not the usual emphasis of End Times Prophecy pundits and groups. Although they may occasionally mention this aspect of Bible prophecy, they are usually much more focused on "figuring out" a chronological scheme for exactly what God is going to do in the near future. And it is here that danger lies for the individual Christian who may be tempted to be swept up into active involvement in such a ministry. For most of the teaching about Bible prophecy is not really about Bible prophecy in general, but on what is termed in theological circles as biblical *apocalypse*.

Prophecy and Apocalypse

A biblical prophet is an individual who speaks on behalf of God, to deliver a message from Him to an individual or a group. Although the common use of the word *prophecy* in modern English implies a "prediction about the future," this is not technically what the message of a prophet is all about. The prophets of the Bible gave many messages to others that were not specific predictions of what was absolutely going to happen. They were, instead, warnings, chastisement, or encouragement from God. Sometimes those messages would include information about the future, but that was not the essence of the prophecy. In many instances, even the predictions about the future were *conditional*. The people of the ancient nation of Israel at Mount Sinai were given a message from God through Moses. It told what would happen to them if they obeyed, and what would happen to them if they disobeyed. Moses was functioning as a prophet to declare the word of the Lord to them.

What most people commonly consider Bible prophecy—the dogmatic, unconditional prediction of coming events—is technically termed *apocalypse*. The word means a *revealing*, and the implication is that these things being revealed are predestined to come to pass no matter what mankind does or doesn't do. Much of the book of Daniel in the Old Testament is apocalypse, as is the book of Revelation. (The Greek word translated *revelation* in the book of Revelation is *apokalupsis*.) In this type of prophecy in the Bible, the future is most often outlined in shadowy metaphors of symbolic beasts and other startling symbolic phenomena. The over-arching, primary purpose of these passages seems to be to reassure the servants of God that, even though evil times are to come upon the earth, the ultimate outcome will be the victory of the forces of God and good over the forces of the Devil and evil.

Thus, in general:

An *apocalyptic* message is not given by a prophet
to **sinners** to **call them to repentance**—
it is given to **saints** to **give them hope**.

47

While *apocalypse* is a **kind** of prophecy,
most prophecy in the Bible **is not** *apocalyptic*.

As noted in this overview, *apocalypse* is the kind of prophecy that is not "conditional" upon the actions and attitude of specific people or nations. It is straight "looking into the future." And thus End Times Prophecy pundits are convinced that, if they just peer hard enough into the apocalyptic passages, they will be able see a crystal clear view of the future. Unfortunately for their listeners and supporters, this view is all too often not **crystal clear** quality, but crystal **ball** quality! For the apocalyptic messages as delivered from God to the biblical prophets were almost all couched in metaphorical terms, employing highly symbolic images, full of fantastic beasts and strange terrestrial and heavenly phenomena.

When ancient King Nebuchadnezzar of Babylon had a strange, symbolic dream, he turned to the Jewish prophet Daniel, whose people were in exile in Babylon at the time, for an interpretation. What did Daniel do in order to understand the meaning of those strange symbols? Did he return to his Babylonian dorm room and get out his scrolls of the scriptures, his concordance scrolls, his history scrolls, his lexicon scrolls, and other research materials ... and try to "figure out" the dream that way? No. He returned to his Jewish companions and asked them to pray with him that God would **give** him the interpretation. And He did.

But what do most End Times prophecy pundits do with material in the book of Revelation—and those portions of the book of Daniel that were not explained to Daniel—in order to understand the future? They get out their Bible translations, their Interlinear Greek/Hebrew/English Bibles, their Greek and Hebrew lexicons, their history books, their newspapers, and their calculators. And they try to humanly crack the code of the meaning of the shadowy types and strange symbolism.

> A thing that strikes one who browses around in the vast literature that has grown up about the book of Revelation is the UTTER DOGMATISM with which so many put forth their opinions, not as opinions, but in categorical statements, as to the meaning of the most mysterious passages, as if they know all about it, and their say so settles the matter. We think a spirit of reverent humility, and openness of mind, would be more becoming in those seeking to interpret a book like this. (Henry Halley, *Halley's Bible Handbook*, 24th ed., p. 684)

Wise counsel! Why has it been so widely ignored among modern commentators? One possible answer: With a limited audience among which to garner supporters for evangelistic ministries, the most dogmatic and bombastic teachers are often the most successful at gathering around themselves the most enthusiastic—and financially generous—followers.

The desire for security mentioned in the introduction to this profile is so strong that many teachers are even able to hedge their prophetic interpretations, sprinkling them with the very occasional use of words like "possibly," "probably," and "maybe." Yet most of their followers filter out these words and hear only "thus sayeth the Lord." The dogmatic and bombastic style of speaking and writing of the teacher in the sections before and after the "hedge words" is so loud that those feeble words are overpowered and forgotten.

This type of teacher has been extant for almost 1900 years now. Each was sure that the events of Revelation and the other apocalyptic passages in the Bible would play out in his own lifetime. Each contrived elaborate proofs that his speculation wasn't just speculation, but trustworthy biblical exposition. Each gathered a following based not on his spiritual maturity as a leader, or the fruits of his service to others, or the soundness of his biblical teaching regarding the Gospel message. He gathered a following based on the enthusiasm engendered by his prophetic speculations.

Most Bible students who become enamored of the speculations of a particular prophecy teacher in our time have no clue that scenarios very similar to that of their teacher may have been dogmatically and bombastically proclaimed to be "imminent" ... decades or a century or more ago. Those earlier teachers may have used some of the same calculations and reasoning regarding Bible passages, and yet arrived at a certainty that the events were just about to happen in 1844, or 1914, or 1972.

Perhaps you have been intrigued by the speculations of a radio or TV prophecy expert, and have been fascinated by what appears to be his incredible ability to interpret obscure passages of prophecy and apocalypse. Maybe you are tempted to begin investing in more and more of this teacher's materials, to drive long distances to hear him speak at a seminar or convention, and even to become involved in fellowship groups that are forming around his teachings. Or perhaps a friend or family member appears about to become deeply involved in a group led by a prophecy pundit. Maybe he or she is even ready to make some drastic life choices that will be hard to "undo," based on the teachings of this guru. If so, you may find the **Examination** section below, which includes an overview of the history of End Times prophetic speculation, of assistance in evaluating the wisdom of your plans, or in dissuading a friend or family member from making foolish choices. And if you would like information on specific End Times Prophecy teachers, see the **Who's Who Digest.**

You may also find it helpful to read the **When Prophecy Fails** chapter that follows, which explains what often happens to followers of self-proclaimed prophets and prophecy interpreters when their prophecies or interpretations are proven false.

Examination

Teachers and groups proclaiming that the fulfillments of major Bible prophecies are imminent have been around since the time of Christ. The following are just a tiny few examples of such up to the 1800s. (Abbreviations of titles in the citations refer to books in the bibliography at the end of this chapter.)

> In the second half of the second century, a Christian convert named Montanus succeeded in convincing many that he had been given a personal revelation directly from God that the Second Coming was at hand. It would happen at Pepuza (near modern Angora). "The prophet's personality and eloquence won him a host of disciples, who flocked in such numbers to the appointed spot that a new town sprang up to house them." (P. Hughes, quoted in *WPF*, p. 6.)

> Joachim of Fiore (ca 1135-1202) a Catholic Abbot, did not believe in a literal second coming, but rather in a new stage of earthly influence on earth by the Church, which would come after the three and a half year rule of the Antichrist. He announced to Richard the Lionhearted in 1191 that the Antichrist had already been born. And he declared the end of the current age would be somewhere between 1200 and 1260, with the rule of Antichrist to immediately follow. A famine in Europe in 1258 and a plague in 1259 led to the rise of the "flagellants" (men who beat themselves in a form of public penance), many of whom were believers in Joachim's prediction regarding 1260. (*TLD*, pp. 50-51)

> An Anabaptist preacher of the early 1500s named Hoffman declared that the events of The End would begin in 1533, and that Strassburg would be the New Jerusalem. "... there the magistrates would set up the kingdom of righteousness, while the 144,000 would maintain the poor of the City, and the true Gospel and the true Baptism [adult immersion] would spread over the earth. No man would be able to withstand the power, signs and wonders of the saints; and with them would

appear, like two mighty torches, Enoch and Elias, who would consume the earth with the fire proceeding from their mouths." (Richard Heath, quoted in *WPF*, p. 7)

In the early 1600s, a common belief of many Jews was that the Messiah would appear in 1648. Just prior to that date, a young Jewish teacher named Sabbatai Zevi declared to his small group of disciples that he was the expected Messiah. Although the 1648 year passed without a public acknowledgement of Zevi's claims, he continued to gather followers. Around this same time, there arose speculation among Christians that the Millennium would begin in 1666, and Zevi seems to have latched onto that date. From 1651-1665 he continued to gather followers, and in the fall of 1665 "... he proclaimed himself the Messiah in a public ceremony in Smyrna: The madness of the Jews of Smyrna knew no bounds. Every sign of honor and enthusiastic love was shown to him ... All prepared for a speedy exodus, the return to the Holy Land. Workmen neglected their business and thought only of the approaching Kingdom of the Messiah."

In an attempt to go to Constantinople and depose the Muslim Sultan there, Zevi was captured and imprisoned by the Muslims. Rather than dampen the enthusiasm for Zevi's Messianic claims, this temporary setback was viewed as just a short time of suffering he must go through before his glorification. "A constant procession of adoring followers visited the prison where Sabbatai held court, and a steady stream of propaganda and tales of miracles poured out all over the Near East and Europe." As one contemporary European Jewess wrote, "Many sold their houses and lands and all their possessions, for any day they hoped to be redeemed. My good father-in-law left his home in Hamelm, abandoned his house and lands and all his goodly furniture and moved to Hildesheim. He sent on to us in Hamburg two enormous casks packed with linens and with peas, beans, dried meats, shredded prunes and like stuff, every manner of food that would keep. For the old man expected to sail any moment from Hamburg to the Holy Land."

The whole Movement came to a screeching halt when the Sultan persuaded Zevi to convert to Islam. (*WPF*, pp. 8-12)

51

Many in Britain were very wary of the year 1666 (1000+666) and thus, "Quaker George Fox wrote that in 1666 nearly every thunderstorm aroused end-time expectations." (*TLD*, p. 68)

Many more examples of this type of prediction are posted on *A Brief History of the Apocalypse*, a website that has a chart, spanning several webpages, of predictions of the End that were made from 2000 B.C to the present.

www.abhota.info/end1.htm

Up to the early 1800s, most prophetic speculators based their scenarios on a number of fairly vague premises. These included personal revelations, or the assumption that current conditions (plague, attacks of barbarians, astronomical phenomena) were so awful that it **must** mean The End was near. Dates were often chosen for mystical significance (multiples of 1000, or 500, or 666 and the like).

But the 1800s brought a new breed of prophecy speculators, with new, more "scientific" methods. Many of the factors that they built into their speculations are still common to this day. They have been compiled into a special chapter of this book called *Aunt Pam's Prophetic Recipe Collection*.

Evaluation

After the Resurrection of Jesus, and before His ascension to heaven, the following dialogue occurred between Him and His eleven Apostles:

> Acts 1:6-8
> So when they met together, they asked him, "Lord, are you at this time going to restore the kingdom to Israel?" He said to them: "**It is not for you to know the times or dates the Father has set by his own authority.** But you will receive power when the Holy Spirit comes on you; and you will be my witnesses in Jerusalem, and in all Judea and Samaria, and to the ends of the earth." (NIV)

Jesus made it clear He wasn't going to reveal the exact details of future events even to His closest followers. So it isn't clear why so many Bible teachers who have come along in the intervening centuries have felt that He **did** reveal to **them** these details. From that day to this there has been a continual stream of prophecy pundits who have claimed to have unlocked the keys to the apocalyptic passages of scriptures which would reveal those things which Jesus said it was not for His Apostles to know. Generation after generation, they have put forth their speculations—never couched in tentative terms, but rather in dogmatic predictions—that He was going to return in their own generation and inaugurate The Kingdom. Some have claimed to have received specific, personal communication from the Lord regarding these matters. Even more have claimed to have special inspiration to interpret the Bible, so that the hidden meanings would be revealed. And all of these have managed to convince others of the validity of their schemes of prophetic interpretation, and thus gather a following of True Believers around themselves.

Some have specifically pin-pointed an exact date for the fulfillment of a prophetic event that would signal the End of the Age. This might be the date for the beginning of the final Tribulation period, the date for the Rapture of the Church, or the date for the actual Return of Christ in glory. More common than this have been those who have set a "time frame" for one of these events, using terms such as "in the next three to five years," or "before the end of this coming decade." And even more common have been those who have merely insisted it would be "within the lifetime of most of those now living." At this point in history, it doesn't really make much difference which one of these styles of date setting that such teachers from past centuries have used. For **all** of their predictions have failed. **All** of the dates have passed, **all** of the decades have passed, and **all** of the generations have passed.

And yet none of this has slowed down the current crop of those in this century who would insist that this time around they really, really have got it all figured out. This time around the keys **will** work—sometimes even the same keys used in the past by others who are now long dead, and whose prophetic ministries died with them! Why can this same pattern keep repeating itself? Because many of these teachers and most of their students have absolutely no historical frame of reference regarding the pattern of failed prophetic speculation. They have no idea that their "air-tight scenarios" have been suggested before, and have been proven false. They have no idea that the systems of calculation they use to connect various obscure prophecies historically have also been used over and over to add up to failure.

Why do they continue to want to make it work? The usual explanation is that the sure knowledge that Jesus will come within your own lifetime should make the average Christian more "diligent" in their Christian walk, and startle the average non-Christian into wanting to "get right with the Lord." Thus many prophetic ministries view their speculations as sure-fire **evangelistic** tools to use on the "lost" and **revival** tools to use on the "saved." This sounds like a good plan perhaps to those with no historic

53

frame of reference. But the record of all the ministries of the past which have used these tools shows that the fall-out from the failure of the speculations can do far more harm than the fruit that is borne for the short time between the prediction and the failure. When a new believer hops on the bandwagon of a prophetic speculation out of fear of the wrath of Jesus at the Return, the commitment he has made is not to the true Gospel, but to the supposed way of escape from a feared event. When that event fails to materialize, what might this do to the commitment?

Sociological and historical studies have shown that there are three typical responses:

1. When the event fails to transpire, some become totally disillusioned, not just with the failed prophecy and the false prophet or prophetic teacher, but often with religion in general and perhaps even with God.

2. Others are unwilling to give up so easily if they have invested much emotionally and physically in participation with the prophetic movement in question. They may attempt to reason around the failure and make excuses for it. The prophetic teacher may explain that he just made some miscalculations and that the scenario is accurate, but the timing just a bit off. Thus the predictions are just moved forward a few months or years, and the most dedicated True Believers will redouble their efforts to get even more converts for the teacher. For, psychologically, if more people can be persuaded to believe what you believe, it gives you more confidence in your beliefs! Of course, eventually the adjusted dates will come and go also. And eventually ministries and groups built on this sort of failed speculation will fade away, with the followers drifting off to find other teachers to feed their need for certainty in the face of troubled times. Many such folks drift from teacher to teacher and ministry to ministry throughout their whole lives.

3. If there were just too many explicit details in the scenario that cannot be shifted to a different timeframe, the prophetic teacher or some of his followers may work hard at creating a *spiritual* fulfillment to explain the prophetic failure. In other

words, they may suggest that everything did happen right on time, but they just hadn't realized that it wasn't to take place in the visible, physical world. The scenario was, rather, symbolic of events to happen "in heaven" or "in the spiritual realm." This makes it impossible for anyone to prove that the scenario was false. Such a turn of events can leave the True Believers the victims of ridicule and criticism by outsiders near the time of the failure. But if they can weather the storm, within a few years their literature can play down the original expectations and play up the spiritual perspective. With the strong emotions of the time of failure in the distant past, this kind of gimmick can become established as part of a religious movement that endures, such as the Jehovah's Witnesses and Seventh Day Adventists.

None of these three outcomes is spiritually healthy for those who have been involved with supporting a speculative End Times prophecy ministry that has, in whatever way, predicted the End to come in a specified period.

What, then, of those ministries which avoid being quite so specific, and merely insist that Jesus is coming "soon"? They claim that they have sorted out all the apocalyptic symbolism that will help their students to see the prophecies unfold "in our time." Since they have not presented a timeframe for their predictions but, perhaps, just an explanation of the "sequence" of coming events, should there be concern about the effect this kind of teaching may have on the spiritual health of those who become fascinated by such a ministry?

The naïve Christian who gets swept up in a specific date, and may thus make some foolish life choices in order to get on board the ministry of one of the date-setters, may suffer the most from making End Times prophecy a centerpiece of their Christian walk. But those who buy into the ministries of one of these "milder" prophecy teachers may also fall victim to a serious challenge to their own walk. The obsession with reading more and more articles and books on End Times prophecy, with watching End Times prophecy programs on TV, and with attending End Times prophecy conferences and seminars may result in the immature Christian being the victim of what can best be termed **Time Wasters**.

Jesus gave a number of parables to warn people to "be ready" when their Lord returned. But what did He indicate was "being ready"? Was it "knowing the day and hour" when He would come? Was it sorting out all the obscure symbolism of apocalyptic passages in the Bible? Was it spending most of one's free time with the study of such things?

Or was it *living out* the Sermon on the Mount and the other teachings of Jesus?

> Matthew 25:31-40
> "When the Son of Man comes in his glory, and all the angels with him, he will sit on his throne in heavenly glory. All the nations will be gathered before him, and he will separate the people one from another as a shepherd separates the sheep from the goats. He will put the sheep on his right and the goats on his left. "Then the King will say to those on his right, 'Come, you who are blessed by my Father; take your inheritance, the kingdom prepared for you since the creation of the world. For I was hungry and you gave me something to eat, I was thirsty and you gave me something to drink, I was a stranger and you invited me in, I needed clothes and you clothed me, I was sick and you looked after me, I was in prison and you came to visit me.' "Then the righteous will answer him, 'Lord, when did we see you hungry and feed you, or thirsty and give you something to drink? When did we see you a stranger and invite you in, or needing clothes and clothe you? When did we see you sick or in prison and go to visit you?' "The King will reply, 'I tell you the truth, whatever you did for one of the least of these brothers of mine, you did for me.' (NIV)

Prophecy is a part of the Bible. Bible study will include a study of those prophecies. This is all good and right. But **studying the endless speculations of supposed "prophecy experts" is not the same thing as studying the Bible**. When someone becomes addicted to the teachings of one or several of these self-proclaimed experts, spending more and more money on their books and tapes, spending more and more time on their broadcasts and conferences, there is a real danger that such a student will have the illusion that he is "pleasing God" with all of this "effort" and "investment." He may never realize that God would be much more pleased if he would invest that same amount of time, money, and energy on doing good to his neighbor, and spreading the **full** Gospel ... not just the shallow "gospel" of one more speculative prophetic scenario that is doomed to fail like all the others of the past 2000 years.

At the end of the Sermon on the Mount, Jesus warned His disciples what to do with the words He had taught them:

Matthew 7:21-24

"Not everyone who says to me, 'Lord, Lord,' will enter the kingdom of heaven, but only he who does the will of my Father who is in heaven. Many will say to me on that day, 'Lord, Lord, **did we not prophesy in your name**, and in your name drive out demons and perform many miracles?' Then I will tell them plainly, 'I never knew you. Away from me, you evildoers!' "Therefore everyone who **hears these words of mine and puts them into practice** is like a wise man who built his house on the rock."

And Paul later put prophetic understanding in perspective also:

1 Corinthians 13:1-13
If I speak in the tongues of men and of angels, but have not love, I am only a resounding gong or a clanging cymbal. **If I have the gift of prophecy and can fathom all mysteries and all knowledge**, and if I have a faith that can move mountains, but have not love, I am nothing. If I give all I possess to the poor and surrender my body to the flames, but have not love, I gain nothing. Love is patient, love is kind. It does not envy, it does not boast, it is not proud. It is not rude, it is not self-seeking, it is not easily angered, it keeps no record of wrongs. Love does not delight in evil but rejoices with the truth. It always protects, always trusts, always hopes, always perseveres. Love never fails. But **where there are prophecies, they will cease**; where there are tongues, they will be stilled; where there is knowledge, it will pass away. For **we know in part and we prophesy in part,** but when perfection comes, the imperfect disappears. When I was a child, I talked like a child, I thought like a child, I reasoned like a child. When I became a man, I put childish ways behind me. Now we see but a poor reflection as in a mirror; then we shall see face to face. Now I know in part; then I shall know fully, even as I am fully known. And now these three remain: faith, hope and love. But the greatest of these is love.

It is impossible to find a Bible passage that praises those who speculate on the meaning of obscure prophetic passages of the Bible. But there is much praise for those who will live out this kind of love in their life.

Personal note from the Author

My interest in failed End Times Prophecy scenarios is not just academic. At one time I was an avid member of a group that was a key player in the End Times Prophecy Movement, the Worldwide Church of God (WCG), led by founder Herbert Armstrong. I have seen first-hand the havoc that can be wrought in the lives of those who get swept up in such obsessions.

When my husband, George, and I first became involved with the WCG in the mid-1960s, three of the main evangelistic booklets distributed by the organization were titled *1975 in Prophecy*, *The United States and British Commonwealth in Prophecy*, and *Will Russia Invade America?* The *1975 in Prophecy* booklet insisted that Christ was going to return to the earth to set up His Millennial Kingdom by 1975, and that prior to this would be a time of terrible trouble called the Great Tribulation. The other booklets declared that the popular prophetic scenario of the time, in which Russia would attack America as part of End Times events, was incorrect. Armstrong was adamant that the final "Beast power" described in Revelation and Daniel would be a united Europe under the leadership of a German leader, and that it would attack and defeat America, taking many Americans to slave labor camps in Europe. Most issues of Armstrong's monthly *Plain Truth* magazine included articles that reinforced these scenarios, as well as other articles presenting many other doctrinal and daily living concepts.

We became official members of the church in 1968, and at that point learned of a prophetic detail that was not publicized in the non-member literature we had been receiving. The Church taught that its members were going to be miraculously transported three and a half years before the Second Coming to a *Place of Safety*, which was strongly speculated to be the site of the ancient abandoned city of Petra in Jordan. (If you have seen the movie *Indiana Jones and the Last Crusade*, Petra is the site of the pink buildings carved out of the cliffs at the end of the film.) There the membership would be in special "training" for their roles as leaders in the Millennium, after their physical bodies were changed to spirit bodies at the Return of Christ.

The proofs offered for all these details of prophetic fulfillments were based on reasonings that I now realize to be quite common in the past 200 years. What I was not aware of was that many of the same elements used in Armstrong's speculations had been used by many other self-styled prophecy experts, with only minor variations, to prove that The End would be in 1844, 1864, 1874, 1878, 1881, 1910, 1914, 1925, and many other dates. I was further unaware that even Armstrong himself had dogmatically announced in one of the earliest issues of the *Plain Truth*, in 1934, that the prophetic time period known as the *Day of the Lord* would begin in 1936, with the Second Coming to follow shortly thereafter.

I was totally naïve regarding religion when I began studying the literature published by Armstrong's ministry. I had never read any of the Bible, and had no historical perspective on religious movements which had preceded Armstrong. As many self-proclaimed prophecy experts do, Armstrong would couch his writings in a way that made you feel you were asking questions and getting solid answers from the Bible. In reality, what was actually happening was that he was feeding you the exact questions he wanted you to ponder, so that he could give you the narrow, canned answers he had prepared.

Looking back now, I can see that the proofs offered for these prophetic predictions were utterly speculative—and often utterly fallacious. But looking around at the current crop of prophecy pundits, I see that many, if not most, of them are using the exact same tactics to this day. And they are successful in gathering followings in the same way Armstrong's teachings drew me into his organization.

Prior to 1972, many members of the Worldwide Church of God made choices about such things as family finances based on the expectation that they would not **need** family finances after 1972! Many gave large amounts of money to Armstrong's organization in the belief that they were helping support his evangelistic efforts "in the gun-lap of preaching the Gospel." Over the years, some even took out loans or mortgaged their homes and sent the money to Church headquarters, at Armstrong's urging, based on his speculations. When 1972 came and went without the Tribulation starting, and without any hint of fleeing to Petra, many in Armstrong's group were bewildered. But most were pacified by the excuses given for the prophetic failures, and many continued to sacrifice their own family's security to support Armstrong's ministry. Thus we stayed on with the Worldwide Church of God until 1978. At that point a major shake-up in the leadership at the Church headquarters disillusioned us totally, and we left to become part of a split-off group formed by Herbert Armstrong's son, Garner Ted Armstrong. (For further details about our personal experiences in the WCG, see the *Afterword: Personal from the Author*.)

In recent years, I have found our experiences in the WCG were quite typical of the experiences of many others who have been swept up by enthusiasm for prophetic scenarios which claim to offer readers, as Armstrong bragged in the title of one of his booklets, *The Key to the Book of Revelation.* After studying the materials of a wide variety of other self-styled prophetic experts, I am fully convinced that **none** of them have that Key. They just seem to have the Key to wasting the time, money, energy, and enthusiasm of naïve people. I am not judging the hearts of any specific prophecy pundits—I don't doubt that many of them believe their own hype. But I do question their methods, their reasoning, and their conclusions—which, in most cases, are just clones of those that have gone before, with only slight adjustments.

In the field of End Times Prophecy speculation, as in many other areas of life, the advice "Let the buyer beware!" is extremely applicable.

Bibliography

The following books, along with many other resources, were consulted in preparation for compiling the information for this section of this **Field Guide**. They provide an overview and extensive documentation regarding a variety of prophetic ministries and teachers. See the **Web Resources and Books for Further Research** chapter for more information on each book.

Apocalypse Delayed: The Story of Jehovah's Witnesses

Armageddon Now! The Premillenarian Response to Russia and Israel Since 1917

The Disappointed: Millerism and Millenarianism in the Nineteenth Century

Doomsday Delusions: What's Wrong with Predictions About the End of the World?

End Time Visions: The Road to Armageddon?

The Gentile Times Reconsidered: Chronology and Christ's Return

The Last Days Are Here Again **(TLD)**

Naming the Antichrist: The History of an American Obsession

The Sign of the Last Days: When?

Soothsayers of the Second Advent

When Prophecy Fails **(WPF)**

When Time Shall Be No More: Prophecy Belief in Modern American Culture

Chapter 10

When Prophecy Fails

From the time that the Gospel of Luke first recorded the description of Jesus Christ returning to heaven after His resurrection, there have been people yearning so badly for His return to Earth that they have pored over the prophecies of the Bible to try to "discern the times" in which they lived. Every generation of Christians has hoped they were living in the time when, as the beloved old hymn "It is Well With My Soul" quotes the Bible, the clouds would "be rolled back as a scroll, the trump shall resound, and the Lord shall descend" to put an end to Man's miserable rule over Man.

And in many of those generations, Bible students have been convinced that they have been able to determine, through the prophetic hints in the Bible, that Jesus was, indeed, coming soon—in the lifetime of most living in their own generation! Not content with just the general hope, many have also worked out elaborate mathematical schemes whereby they could pinpoint not just the generation, but the decade, the year, the month, perhaps even the day that their "blessed hope" would be fulfilled.

This phenomenon has increased greatly in the past two centuries, and even more in the past two decades. Teacher after teacher, group after group has arisen to publish magazines, books, pamphlets, study guides, and more to convince others of the certainty of their predictions of chronological details of the Return. Thousands of lectures and sermons have been given, and thousands of TV and radio programs have been recorded, all with the primary aim of persuading the public to get on the bandwagon of the latest prediction of the year of the start of the Great Tribulation, or the Rapture, or even the Coming of the Lord Himself.

The pace of this speculation grew even more frantic in some religious circles as the year 2000 approached. Even those who didn't normally focus on dates seemed to be mesmerized by the number of zeros after the 2! Surely, thought many, the Lord will tarry no longer than the end of the millennium. Thus dogmatic pronouncements regarding specific dates were plastered on websites, trumpeted on radio talk shows, and circulated in newsletters. Many ministries have arisen with the primary goal of bringing together in fellowship, under one teacher or group, those who were convinced of the prophetic scenario of that teacher or group. Each of these may have also taught elements of the Gospel and truths from the scriptures, but in many settings these almost seemed to be an afterthought. The biggest publicity, the most printed material, the most time on radio and TV, the most "bandwidth" on the Internet was devoted to endless feeding of the desires of followers for more and more details about the prophetic scenario.

To date, **all** of these many, many, many prophetic pronouncements of the past 2000 years have failed.

"When prophecy fails," what happens to all those faithful supporters whose generous tithes and offerings made the programs, publications, and personal appearances to promote the prophecies possible? *Common sense* would suggest that they would abandon the ministries that had misled them. *Common sense* would indicate they would accept the reality of the failure and get on with their lives, adjusting their priorities to give more attention to Bible basics and daily Christian living.

Common sense would be incorrect.

Cognitive Dissonance

There is a famous book from the 1950s, required reading in many Social Psychology courses for decades, titled *When Prophecy Fails*. The researchers preparing the book, led by social psychologist Leon Festinger, stumbled on a "flying saucer cult," just then forming, which was predicting The End. They had previously studied the historical records regarding doomsday groups of the past 2000 years that had dogmatically predicted dates for the Return of Christ or the End of the World. As a result, they had developed some theories about what happens to members of such groups when their expected prophecy fails. They outline those theories in the beginning of the book, and then describe their case study of the new cult, to clarify for the reader their conclusions regarding whether their theories applied to it. They did, perfectly.

One of the major innovations to psychological thought pioneered by this book was author Festinger's proposition of the theory of *cognitive dissonance*. This theory has since been applied to other modern groups, and found to be amazingly accurate much of the time. Below is an excerpt from a website that very effectively uses the theory to evaluate what happened in the Jehovah's Witness denomination in the late 1970s. The leadership of the Witness organization dogmatically insisted that the beginning of the visible Kingdom on earth would occur in 1975. The year 1975 came and passed with no fulfillment of the expectations promoted by the organization. The excerpt here is introductory material that explains the basis of the cognitive dissonance theory. The whole document, explaining how the theory applies to the Witness experience, is available on the Internet at:

www.freeminds.org/psych/propfail.htm

Leon Festinger's Theory

In studying this phenomena, credit must be given to Leon Festinger for his *cognitive dissonance* theory, as developed in his book

When Prophecy Fails, originally published in 1956 and co-authored by Festinger, Henry W. Riecken and Stanley Schachter. The authors comprised a research team who conducted a study of a small cult-following of a Mrs. Marian Keech, a housewife who claimed to receive messages from aliens via automatic writing. The message of the aliens was one of a coming world cataclysm, but with the hope of surviving for the elect who listened to them through Keech and selected other mediums. What Festinger and his associates demonstrated in the end was that the failure of prophecy often has the opposite effect of what the average person might expect; the cult following often gets stronger and the members even more convinced of the truth of their actions and beliefs! This unique paradox is the focus of attention in this article, and will be later applied specifically to the Jehovah's Witness movement.

Festinger observes:

A man with a conviction is a hard man to change. Tell him you disagree and he turns away. Show him facts or figures and he questions your sources. Appeal to logic and he fails to see your point. We have all experienced the futility of trying to change a strong conviction, especially if the convinced person has some investment in his belief. We are familiar with the variety of ingenious defenses with which people protect their convictions, managing to keep them unscathed through the most devastating attacks. But man's resourcefulness goes beyond simply protecting a belief. Suppose an individual believes something with his whole heart; suppose further that he has a commitment to this belief, that he has taken irrevocable actions because of it; finally, suppose that he is presented with evidence, unequivocal and undeniable evidence, that his belief is wrong: what will happen? The individual will frequently emerge, not only unshaken, but even more convinced of the truth of his beliefs than ever before. Indeed, he may even show a new fervor about convincing and converting other people to his view.

When Prophecy Fails focuses on the failure of prophecies to come true, termed *disconfirmation* by Festinger, and the accompanied renewal of energy and faith in their source of divine guidance. His theory presupposes the cult having certain identifying features, such as: (a) belief held with deep conviction along with respective actions taken, (b) the belief or prediction must be specific enough to be disconfirmed (i.e., it didn't happen), (c) the believer is a member of a group of like-minded believers who support one another and even proselytize. All of these characteristics were present in the saucer cult.

Of particular interest in Festinger's book is how the followers of Mrs. Keech reacted to each disconfirmation (failed date). Little attempt was made to deny the failure. The strength to continue in the movement was derived, not largely from the rationalizations , but from the very energy of the group itself and its dedication to the cause. This explains why proselytizing was so successful later in reinforcing the group's sagging belief system. Festinger relates:

But whatever explanation is made, it is still by itself not sufficient. The dissonance is too important and though they may try to hide it, even from themselves, the believers still know that the prediction was false and all their preparations were in vain. The dissonance cannot be eliminated completely by denying or rationalizing the disconfirmation. But there is a way in which the remaining dissonance can be reduced. If more and more people can be persuaded that the system of belief is correct, then clearly it must, after all, be correct. Consider the extreme case: if everyone in the whole world believed something there would be no question at all as to the validity of this belief. It is for this reason that we observe the increase in proselytizing following disconfirmation. If the proselytizing proves successful, then by gathering more adherents and effectively surrounding himself with supporters, the believer reduces dissonance to the point where he can live with it.

In the end, the members of the flying saucer cult did not give up their faith in the Guardians from outer space with their promises of a new world. Despite numerous prophecies and the resultant disappointment accentuated by many personal sacrifices, the group remained strong.
(End of excerpt)

Personal from the Author

I first encountered Festinger's book, and the theory of cognitive dissonance, while taking a course in Social Psychology at Michigan State University in 1974. The book was required reading. At the time, my husband and I had been members of the Worldwide Church of God (WCG) for six years, and we had been diligently studying the group's literature for several years before that. Founder Herbert W. Armstrong had been bombastically declaring to his supporters that the year 1972 was the deadline for The Church to be whisked to "The Place of Safety" prior to the Great Tribulation, which would be followed by Christ's Return in 1975. When the dogmatic 1972 prediction failed, a number of followers had become disillusioned and left the organization, but a large percentage had not. At the time, it did not occur to me to apply the information I was learning in the course to my own personal circumstances! But it surely did apply.

In looking back and examining why I was not totally disillusioned by the disconfirmation in 1972, I can only assume it was in part because, just as Festinger and his associates had concluded, my husband and I had already invested so **much** of our time, efforts, emotions, and financial resources in the organization. In addition, the level of discomfort and confusion at the single event of the disconfirmation was not high enough to off-set what we viewed as positive aspects of our involvement. These included our positive experiences in the organization; the level of doctrinal truth which we had thought we learned from the group and which we didn't believe was available elsewhere; and the many personal relationships which had been built with church members—which we knew would end if we were to leave the organization.

This off-set was upset, however, in 1978. For details of the circumstances which led to our departure from the WCG, see the *Afterword: Personal from the Author* chapter. In summary, in that year there was a huge upheaval in the church leadership. Herbert Armstrong disfellowshipped his own son Garner Ted, who had been the primary spokesman for the church on television and radio, and managing executive of most of its operations, for many years. I saw confusion all around me. I saw outright lies published by the church headquarters, and mountains of evidence of corruption, greed, profligate extravagance, and distortion of the facts. I was unable to just gloss over all of this in order to resolve the dissonance and bring my mind into a peaceful state again. I had to have answers. And even though the answers were painful, I found facing them more tolerable than staying in ignorance, and having my mind in a state of perpetual cognitive dissonance.

After our departure from the WCG in 1978—and later Garner Ted Armstrong's Church of God, International (CGI) in 1988—I began a study of groups that had predicted The End to come in their own time, or that had claimed an exclusive position as the only true expression of the Church on earth. While studying the Jehovah's Witnesses, the Latter Day Saints (Mormons), and the Seventh Day Adventists, I discovered that many in these organizations also had been subject to incredible inner turmoil from about 1970 on. This had happened because of failed prophetic speculations and/or revelations about some of their cherished teachings—and foibles of their founders and current leadership. The same sort of internal politics that I experienced in the WCG and CGI, that forced me out of those organizations, were rampant in these other groups. And thus thousands upon thousands of folks—including long-time ministers—were forced out of the official organizations of the Jehovah's Witnesses, the SDAs, and the Mormons. For if they had not been removed, the presence of dissidents and their questions would have increased the level of cognitive dissonance present in the minds of those members who did not have immediate knowledge of the many issues. Thus the disconfirmations that upset some in these groups did not lead to reformation or dissolution of the groups. Instead, the attempts by the groups to make more new converts increased greatly after those who were upset were removed.

65

End Times Fever

We live in confusing, troubling times. Sure answers to the question "What will happen next?" give people a secure anchor in the stormy sea of life. In addition, being "in the know" about mysterious prophecies gives many people the heady feeling of being one of the elite, an assurance that they are among God's Chosen, which further strengthens their anchor.

For several years preceding 1975, the leaders of two major religious sects—Jehovah's Witnesses and the Worldwide Church of God (WCG)—promulgated the concept that the year 1975 would be cataclysmic in some way. The **strong** suggestion was that it would bring the Battle of Armageddon and usher in the Millennium. In addition, the WCG emphasized that the evangelistic work of that church would end in 1972. The Great Tribulation (which was to last 3 1/2 years by their calculations) would begin that year, and their members would be miraculously taken to what they termed *The Place of Safety* to await the Second Coming.

Both groups published numerous articles and booklets about these events, complete with detailed chronological charts—and sometimes gruesome line drawings of the coming horrors. The WCG even published a booklet in the 1960's titled *1975 in Prophecy*, which covered the prophecies regarding the Great Tribulation and the Battle of Armageddon. Of course, when 1975 came and went with no great cataclysm, the WCG leadership denied the title was ever meant to be taken as a specific prophecy. They claimed the title date was merely chosen as a "literary device," in response to a popular article in a secular publication in the 1950s, which spoke glowingly of man's technological advances predicted for 1975. This was news to most of the members, who also remembered many sermon, articles, and prophetic charts that all pointed to that date!

The same confusion reigned among Jehovah's Witnesses. The following comments appeared in the October 8, 1968, issue of their publication *AWAKE*:

> According to reliable Bible chronology, Adam and Eve were created in 4026 B.C.E. ... This would leave only seven more years from the autumn of 1968 to complete 6,000 full years of human history. That seven year period will evidently finish in the autumn of the year 1975...
>
> How fitting it would be for God, following this pattern, to end man's misery after 6,000 years of human rule and follow it with His glorious Kingdom rule for a thousand years! (from a photo-duplicate reproduced in *Questions for Jehovah's Witnesses Who Love the Truth* by William Cetnar, p. 36)

The lay members of that organization should certainly be forgiven for assuming that this article, along with many other articles, charts, and sermons, was encouraging them to look to 1975 with expectation. But for them also, 1975 came and went with no cataclysm.

And what was the response of the leadership of both organizations to this failure of prophetic interpretation? WCG founder Herbert Armstrong, in a letter to his followers dated 3/25/75, wrote the following (capitalization was in the original):

"Some years ago I saw factors INDICATING the POSSIBILITY that our work might be completed by early 1972, and immediately followed by the [3 1/2 year] Great Tribulation. I NEVER SET A DEFINITE DATE. I NEVER SAID IT WOULD DEFINITELY HAPPEN—but cautioned there were indications of the possibility. Yet some misunderstood and took it as a definite prophecy for a definite date."

This same general approach was adopted by the Witness leadership as well. As one member wrote after 1975:

I have been associated as a baptized Witness well over 39 years and with Jehovah's help I will continue to be a loyal servant. But to say I am not disappointed would be untruthful, for, when I know my feelings regarding 1975 were fostered because of what I read in various publications, and then I am told in effect that I reached false conclusions on my own, that, I feel, is not being fair or honest. (Robert Warren, quoted in *Crisis of Conscience* by Raymond Franz.)

One would think that after such disappointments the lay members would have become more wary. Although this was true for some, the desire of most to be reassured that their leaders had an inside track on God's timetable encouraged the leaders of both organizations to continue resetting "possible" time interpretations of prophecies. This is not really surprising, as both organizations had successfully weathered **many** unfulfilled prophecies over a period of decades. The Witnesses had set many dates in their publications for the "probable" beginning of the Millennium, including, particularly, 1914 and 1925. Each disappointment led to some drop in membership, but many members soon developed a psychological amnesia about the incidents. New proselytes were seldom aware of past Witness failures. And thus the organization soon picked up momentum in growth again. For instance, in 1969, the total U.S. membership of Jehovah's Witnesses (as reported in the *World Book Encyclopedia Year Book*) was about 334,000. Below is a chart showing the **net change** in membership for each year from then until 1980. (If a group

gains as many new members as it **loses** old members in one year, its **net change** in total membership for that year would be **zero**.)

Note the huge **net increase** for 1975. In that year, they gained enough **new** members to make up for any lost to death or disaffection, **plus** another 66,000. It would be logical to attribute this unusually high increase in total membership to the urgency of the door-to-door preaching by Witnesses who felt "The End" would come that year in the fall. This urgency may well have had a panic effect on susceptible converts, who were frightened by the preaching into joining the ranks of those who claimed that only Jehovah's Witnesses could be assured of safety in the perilous times about to begin. But note the rapid drop almost immediately! The trend down, starting in 1976 and hitting a low point in 1979, was likely directly related to the disillusionment and defection of many current members, deeply cutting into missionary efforts of the group. At the bottom point in 1979, they had **lost** as many members as they gained, **plus** losing 35,000 beyond that! But they rebounded—now, more than 30 years after the end of this chart, there are over 7 million Witnesses regularly going door to door in the U.S., and over 18 million in attendance worldwide at their most important annual memorial gatherings.

JEHOVAH'S WITNESSES:
Net change in membership 1971-1980

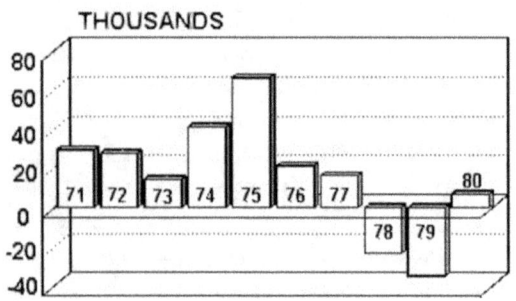

As for Herbert W Armstrong (HWA), he began his publishing career by insisting in the very first issue of his *Plain Truth Magazine* (PT) in February, 1934 (p. 3):

> "...we may be absolutely certain that we are in, and for about three years have been passing through, this great world-wide tribulation ... We have seen that the "day of His wrath" is the "Day of the Lord," which is a day of DESTRUCTION. WHO will be able to stand it? Will

YOU, brother, sister? You can't escape it. It is just as CERTAIN as are all these other events which have happened right on schedule."

In a hand-drawn time chart in the June/July 1934 issue of the PT, 1936 is **clearly** marked by HWA as the "end of the age," to be immediately followed by the "heavenly signs" and the "Day of the Lord."

Even those these dogmatic predictions failed totally, Armstrong went on bombastically announcing erroneous "probablies" for almost 40 years, including these gems from the *Plain Truth* during World War II. (Capitalization is in the original.)

> We cannot imagine Hitler, ruler over a German nation twice as great in population as Italy, turning all his vast power over to Mussolini ... yet Bible prophecies [show] ... most if not all of the nations now coming under Hitler's influence, finally giving their armed power over to [Mussolini] the Roman leader ... Possibly Hitler will die or be killed within the next eighteen months. (Feb-Mar 1939 PT issue)
>
> Democracy went, yesterday, in England! Today England is a dictatorship, as absolutely as that of Adolph Hitler or Benito Mussolini ... And when the United States gets into the war ...THE SAME THING WILL HAPPEN HERE! ...the president will become dictator absolute and not only soldiers, but factory workers, farmers, every dollar of our money and wealth—all will be CONSCRIPTED! And it is THEN ... [that] the Great Tribulation shall come, and the MARK of the Beast will be enforced! THE TIME IS AT HAND. IT IS time for us to AWAKE! ... Armageddon, we believe, must be at least [only] three or four years away ..." (Apr-May 1940)
>
> It is part of God's prophesied plan that Britain shall be invaded and conquered ... It is in the prophesied course of the war that the main fighting shall be in the Mediterranean and the Near East. (Sep-Oct 1941)

Armstrong's organization, in the years after 1972 and prior to his death in 1986, did not grow with the kind of numbers the Jehovah's Witnesses have sustained. But, in spite of frequent repeats of the type of dogmatic mistakes quoted above, it did manage an impressive growth record for a small, obscure start. Attendance at the church's annual fall convention of the Feast of Tabernacles was a few hundred, held at one site, at the beginning of the 1950's. In 1988 the church announced an attendance of about 144,000 (total), attending scores of sites around the world.

After Armstrong's death in 1986, the organization underwent many major changes in doctrine under new leadership, and suffered numerous splits, with membership eventually only a fraction of the figure at its height.

69

But the immediate causes of this did not include disillusionment over Armstrong's prophetic speculations. In fact, a majority of those who left the organization did so because the leadership did **not** continue to promote Armstrong's speculations! And a number of the groups that ex-members and ministers have formed have made those speculations the centerpiece of their reason for existence. They have merely adjusted the references to specific dates, making them a bit more generalized.

Observing the kind of embarrassing failures endured by such groups as the WCG and the Jehovah's Witnesses, leaders of other church organizations that emphasize prophecy became much more wary in the following decades about speculating on specific dates. While "selective amnesia" may work in organizations such as the WCG and the Jehovah's Witnesses, it is obvious to many that this is because those organizations are strongly authoritarian, and their members are used to accepting **many** discrepancies, because they are used to being obedient to leadership. In less authoritarian organizations, the members might be less forgiving of radical failures in prophetic timetables!

Does this mean that teachers in these less-authoritarian organizations are less prone to prophetic dogmatism? **No**! It is just that they reserve their dogmatism for aspects of prophecy that are less "testable" than dates. When it comes to identifying mysterious biblical symbols such as the beasts in the prophetic books of Daniel and Revelation, many teachers are just as dogmatic as the leaders of the Witnesses and the Worldwide Church. And, until the actual prophecies come to pass, they can usually safely expect that no one can really prove their interpretations false.

This trend is now undergoing a reversal, and an increasing number of budding ministries are coming forward to declare the certainty of their speculations, to sometimes even set dates, and to build their organizations through the zeal of those supporters who are True Believers.

A number of teachers and groups, past and present, which have either set specific dates for The End, or have come very close to it, are profiled in the *Who's Who Digest* chapter.

Bibliography

The following books contain useful information for deeper study into the concepts covered in this chapter. See the chapter on *Web Resources and Books for Further Research* for detailed information on each.

The Social Psychology of Social Movements, Hans Toch
The True Believer, Eric Hoffer
When Prophecy Fails, Leon Festinger et al

Chapter 11

Aunt Pam's Prophetic Recipes

How many different recipes do you think a professional chef could make with just some or all of the following five basic ingredients: flour, sugar, eggs, butter, and chocolate (along with a tiny bit of salt, vanilla, baking soda, baking powder, and yeast)?

Why, such a chef could concoct almost unlimited delicacies—everything from an Angel Food Cake to a Devil's Food Cake!

And with just the addition of a few more accessories, such as fruit pieces, nuts, sour cream, and flavorings such as almond liquor, you could fill many recipe books.

It is truly amazing that the same few ingredients, with merely the amounts, blending methods, and cooking temperature slightly adjusted, can take so many forms, all the way from croissants to chocolate chip cookies, and from soufflés to cheesecakes.

By analogy, it is truly amazing to see the wide variety in the End Times prophetic scenarios that "prophecy chefs" have been cooking up for the past two hundred years, all using basically just a few of the same ingredients! They have each merely slightly adjusted the amount of each ingredient, the blending method for putting these ingredients together, and the amount of "heat" they use in promoting their idiosyncratic scenario.

Unfortunately, most of these scenarios have been half-baked. And in spite of the culinary failures of the chefs who have gone before, new contenders for the Bake-Off rise up all the time.

Cooking up a Prophetic Scenario

Are you are one of those who have recently started studying speculative prophetic scenarios? Have you picked a favorite "prophecy expert," and been just amazed at how wise and clever he is to come up with all his explanations? If so, you may be surprised at just how little is truly "new" in his teachings. You may find that, just as a housewife out of sugar may run next door to borrow a cup to make cookies for tonight's dessert, he has just borrowed his ingredients from those who have gone before—those who used the same ingredients to concoct a scenario that failed. And once you see how many such "experts" have tried to doctor up a failed recipe with just an extra teaspoon of this or that, or with stirring or baking it just a minute or two more, you may realize that your favorite chef's Amazing New Recipe ... may just be one more recipe for failure.

What are the basic ingredients which most self-appointed End Times prophecy experts whip up into their scenarios? Here are the most popular elements for the past 200 years. Not every contender will use all of these, but most have used several of them.

Attempts to correlate the chronology of the apocalyptic sections of the Book of Daniel with similar sections in Matthew 24 and the Book of Revelation.

Attempts to assign the identity of modern nations to nations mentioned in the prophetic passages in the Bible.
Gog, Magog, Meshech, and Tubal in the Old Testament are often assigned to Russia or the former USSR. The Roman Empire, it has often been speculated, will be "resurrected" as a modern combine of European nations. Prophecy speculators who subscribe to the *British Israel* theory often identify Israel in prophecy with the U.S. and Great Britain. They consider that the modern nation of Israel in the Middle East is actually made up of the descendants, not of the northern tribes of the Kingdom of Israel, but of the southern tribes of the Kingdom of Judah.

Attempts to assign historical dates to key chronologies in the books of Daniel and Revelation. Various schemes for the start and ending of historical periods of 490, 1260, 2300 years, and 2520 years are proposed.

An assumption that there is a *prophetic principle* according to which a symbolic **day** in a prophecy must be taken to be an actual **year** in fulfillment. This is based on the specific instance in the book of Ezekiel in which Ezekiel is ordered by God to perform symbolic acts that last a number of days, which foreshadow events that will actually last that number of years.
An assumption that there is another prophetic principle according to which, at times, a **day** in prophecy is equal to **1000 years**. This is based on 2 Peter 3:8 which states that "… one day is with the Lord as a thousand years." This principle is particularly assumed to establish that, just as God took six days to accomplish the Adamic creation, and then rested the seventh, the world is scheduled to have six thousand years— six millennia— of struggles under the rule of Man. And then will come the seventh millennium. This will be the Millennium of God's Kingdom, when Christ and the Saints will rule over the Earth and bring a type of "rest."

An assumption that Jesus' comments in the "Olivet Prophecy" in Matthew 24, regarding "wars, rumors of wars, famines, and earthquakes" can be applied to the lifetime of the prophecy speculator as being a **unique** time of such elements.

An assumption that the presence of the Jews back in the area of Palestine indicates the human generation in which The End will come. In the early 1900s, the mere return of some of Jews to the area in relation to the Balfour Declaration was enough to fire speculation that the last generation had begun. In 1948, with the formation of the Jewish nation, speculation again suggested **this** was the "sign of the last generation." Then when the Jews took Jerusalem from Arab control in 1967, other teachers suggested **that** was the sign instead.

Fruits and Nuts and More

The above items have been the main ingredients used by self-proclaimed prophecy experts for the past 200 years to establish their scenarios. These have often been spiced up, however, with a number of lesser ingredients. Many such experts have also incorporated one or more of the following into their speculations:

1. A belief that the **measurements of the Great Pyramid** of Giza in Egypt have prophetic significance.

2. A belief that **contemporary astronomical events** are, or may be in the near future, either a fulfillment of a prophecy, or *signs* of the end. This would include things such as Halley's Comet and the more recent Hale-Bopp Comet, the so-called Jupiter Effect of the 1980s (that was predicted to cause great earth-wide catastrophes when the planets "lined up"), eclipses of the moon in which it appears red, and unexpected meteor showers.

3. A belief that there are **"hidden messages" in the Old Testament**, either disguised directly in the content of passages, or in a coded arrangement of the letters in ancient Hebrew. This would include the so-called *Bible Codes*, as well as such speculations as those of TV prophecy pundit J.R. Church, who claimed to have found hidden prophecies in the Psalms.

4. A belief that **current events provide clues** that can establish the identity of the Beast/Antichrist of Revelation.

5. A belief that the **Seven Churches of Asia in the Book of Revelation** are actually intended to be prophetic references to a sequential series of "church ages," leading up to The End.

73

Under this scenario, the group that the prophecy speculator belongs to (or has founded) is most often viewed as being the Philadelphian Era—the sixth era—of the Historical Church. Thus his group is destined to be either raptured to heaven or whisked to a place of safety before the Tribulation period. And any who leave, or refuse to belong to, that group are often viewed as the Laodicean Era of the Church—the seventh era—who are destined for suffering and martyrdom during the Tribulation.

6. Attempts to **correlate passages in the Book of Ezekiel** with current events and current world nations.

7. A belief that certain **visionary elements of the Book of Revelation** are not symbolic at all, but rather representations by John of glimpses he had into the actual physical future. Under this sort of scenario, John's description of locusts is assumed to be his feeble attempt to describe helicopters, and some of the details of the plagues to come upon mankind are viewed as vivid descriptions of the aftermath of nuclear warfare.

There are a number of other typical ingredients that some self-proclaimed prophecy experts mix into their recipes. But the above should give the reader a sufficient sense of how common—and long-lived—some of the elements are which are presented by many modern prophecy pontificators as fresh, amazing new insight that will allow the "Secrets of Bible to Be Revealed At Last!"

As the old saying goes, "Those who do not learn the lessons of failed prophecy are doomed to keep using the same flawed recipes."

And as another old saying goes ... "It's best to take **all** of these recipes with a grain of salt."

No—maybe a whole salt shaker would be best! A BIG saltshaker!

Chapter 12

The Word Faith Movement

The Claims

The *Word Faith Movement* is a branch of the general Charismatic movement. Not all Charismatics accept Word Faith teachings. But Word Faith Charismatic teachers have, in the past decade, become the most publicly prominent representatives of the Charismatic movement. Trinity Broadcasting Network (TBN), the most powerful and pervasive of the televangelistic outreaches in American religion (it has claimed to be available to 92% of the homes in the U.S.) features and promotes Word Faith teachers almost exclusively.

Teachers in the Word Faith Movement (sometimes called the *Word of Faith Movement*) claim that the Bible promises perfect health and unlimited prosperity to all believers. Therefore, if any believers are sick or in poverty, it must be because they do not understand how to "appropriate" these promises for themselves. According to Word Faith teachers, the way to appropriate that health and wealth is through the "power of the tongue" to "confess" the believer's faith in what he determines to be the biblical promises of God. This creates, according to the teachings of many in this movement, a "legally binding" requirement for God to act. And thus, in their perspective, **God Himself** is controlled by the power of the human tongue when it speaks "the word of faith." Just as God created the world and all in it by His Word, Word Faith teachers assume that God grants human believers the same kind of creative power in their words.

Such teachers warn their students **never** to pray prayers of petition to God with the conclusion "If it be Your will, Father." For that would indicate you haven't studied your Bible well enough to know all of His promises. If you know the promises, they insist, you know His will at any moment, and need only speak that word. Anything less is evidence you lack faith in His promises. They also insist that their students should never "pray the problem," but rather "pray the solution." Speaking to God about your problems is tantamount, in their eyes, to not believing that God will take care of your problem immediately if you will only "pray the solution" exactly as you find it in the Bible.

The Allure

The prosperity teachings of the Word Faith movement are particularly popular with those who feel disenfranchised from the system of prosperity which many in the Western world enjoy. The solution proposed by Word Faith teachers for a low standard of living does not include either hard work or education. The first part of the solution is a series of verbal affirmations, called positive confessions. And equally important to the solution is a process usually described as sowing and reaping, in which believers are encouraged to give money—"planting a seed"—into a particular ministry, in the hopes that God will miraculously grant them a prosperous "harvest" from that monetary seed. Many Word Faith teachers even use a gimmick that they call the hundred-fold blessing to induce larger offerings from their audiences. They will declare that God has revealed to them that there is a special window of opportunity for an unusual blessing for those who will respond to the immediate request for donations—He will give back to any who donate a certain amount a "hundred-fold return" on their donation. This can particularly appeal to the person who is despondent over his finances—if he can only scrape together a sacrificial offering, he can hope for a huge return on it.

The **health teachings** of the Word Faith Movement are particularly popular with those who have physical problems for which medical help has been ineffective. The solution proposed for ill health does not include improved diet and exercise, or anything that requires personal self-control, but merely "claiming" healing for any and all afflictions.

Concerns

Although these promises of health and wealth are surely appealing, they do not line up with the reality of the Bible.

1. **The Bible does not offer unlimited prosperity as a guarantee to all believers in this life**. In order to establish that all believers are entitled to unlimited wealth, scriptures must be ripped from their context by Word Faith teachers, and twisted to fit a pre-conceived notion of God's will.

2. **The Bible does not offer perfect health and freedom from injury to all who believe.** Only in the resurrection will believers have such perfection. Although there are miraculous healings described in the scriptures, many great servants of God have suffered injury or illness, with no instantaneous relief. Word Faith teachers often insist that believers must "confess" that they are healed from their

76

affliction, even though all of the symptoms of their affliction, such as cancer or diabetes, are still present. And they must avoid any mention of these symptoms lest they hinder the reality of their healing from "manifesting." Some believers are thereby convinced to abandon all conventional methods of dealing with such afflictions, such as taking insulin for diabetes. And many others, who are unable to experience healing despite their dedicated, positive confession, are led to the point of despair because they assume that the lack of healing indicates a deficiency in their faith.

3. The manifestations of healings among Word Faith believers are frequently described as "gradual," and it is even declared possible for those who believe that they have been healed to "lose their healing" if they falter in their positive confession. There is no indication anywhere in scripture that true, divine, miraculous healing is limited by such stipulations. **Every instance of healing in the Bible is instantaneous, and the recipient does not do anything to "maintain" the healing. It is permanent.** People in modern times do, indeed, get better gradually at times in a way that seems to indicate that God did intervene in their circumstances. This might include lessening of pain or a speedier recovery than was expected by medical doctors. But this is not the same thing as dogmatically claiming the sort of instantaneous divine healing administered by Jesus and Paul and Peter—while the reality is that the healing is not at all of the sort experienced by those touched by Jesus, Paul, and Peter.

4. The Bible does admonish believers to be generous to others, and to serve God by investing their resources of time, money, and goods into worthy causes, such as helping the poor and spreading the Gospel. But **nothing in the Bible supports the notion that donation of money to a particular teacher or group binds God to a promise to financially bless the donor with increase.**

5. The concept that God can be regularly counted on to intervene with financial miracles appeals to precisely the same attitude in people who are drawn to casino gambling or buying lottery tickets. Christians can surely rely on God to intervene on occasion in their circumstances, in times of crisis. But **the promise by a televangelist that God is bound by the televangelist's words to do a financial miracle for everyone in the audience during a given**

telethon is pure presumption on the part of such televangelists.

6.   The notion that God is somehow bound by the words of the mouths of fallible humans is blasphemous. God is sovereign, and can do anything He wishes any time He wishes. The true believer is a child of God and can come boldly before Him and *make requests*. But **only God knows what is best for His children at any given moment—and what may be best for them at times is to deny their request.** Just because they believe a request is based on a scripture which seems to guarantee that they are promised the thing that they are asking for **does not make it so**.

Nuggets of Truth

Some Bible students have a hard time resisting the teachings of the Word Faith Movement because Word Faith teachers do, indeed, focus on some scriptures and biblical principles that are ignored at times by other Bible teachers.

1.   We are told in the Bible that, as children of God, we now have direct access to Him, and can "come boldly unto the throne of grace to make our petitions." Many Christians are timid with their prayers. There is a fine line between boldness and presumption. The Word Faith teachers definitely go over that line into presumption at times. But understanding that we need to avoid such presumption should not deter us from **godly boldness**.

2.   Many Christians conduct their lives as if they are utterly convinced that God no longer interacts with His creation. They do not expect **any** miracles from God, they do not expect Him to guide them personally through the Holy Spirit, and they do not expect Him to intervene in circumstances in the world around them. They view Him as a God who is "afar off," and although He will one day again send Jesus to the Earth, that Jesus is only a figure on a throne in heaven at this point in time. Yet Jesus said, "Lo, I am with you always, even unto the End of the Age." It is certainly possible to understand that **God takes a very intimate interest in our daily lives, interacts with us,**

and intervenes actively at times in our circumstances, without insisting that we control Him with our words.

3. The scriptures do not promise that every affliction that Christians will endure in this life will be lifted miraculously and instantaneously from them if they can just grasp the proper "keys" to such miracles. However, the Bible most certainly does claim that **God can and does intervene miraculously at times** to fulfill His own will in the lives of His people. And it thus admonishes us to pray for one another in such circumstances, and directs an individual who is sick to call for the elders of the church to anoint him. It is obvious from the letters of Paul that healing did not happen for everyone all the time. For instance, in one place he notes that he "left Timothy sick at Miletus." And in another place, he suggests to Timothy that he drink a little wine to help his stomach problems. These were both men of great faith, who served God mightily. No doubt such sickness interfered with Timothy's ability to accomplish as much as he would like in his ministry. Yet neither he nor Paul was evidently able to "claim" a healing for Timothy. At the same time, there is absolutely no indication that either stopped believing that God could and would perform future miracles, including healing. Nor should believers of our time doubt this.

God does heal, and even if the Word Faith teachers presumptuously insist that we can force Him to do so according to our own will, this does not negate the fact that sometimes it is His will to heal miraculously and instantaneously.

The Word Faith movement insists that following certain "faith formulas" will guarantee health, healing, and wealth from God. The next chapter profiles a related movement that also promises healing. But in the Healing Ministries Movement the spotlight is on specific individuals, who claim the authority to dispense healing from God.

Chapter 13

Healing Ministries Movement

James 5:14-15
Is any one of you sick? He should call the elders of the church to pray over him and anoint him with oil in the name of the Lord.
And the prayer offered in faith will make the sick person well;
the Lord will raise him up. If he has sinned, he will be forgiven.
(NIV)

There are likely very few people who claim the designation "Christian" who do not believe that God can and does heal people miraculously on occasion. And reports of such healings are not confined to religious circles. Secular publications such as *Reader's Digest* or *The National Enquirer* occasionally contain stories of amazing recoveries from sickness or injury which even medical doctors describe by the term "miracle."

The Bible is absolutely clear that God can heal, has healed, and will heal individuals at times. Thus the questions and concerns that will be addressed in this profile of the **Field Guide** are not directed at God's ability or willingness to intervene in the health of individuals at times. Rather, the questions and concerns relate to specific claims by some teachers and evangelists and groups that they have a special calling from God to in some way "dispense" His healing through their own ministry. This role of intermediary between the individual seeking healing and God is not the same as that noted in the passage from James above. James specifically directs the individual believer to contact the "elders" in his own local congregation of fellow believers, those who are part of his own spiritual "family," and to request that they come and "anoint" him. There is no indication in this passage of a specific "gift of healing" that will be held by one or more of those elders which will be brought into play. The issue is fellowship, prayer, and faith.

The Bible also is clear that the ministries of both Jesus and the Apostles were confirmed by a number of miraculous signs including, in particular, many physical healings done in public. These healings at times drew attention to the preaching done by these men, and then provided a confirmation of the credentials of the speaker because he was able to be the instrument of such notable miracles.

The Claims

In the Healing Ministries Movement, the local church is totally by-passed. Individuals seek out an external religious figure, convinced that if they can just encounter him at the right time and place, he will be the "connection point" between their desire and hope for healing—and the power of God to bring that healing to pass. The setting for this transaction is often called a "healing crusade," or a "healing revival." This is a public meeting, sometimes with those in attendance numbering into the thousands or tens of thousands, led by a religious figure believed by most in attendance to have a special *gift of healing* or an *anointing* from God. Sometimes the element of healing is used as only one portion of a program particularly designed to preach the Gospel to the "unsaved." But it is perhaps more typical for the claims of healing to be the primary focus of the meetings, with very little biblical teaching or preaching available.

The "healing evangelist," as he or she is often styled, may line up people seeking healing at the front of the meeting facility, and then go down the row, touching each one and declaring that they are now healed. (Some may fall over backward as he touches them, in an evident "swoon" which is referred to as being *slain in the spirit.*) This style of meeting has been typical for a hundred years or more.

Another common procedure (used by a handful of ministers as early as the 1940s, but much more typical today) has been the exercise by some evangelists of an alleged gift of a *word of knowledge*. In this type of meeting, the Lord has allegedly revealed to the evangelist the malady of specific members of the audience. These individuals are *called out* of the audience to come to the front to "receive their healing." Sometimes the evangelist will issue a general invitation such as urging "someone in the back row with a heart problem" to identify himself. At other times he may use a more specific designation such as ordering "the woman in the fourth row in the red dress" to come forward.

In recent decades, a different method has been used by some healing evangelists. In this procedure, the audience is primed at the beginning of the meeting to "expect their miracle tonight." After an extended period of singing and exhortation, audience members are invited to come forward if they believe that they have miraculously received their healing while in their seats. They are then brought on stage one at a time to give their "testimony" of healing to the evangelist—and, via a microphone, to the whole audience.

With the advent of television, the audiences of many healing evangelists have expanded. And thus another method has been adopted by some. As in the *calling out* done in some crusades, they will declare that they have a *word from the Lord* that someone in the television audience has a particular malady. They assure that person that the Lord is indeed healing

81

them at that moment, and they should contact the ministry by phone or mail and confirm that they received the healing.

Specific statistics would be hard to come by of what percentage of the audience at most healing crusades consists of committed believers, and what percentage is made up of guests or curiosity seekers. But it would likely not be an exaggeration to speculate that the vast majority of any given audience would describe themselves as "born again believers." The parking lots of many convention facilities hosting crusades contain numerous buses belonging to or chartered by area churches, bringing groups of their own members to the meetings. And many more in attendance are likely regular supporters or followers of the ministry of the evangelist, including watching him on television, getting his newsletters and magazines, and purchasing his books. Although the larger meetings, such as those featuring Charismatic super-star Benny Hinn, are advertised in the local media in the cities where they are to take place, they are also heavily promoted on the weekly TV programs and in the newsletters for supporters (often called "Partners") of the ministry.

Theologies of healing

Within the Healing Ministries Movement of the past one hundred years, there have been a number of approaches to just what the "underlying theology" of healing should be.

1.   For some, supernatural healing is viewed as an evidence of a "restoration of the spiritual gifts" of the first century. Thus the emphasis is on the fact that the individual healing evangelist has a special *anointing* from God and is using it to benefit others.

2.   In another approach to healing, it is declared that the promise of healing for all believers is "in the Atonement." In other words, it is alleged that Jesus' suffering and death accomplished two things: the spiritual redemption of individuals for all eternity, and the conquering of physical ailments in this life. This concept is usually based on one scripture

> 1Peter 2:21-24
> 21 For even hereunto were ye called: because Christ also suffered for us, leaving us an example, that ye should follow his steps:
> 22 Who did no sin, neither was guile found in his mouth:
> 23 Who, when he was reviled, reviled not again; when he

suffered, he threatened not; but committed himself to Him
that judgeth righteously:

24 Who his own self bare our sins in his own body on the tree,
that we, being dead to sins, should live unto righteousness:
by whose stripes ye were healed.

3.   Many groups who believe in following the precept of James
5:14 and "calling for the elders" to anoint the sick also use
the 1Peter 2:24 scripture to explain why the believer can
expect healing. But within the Healing Ministries
Movement, the emphasis is shifted from calling for the
elders to some other "act of faith" which will "release" a
guaranteed healing for the person with physical afflictions,
whether illness, injury, or congenital deformity. If a healing
evangelist will be nearby at a crusade in the near future, the
afflicted one is encouraged to attend. The implication is that
the likelihood of healing is greater in the actual presence of
the evangelist. However, in recent years many such
evangelists also have their own television programs. And
they use a number of incentives for the afflicted to contact
them by mail in order to "receive their healing." Examples
of some of these incentives are given in the *Examination*
section below.

4.   Another approach to healing is to view it as a "tool"
provided by God to the minister for *power evangelism*. In this
approach, healing of individuals in an audience is viewed as
a *sign gift* that can validate, in the minds of the audience, the
ministry of the evangelist.

In each of these approaches, the actual "level of faith" of the person
afflicted may be viewed as playing an important part in whether they are
healed. But particularly in approach number 2, there is a definite emphasis
on a connection between level of faith and expectation of healing—and
"preservation" of the healing. For many healing evangelists, particularly
those in the *Word Faith Movement*, propose that all supernatural healings are
"conditional." The recipient of the healing is expected to first believe
unconditionally that God wills to heal through the ministering of the
evangelist. And then, regardless of their physical state, they are to "declare"
that they are healed and keep on declaring and believing that. If, on the
initial touch from the evangelist, they feel better immediately, and have
some of their symptoms relieved, they are not to rely on that for conviction
of their healing. If they later begin to exhibit symptoms of the illness, they
are to deny them, and continue in a *positive confession* of their conviction that

they have been healed. If they waver in that conviction, many healing evangelists will warn them that they can "lose their healing."

The result of this approach is obvious. If a person truly seems to get better after contact with the evangelist (either in person or by letter), they will likely attribute their improvement to that evangelist's ministry. But if they do not get better, or improve only temporarily, they are encouraged to attribute the failure to their own level of faith. Thus there is no objective standard whereby to evaluate the "success rate" of the evangelist. He or she is held to no standard of performance at all. **They get to claim all successes, and wash their hands of all failures!** There is no system of accountability for the healing evangelist.

The Allure

It is sometimes noted by those opposed to the very concept of "supernatural healing" that medical science has progressed to such an extent that we no longer need the kind of divine intervention that was at times present to heal in the first century. They view supernatural healing as having been a sort of "stop-gap" measure by God until mankind could progress enough to understand the causes of illness and develop cures.

It is difficult to understand this perspective—for in spite of increased life expectancy and the conquering of a number of communicable diseases such as polio, people get sick and die every day—even in the most advanced, affluent countries. Even young children die of cancer. Although many diseases do now have cures, many do not, or merely have methods to control the severity of symptoms. Even debilitating arthritis and other common conditions have not been conquered by modern medicine. And accidents and congenital birth defects leave many without "whole" bodies. So while the **percentage** of people needing healing may be smaller now than in the first century, the number of people with chronic, untreatable conditions is huge.

Thus the allure of the healing evangelist and the healing crusade: They offer hope to the hopeless.

Concerns

At first glance, it might seem both heartless and foolish to criticize, in any way, individuals who offer hope to the hopeless. If just one person is truly healed at a healing crusade, isn't that worth the effort? Even if some charlatan, who knows he doesn't have a gift of healing at all, comes to town, and is only there to bilk the unwary of their offerings in exchange for a good show, doesn't he do some good by offering a few moments of hope to the hopeless, a bright spot in their drab life?

Field Guide readers are encouraged to consider the concerns below and come to their own conclusions regarding the answers to the questions above.

Areas of concern regarding the Healing Ministries Movement:

1. In spite of the unending hype claiming numerous healings that comes via newsletters and TV programs of the ministries involved in the Healing Ministries Movement, actual solid documentation establishing the truth of these claims is almost non-existent. Healing ministry crusades have been photographed and captured on motion picture since the 1940s, and videotaped in recent decades. In spite of this, there are no video records available of astounding healings of the type that Jesus performed—those born blind seeing clearly, those with withered limbs made instantaneously whole. In spite of the many claims, there are no videotapes of tumors visibly shrinking or falling off, or of paraplegics getting up out of wheelchairs. And, as for documentation of the less visible alleged healings such as internal cancer—a number of sincere researchers have contacted numerous such ministries in the past fifty years and more, attempting to get such documentation. They have been thwarted at every turn. The reality is that most ministries do not in any way "follow up" on any claims of healing made at their gatherings. They merely "report" them to their supporters. If questioned, they will insist that they, personally, never claim that someone is healed, but that they just accept the reports of those who wish to make such a claim.

2. In spite of the focus on a few alleged healings at every such crusade, mention is never made of the hundreds or thousands in attendance who were not healed on any given night. Many healing evangelists make a point at the beginning of such an evening to bombastically assure their audience that "tonight is the night for your miracle!" Is it really logical to assume that only those who were brought forward to the stage and pronounced healed had faith for healing on that night? Many others—sometimes thousands—may have made extreme efforts to get to such a meeting, obviously because they **did** believe that healing would be available. Watching others go forward to claim a healing should, even just psychologically, give them more hope and confidence. What, then, are they told when they go home in the same condition as they arrived? They are told nothing. For each one is only one among thousands, and their private, personal anguish is not evident among the throngs.

3.	In spite of the occasional claim of outstanding miracles such as a blind person receiving their sight, most healings claimed by healing ministries are of such a nature that they are not obvious to the observer. Someone can claim that an internal cancer was healed, but without an x-ray, it will be impossible to verify this claim. Someone can claim a pain has left their body, but that cannot be seen either. And in many cases, such claims have nothing to do with an actual healing, but with a temporary alleviation of a symptom, that can be attributed to the excitement of the evening. The real issue is ... what about the people who came with obvious external maladies—deformed legs, withered hands, multiple sclerosis, Down Syndrome? Where are the videotapes of healings of these kinds of maladies? They do not exist. If one accepts the theology mentioned above that healing is "guaranteed in the Atonement," that ought to be healing of every kind of physical problem. Is it possible that no person at any of the modern healing crusades with a serious, obvious deformity has ever had the level of faith necessary for healing?

4.	In spite of the reality of point 3 above, many healing evangelists continue to imply to their audiences that they should expect healing of every problem—at the same time that they make sure to keep any individual cases of obviously crippled or deformed people out of range of the cameras capturing the events of the evening. A person with a slight limp walking with a cane is one thing. They may well toss their cane aside later in the evening and stride across the stage to the cheers of the audience. Some people may even get up out of wheelchairs and walk, also to the cheers of the audience. However, it has been documented that a number of prominent healing evangelists have crews which direct people to sit in wheelchairs provided by the crusade itself at the beginning of each service. The person may have a condition that has left them weakened but actually able to walk on their own. Thus the fact that, in a situation of excitement, a rush of adrenaline would allow them to walk energetically across a stage is not surprising. The audience does not realize that the person was not "wheelchair bound" at all, so this seems like a notable miracle. But a person with a withered leg, or an orthopedic shoe with a three-inch sole, is quite another issue at most healing revivals. They will likely find themselves sitting back in the shadows, well out of sight.

5.	There is an obvious factor of statistical time and chance that enters with such methods as the *word of knowledge* used on the television programs of healing evangelists. The audiences for the most popular programs, such as the *700 Club* or Trinity Broadcasting's *Praise the*

Lord, are likely in the tens or hundreds of thousands. Thus the host on such a program can proclaim that "someone" in the television audience has a hearing problem, or a sore back, or any other malady, and know that the odds are in his favor. Just by the law of averages, someone in the vast television audience will indeed be suffering from just such a problem. The conditions described are usually those most common, and the chances are that hundreds or thousands might fit the profile. That one of those might have their condition improve in the time period near the proclamation is not a matter for astonishment. This is not at all to deny that God can intervene and heal someone who is sincerely seeking such a healing at the same time as the television evangelist is declaring that "someone out there in TV land is being healed this very moment." But when such time and chance occurrences are used to "validate" the ministry of the evangelist, and particularly to encourage supporters to send donations, the claims stretch credibility.

6.   One of the most disturbing aspects of some of the ministries involved in the Healing Ministries Movement is the methods and gimmicks they use in mass mailings to their supporters. Rather than encouraging believers to follow the admonition of James 5:14 if they are ill, they encourage them to follow some man-made "faith formula" that will guarantee that God will be forced to give them their healing. Or they will encourage them to become involved in some physical scheme connected to the healing evangelist. They must request an anointed cloth, accept a vial of alleged "holy oil" or "holy water," place their hand on a paper outline of the evangelist's hand (or on his hand on the TV screen) as a "point of contact," and many, many similar gimmicks. Inevitably, these gimmicks also include an admonition that the one seeking healing (or a "financial miracle" or other type of divine intervention) include with their request the largest *seed faith* donation possible to the ministry.

The New Testament examples of healing by Jesus and the Apostles **never** included any request for money. In fact, in the one instance that money is mentioned, it is of a crippled man begging money from Peter.

> Acts 3:2-8
> Now a man crippled from birth was being carried to the temple gate called Beautiful, where he was put every day to beg from those going into the temple courts. When he saw Peter and John about to enter, he asked them for money. Peter looked straight at him, as did John. Then Peter said, "Look at us!" So the man gave them his attention,

expecting to get something from them. Then Peter said, "Silver or gold I do not have, but what I have I give you. In the name of Jesus Christ of Nazareth, walk." Taking him by the right hand, he helped him up, and instantly the man's feet and ankles became strong. He jumped to his feet and began to walk. Then he went with them into the temple courts, walking and jumping, and praising God. (NIV)

There is not one healing evangelist of the past 100 years who has had the ability to tell a man **crippled from birth,** "walk"... and be absolutely confident that it would happen. There is no hedging by Peter that the man needed great faith. In fact, the man had no faith at all! He wasn't expecting a healing, and he didn't ask for a healing. And there is no insistence by Peter to the man that he'd better be sure to stay in *positive confession* about his healing or he would lose it.

When Jesus and the Apostles healed people, they stayed healed.

As noted in the introduction to this profile, there is no question that God can heal miraculously, and that He has done so down through the ages. The question is whether the grandiose claims of healing crusade ministries can be established as fact, whether the underlying assumptions of the theology of healing that they promote are biblical, and whether the methods they use are inspired by the Holy Spirit. Or is it possible that those methods are inspired by human reasoning and human psychology at best—and greed at worst? And then there is the biggest question: Are their ministries, as a whole, doing more harm than good to the cause of the Gospel?

Bibliography

An excellent overview, history, examination, and evaluation of the "guaranteed healing in the Atonement" position is contained in an article by David W. Cloud titled *Is Healing in the Atonement?* It is available from:

Way of Life Literature, P.O. Box 610368, Port Huron, MI 48061-0368, fbns@wayoflife.org

And it is posted on the Net for free download at:

www.wayoflife.org/fbns/ishealing01.htm

The following books, along with many other resources, were consulted in preparation for compiling the information for this profile. They provide an overview and extensive documentation regarding a variety of Healing Ministry Movement ministries and teachers of the past and present. See the chapter **Web Resources and Books for Further Research** for more information on each book.

Charismatic Chaos

Counterfeit Revival: Looking for God in All the Wrong Places

A Different Gospel

The Faith Healers

The New Charismatics

Chapter 14

Hebrew Roots Movement

There are a wide variety of groups and teachers which use the term *Hebrew Roots* (or, in some cases, *Jewish Roots*) to describe an aspect of their ministry. They differ widely in how they apply the term. Therefore, it is not accurate to speak of them as if they all belonged to one monolithic movement with a shared theology.

But they do share a few specific concepts in common.

➢ They emphasize that Jesus of Nazareth was a Jew, and His original Apostles and disciples were Jewish. The logical conclusion they draw from this is that, in order to fully understand the life and teachings of Jesus, it is necessary to understand the Jewish culture in which He lived in the first century.

➢ They emphasize that the authentic Christian way of life and beliefs, and the writings of the New Testament, are not an outgrowth of pagan religions, but an outgrowth of the religion of the collection of writings called by Jews the Tanakh and by Christians the Old Testament.

➢ They emphasize that the New Testament is not a separate document unrelated to the Old Testament, but rather a continuation of the Old Testament, making one whole collection of writings that Christians refer to as the Bible.

➢ They emphasize that much of the New Testament, from the Gospels, to the Epistles of Paul, to the Book of Revelation, cannot be understood fully without realizing how much in it either directly quotes or makes clear allusions to people, places, events, ideas, and prophecies in the Old Testament.

There are few Bible scholars and serious Bible students who would disagree with any of the points above. Many "Bible helps" such as commentaries, study Bibles, lexicons, Bible dictionaries, and specialized handbooks covering such topics as "Bible times and customs" have been created over the centuries to provide just the assistance needed to address the concerns stated above. While it may be true that many Bible teachers in Protestant and Catholic churches have not adequately incorporated this perspective in their own teaching, it has not been for lack of teaching and research materials on the topics.

In addition, there are a number of groups that do not refer to themselves as being part of the Hebrew Roots Movement but which might be considered such by outside observers. These groups may observe the seventh day Sabbath, and even the same annual Holy Days as the Jews. However, they do not view this as returning to Jewish Roots but, rather, **biblical** roots. For after all, the Sabbath is part of the Ten Commandments, and the annual Holy Days are described in Leviticus. Some Christian groups believe these days were intended only for the Israelites, and that their observance has no relevance for Christians. But Paul did write about biblical observances to a Gentile church in Corinth:

> Christ our Passover is sacrificed for us. Let us therefore keep the Feast, not with the old leaven, the leaven of malice and wickedness, but with the unleavened bread of sincerity and truth. (1 Corinthians 5:7b-8)

It would appear from this passage that the church at Corinth was observing, in some fashion, both the Passover and the Feast of Unleavened Bread. Otherwise, it would make no sense for Paul to use these analogies in writing to Gentile believers. Paul later notes that the Sabbath and Holy Days are shadows pointing to Christ. Therefore, some Christian teachers and groups have concluded that the annual biblical Holy Days are relevant to Gentile Christians as well as Messianic Jews. And they observe them, not necessarily with specific Jewish customs, but as Christian celebrations rooted in the Bible, that teach and remind observers about the plan of salvation through the Blood of the ultimate Lamb, Jesus Christ.

So what is the point of a new set of religious teachers and groups which purport to emphasize the Hebrew Roots of Jesus or the Hebrew Roots of the Christian faith?

The Claims

As noted above, there are a wide variety of ministries that have what they term a Hebrew Roots emphasis. For the purposes of this profile, most can be grouped on a continuum from those which emphasize the centrality of faith in Jesus to those which, at best, minimize the role of Jesus in the Faith of the believer—and at worst totally undermine belief in Jesus at all. The following list of the various types of groups moves from the least problematic to the greatest.

1.   Some Hebrew Roots ministries seem just to be convinced that not enough emphasis is made by the average Bible teacher regarding the

Hebrew/Jewish background of Jesus, the culture of the first century, and the connection between the Old Testament and the New Testament. Thus, they direct their teaching to "consciousness-raising" on this topic. They may point out in their writings how often Paul or the Gospel writers quote Old Testament passages. Or they may emphasize how difficult it is to get any sort of grip on New Testament prophecies such as the book of Revelation without having a background in the books of Daniel and Ezekiel.

It is the position of this *Field Guide* that the approach of this type of ministry is not harmful, and may actually be helpful, to those who enjoy detailed Bible Study.

2. Some Hebrew Roots ministries seem convinced that the material in most common Bible helps is just not detailed enough when it comes to first century customs. They feel most Christians don't understand enough about the Jewish theology that may have affected the New Testament writers, and the possible foreshadows of the ministry of Christ in various Old Testament events, objects, and activities. Thus, they may embark on their own detailed research in Jewish writings, such as the Talmud, in order to discover more and more information which they believe will shed light on important aspects of Christian life and belief.

It is the position of this *Field Guide* that the approach of this type of ministry can be misleading, as the writings of the Talmud and other Jewish literature may be as riddled at times with non-biblical material as are Gentile pagan sources. The speculations of the Rabbis down through the centuries are just that—speculations. A Rabbi who lived a thousand years after the time of Jesus may have no more insight into exactly what was going on in Old Testament times in the ancient religion of Israel, or in the first century during the time before the destruction of the last Temple, than a modern Protestant commentator. Both have equal access to the same ancient documents upon which to speculate. Dabbling in unending speculation doesn't necessarily cause great spiritual harm. But if it leads to an obsession with wanting to know more and more about more and more obscure information—it can be a major distraction for a Christian.

3. Yet another type of Hebrew Roots ministry may encourage Christians not only to study Jewish customs of the first century (about which extra-biblical sources of information are very scanty), but study and regularly participate in Jewish customs of the present

in order to somehow be more authentically Christian. They may even imply that this sort of study and participation will lead to "deeper spiritual understanding" which will bring one "closer to God."

It is the position of this *Field Guide* that the approach of this type of ministry can very easily distract Christians from the importance of scripture in forming the foundation of the Christian Faith. There is absolutely no documentation to establish that most modern Jewish customs were inspired by God, nor that they were even in place in the first century. Many customs have obviously evolved over the centuries, in the same way many Protestant and Catholic customs have evolved. Those who are trying to avoid superstitious customs in Christian settings by adopting Jewish customs may find that they are merely exchanging one set of man-made superstitions for another. In addition, many elements of modern Jewish ritual and thought have obvious mystical and/or occult roots.

It is not surprising that a Christian might look into the Bible, see the Sabbath rest described in the Ten Commandments, and conclude that it is applicable to Christians, since Jesus even said that "The Sabbath was made for man"—not just "made for the Jews." Most Sabbatarian Christians do not base their Sabbath observance on the customs of the Jews, but on the guidance of scripture. Therefore, they have very few if any customs or rituals involved in their Sabbath observance. They merely view it as a blessing from God, resting and being refreshed from their regular work on that day, and perhaps using the day for Christian fellowship and worship. They may even develop their own family traditions over the years for the Sabbath. But these are not confused as being inspired ritual or custom necessary for **properly worshipping** God.

And there is certainly nothing wrong with Messianic Jewish believers choosing to keep the traditional customs of their families as part of their cultural heritage. (Although they may find it helpful to look into the roots of some of the customs and decide if they wish to perpetuate those which have pagan origins.) Nor is there anything inherently wrong with non-Jewish believers adopting some of these traditional customs if they find them meaningful and pleasing. But these traditional customs should not be confused as being inspired ritual or custom necessary for **properly worshipping God**. The type of Hebrew Roots teaching that would insist that a variety of man-invented rituals need to be imposed on such observances in order to "get closer to God" or have "deeper spiritual understanding" is a real distraction from the centrality of salvation through Jesus.

But the above is not the most problematic of the types of Hebrew Roots ministries ...

4.   Some Hebrew Roots ministries go beyond mere suggestion that Christians should "try out" various religious practices and customs of the Jews. They actually teach that the only way to be authentic disciples of Jesus (they would call Him by the Hebrew name "Yeshua" or "Yashua" or perhaps "Yahshua") is to become Jewish believers in Messiah. This would include adoption of most Orthodox Jewish practices, such as wearing prayer shawls for worship, wearing blue tassels on the corners of a special garment worn at all times, using the traditional Jewish "blessings" throughout the day, and, for some males, even undergoing circumcision if necessary. All of these things are adopted in order to be more spiritual and to be more acceptable to God.

It is the position of this *Field Guide* that this type of approach leads away from true biblical, spiritual faith and practice rather than toward it.

5.   There is one final type of Hebrew Roots ministry that has begun to develop in recent years out of the last type mentioned above. This ministry **poses** as one that offers to help Christians explore the Hebrew roots of Jesus and the Hebrew roots of the New Testament Faith. But under this benign surface, its goal is to totally undermine the faith of believers in both Jesus and the New Testament. One type of this branch of the Hebrew Roots movement downplays the role of Jesus in salvation, implying strongly that He was just a good Jewish Rabbi of the first century, rather than the unique Son of God. And they teach that the New Testament, while containing some inspirational material, is unreliable as the written Word of God. Out at the farthest reaches of this branch of the Hebrew Roots movement is a position even more radical, which attempts to draw Christians to such conclusions as:

- The New Testament was a forgery of the early Roman Catholic Church.

- The Apostle Paul sought to undermine the teachings of Jesus, and created a false religion.

94

- Jesus of Nazareth didn't exist at all—or, even worse, was not the Son of God, but was an incarnation of Satan the Devil himself.

It is the position of this **Field Guide** that both of the approaches described in point 5 are not just distracting to Christians, but are in fact Anti-Christ.

The Allure

Various aspects of the different branches of the Hebrew Roots movement have appeal to diverse audiences. The allure to individuals who come from a Christian Sabbatarian background (those who observe Saturday as the Sabbath) may be quite different from the allure to individuals of a general Protestant, or a specific Charismatic, background.

Christian Sabbatarians may already have a sense of "kinship" with Judaism because of their shared belief in the observance of the weekly Sabbath. Several Sabbatarian denominations have experienced turmoil and break-up in recent years. Quite a few former members have found themselves without any regular setting for fellowship on the Sabbath. Many such people have ended up exploring the Messianic Jewish culture. A large number of Messianic Jewish groups retain little of their Jewish cultural background, perhaps no more than a few surface family customs for the Jewish Holy Days. They might be more accurately described as Protestants with a few Jewish customs. But there has been an increasing development in recent years of ethnically Jewish groups which profess belief in Jesus as Messiah yet retain a strict adherence to their religious traditions, customs, and what they believe to be commandments of the written or oral Law. A number of these groups identify specifically with branches of the Hebrew Roots movement. And some Christian Sabbatarians have found such groups to be particularly appealing. Why?

Hebrew Roots Appeal to Sabbatarians

One such Sabbatarian group that has undergone turmoil is the Worldwide Church of God (WCG). Under founder Herbert Armstrong, the members of the organization accepted the observance of the annual biblical Holy Days, outlined in Leviticus 23, as being applicable to Christians, and rejected the observance of holidays such as Halloween, Christmas, and Easter because of the pagan origins of many of their customs. However, the Bible gives almost no details (other than the ancient sacrificial system, which ended with the destruction of the Temple in Jerusalem in 70 AD) on **how** to observe the Holy Days. The Old Testament makes it clear that they were to be days of rest from regular work, and days of assembly for religious worship. But only the prescribed Temple sacrifices and ceremonies are described. By the time of Christ, the Jews had developed many elaborate customs in connection with the Holy Days. However, the WCG did not get its impetus to observe the Holy Days from the Jews, but rather directly from the Bible.

The appeal to many, both Christians and agnostics, of Christmas and Easter are the beautiful decorations, the festive celebrations, and the quaint customs connected with them. When individuals joined the WCG, they gave up all of these customs and such, but there was nothing to replace them with in the observance of the Holy Days. The WCG culture never developed any traditions, customs, or decorations in connection with the Holy Days. And thus Holy Day gatherings were almost identical to any other church gathering, just "more of the same." With the break-up of the organization, many began wondering if there couldn't be a way to have more festive observances, and the obvious place to look for such possibilities was to the Jews. Wanting to keep Jesus at the center of Holy Day observances, most did not turn to Orthodox or Reform Jews, but rather to branches of the Messianic Jewish Movement. And through that connection, many have been exposed directly to specific Hebrew Roots ministries.

The WCG also emphasized the Old Testament in its teachings far more than most Protestant organizations traditionally have. Former WCG members have thus been more inclined to be interested in topics which pertain to the Old Testament than the average member of most Protestant denominations. Typical popular (not necessarily technical or scholarly) Christian literature, before the advent of the Hebrew Roots movement, has spent little focus on elaborating the connection between the Old and New Testaments. So there had been historically little material outside of WCG denominational literature for WCG members to study to feed their interest in the Old Testament. With the breakup of the WCG, many Bible students from that background have sought other sources for popular study materials. They have often been extremely attracted to the sort of technical Old Testament studies which are typical in material offered on recordings and in print by Hebrew Roots ministries.

One last emphasis in the ministry of Herbert Armstrong and the WCG which has primed many former WCG members to find Hebrew Roots material appealing was Armstrong's frequent claims to be restoring "forgotten" understanding of obscure Bible analogies and prophecies. WCG members could count on an endless stream of such "fresh" material, which made them feel as if they were privy to "inside information" not available to the average member of other denominations. With Armstrong's death, this source of "astounding new truth" (as he often described his latest teachings) dried up. For many, just plain old mundane study of the scriptures to find inspiration and guidance for Christian daily living was not satisfying. For this reason, some have found the teachings of various Hebrew Roots ministries to be just the source of fascinating tidbits of insight into obscure passages that they have missed.

Hebrew Roots Appeal to Non-Sabbatarians

One of the first appeals made by some Hebrew Roots proponents to Protestant or Catholic believers is an emotional one—they point to the persecution of Jews throughout history by Christians. Once someone realizes that Jesus was, indeed, a Jew, and lived in a Jewish society, it can seem only "fair" that Christians should right the historical wrong done to His physical brethren by studying into Judaism.

Many serious Bible students have never closely considered the history of religion of the past 2000 years, and the significant departure in most Christian settings from the evidence in the New Testament of what the first century Church was like. Because of this, some Hebrew Roots teachings may well appeal to their sense of logic. Ornate church buildings; a hierarchical "clergy" class separate from other Christians; liturgical schemes of worship with special clothing for those officiating (and with rigid repetition of the same few rituals week after week); "worship services" in which most participants are spectators and one man holds forth for an extended period with a prepared message—all of these things are not in evidence at all in the New Testament. Many Hebrew Roots teachers emphasize a completely different way of fellowship and worship for believers, and a number of students may find their alternative highly attractive.

For those Christians who have never used many Bible helps, such as commentaries and handbooks, the first Hebrew Roots lecture they hear may seem full of amazing biblical insight. The fact that the speaker represents either Messianic Judaism or some sort of specific Hebrew Roots ministry often gives such a speaker an aura of biblical authority. There is a mistaken assumption among many Christians that the average Jew is particularly learned in matters pertaining to the understanding of the Old Testament and the customs of the Jews of Jesus' time.

As with some of the followers of Herbert Armstrong mentioned above, many non-Sabbatarian Bible students are particularly fascinated by "astounding new revelations" in matters of biblical prophecy, metaphors, ancient history, and the like. A number of Hebrew Roots ministries specialize in presenting their material as hidden or lost facts, or "amazing truth restored to the Church."

Personal from the Author

A Search for Jewish Roots

In many families, even in "melting pot America," weddings are "ethnic" events, with lots of tradition and custom handed down from generation to generation. For instance, in American Polish communities, a wedding reception will likely include familiar traditional music—perhaps a polka band led by an accordion, favorite traditional foods, maybe even guests in traditional costumes from the Old Country. The same could be said for many other cultural groups in this country, such as those with roots in Mexico, Germany, and Italy.

However, when my husband, George, and I got married, in 1965, there were almost **no** traditions involved. Neither of us had roots in a particular ethnic, religious, or cultural group. Although we each had some background in our youth of religious affiliation, neither of us was actively involved in any religious community by the time of our wedding. Nor were we even close to our own immediate families—we decided to get married quietly in our college town without even telling our parents of our plans. Thus our "generic" ceremony was held in a side chapel of a non-denominational church, officiated by a minister whom we had chosen out of a phone book. And the tiny event was truly "ecumenical"—George's best man was a Russian expatriate (likely a member of the Russian Orthodox Church), my maid of honor was an Italian Roman Catholic, and the only guests were my Jewish roommates.

The **one** area in which we shared common cultural experiences with most Americans was in the general customs involved in the observance of Christmas, Easter, and other traditional holidays. But in our very first year of marriage, we studied together the literature of the Worldwide Church of God (WCG), and became convicted that these were non-biblical observances in which we could not, in good conscience, continue to participate. Becoming official WCG members in 1968, we soon found that even religious music of any kind not specifically endorsed by the Church was forbidden for our home. The church observed the annual Holy Days of the Bible, the same ones observed by the Jews, but with an emphasis on their significance pointing to Jesus Christ. Yet the church had no specific "customs" involved in the observances—Holy Day gatherings were basically the same kind of church service as our weekly Sabbath meetings, with perhaps the addition of more pieces of "special music" performed by a choir or soloists. There were no specific foods associated with the days (as there would be in Jewish homes), no traditional songs, no festive costumes or decorations. And thus we entered into a way of life taken up with many church activities, but accompanied by almost no replacements for the customs, traditions, music, festive decorations, or any other thing that would define special times for most Americans.

By the mid-1970's, we were beginning to really feel an emptiness inside that seemed to cry out to be filled with music, tradition, custom, and beauty. We were strongly committed to the doctrines of our church, but felt it was sadly lacking in all of these more aesthetically and emotionally satisfying elements in its gatherings and in our home life.

So where to turn? The church organization was very exclusivist, viewing itself as the "One True Church" and all other church organizations as "apostate." Thus we knew we couldn't dabble in any non-WCG Christian sources, no matter how non-denominational or doctrinally neutral, as that would get us in trouble with the WCG leadership. So we thought, "What about Judaism?" It had many things in common with our belief system, particularly the Sabbath and Holy Days. And it certainly had lots of traditions, customs, decorations, music, and so on! In the mid-1970's, outside major metropolitan areas, "Messianic Jews" were almost unheard of, so our only option for exploring the possibility of "borrowing" some things from Jews was to look into the non-Messianic Jewish community. We later ran across the ministry of Zola Levitt, a Messianic Jew, as well as the *Jews for Jesus* group. But we soon found out that both Zola and the Jews for Jesus do **not** represent a "Torah-observant" branch of Judaism (one that attempts scrupulous observance of all Old Testament laws). Although observing some Jewish customs, they also graft on such things as Christmas and Easter celebration to the Jewish customs of their converts to belief in Y'shua the Messiah (Jesus Christ). And this was not compatible with our beliefs. So we decided upon investigating the customs of non-Messianic Judaism.

Our daughter, Ramona, was very young at this time. Determined to see if we might find the roots we were looking for, and might pass on to her, in a more Jewish lifestyle, we began looking for sources of information and materials. Our first stop was the local public library, which happened to have an LP recording of Jewish traditional Sabbath and Holy Day music. Most of it was in Hebrew, but we were so excited to have something other than the WCG hymnal's music! That hymnal had been purged recently of all but a handful of Protestant hymns, replaced by a number of the gloomiest of the Psalms set to boring tunes written on commission by Dwight Armstrong, the brother of WCG founder Herbert Armstrong. So we taped the Holy Day music record to play over and over on Friday evening at the beginning of the Sabbath—even though we weren't sure what all the words were about.

One of the first books we purchased was titled *The First Jewish Catalog*. It was modeled on the *Whole Earth Catalog*. It was a big handbook aimed particularly at young Jewish people who may have become secular as they moved out on their own away from their more religious parents, but who were now looking to "return to their roots." It included everything from a detailed description of the meaning and traditional observance of the Sabbath and Holy Days, to how to keep a kosher kitchen, and how-to instructions for making beautiful Hebrew calligraphy. It also included information on how to go about creating your own personal library of Judaic materials. I tried their *hallah* (traditional Sabbath bread) recipe, and we pondered how we might add some of the customs to our Holy Day observances.

There was an address for the Jewish Publication Society, so we wrote to them, and joined their organization by paying an annual dues/fee so that we could get discounts on various Jewish publications. We purchased a number of books from them, hoping that perhaps they would not only provide us hints for the area of customs, but also help us in biblical understanding. We bought the Society's new translation of the Tanakh (what Christians label the Old Testament), an abridged version of *Maimonides' Mishneh Torah*, a thick *Encyclopedic Dictionary of Judaica*, and numerous other volumes.

We also ordered a copy of *The Second Jewish Catalog*. It covered even more details on Jewish lifestyle, including everything from circumcision rites for baby boys, to choosing a rabbi when you move to a new town. And in the back it included *The Jewish Yellow Pages*, which was literally a phone book for Jewish businesses and organizations throughout America.

From that we found some supply houses for decorations, children's materials, and so on. We sent away for a set of Purim hand puppets for Ramona. Purim is the holiday described in the biblical book of Esther. It is celebrated in Jewish communities by festivities particularly aimed at children. The story of Esther is retold in plays and musicals in local synagogues with much merriment and enthusiasm. Traditionally, the audience members use loud noisemakers and vocal jeers to drown out the name of the "bad guy" Haman each time it is mentioned in the play. That year on the evening of Purim, Mona and a little friend whose family also belonged to the WCG joined their dads watching a Purim play put on by their moms. Since the set of puppets we ordered only included Esther, Ahasuerus, Haman, and Mordechai, we had to improvise the rest of the cast. Re-enacting the part of the story of Esther where Mordechai was led around the city on the back of a horse, we pressed into service a plastic horse that came with Ramona's "Jane West" fashion doll. For the narrator, we had Mona's *Sesame Street* Cookie Monster hand puppet!

We really appreciate the exposure we thus had to many things Judaic. We came to understand more of the Jewish culture and community. We were fascinated to see in our *Jewish Directory and Almanac* how many famous folks are Jewish that you might never guess, given their "stage names" or Americanized names. Most folks realize that Steven Spielberg and Woody Allen are Jewish, and perhaps Milton Berle, and even Richard Dreyfus. But how about: Herb Alpert, Alan Arkin, Ed Asner, Lauren Bacall, George Burns, Jill Clayburgh, Neil Diamond, Kirk Douglas, Lorne Greene, Henry Winkler, Howard Cosell, and ... the Three Stooges!

In later years we attended a Jewish Passover *seder* (traditional dinner) put on by a lady in our Church of God congregation who was also attending a Reformed Jewish synagogue. (She later married a Jewish gentleman and converted to Judaism.) George was given a fancy *kippah* to wear (the skull-cap worn by observant Jews) which he still has, and Mona was invited to say the traditional blessing on the candles opening the evening's activities. (She still remembers the Hebrew words she memorized for that.)

However, that event was perhaps the culmination of the journey we had been on. We realized that night that, for all our attempts to graft on the customs and trappings of Judaism, we still felt no sense of roots in all of it. It was, in the final analysis, an attempt to "work up" feelings that those who are **born** into a Jewish community experience just as they experience breathing—naturally. We could **enjoy** the music, we could **respect** the meaning that others found in the customs. But we could not "tap into" the root in a way that would give us the sense of belonging and rejoicing we were looking for. We couldn't somehow "become Jews" by acting Jewish! For the Jews are not "acting"— they are **living** it because they were **born into** it.

We are aware that there are many from the same background that we have in the WCG who are just now beginning to look into the customs of Judaism in almost the same way we looked into them over thirty years ago. Perhaps some have the same yearnings we had for roots. We wish them well in their quest. Perhaps it **will** give some of them what they are looking for. At the same time, we hope they will understand our choice not to pursue that avenue for our own lives.

We have not been affiliated with the Worldwide Church of God or any of its off-shoots for over 20 years. Now that we are no longer hampered by the control of religious leaders, we are free to explore other options for making our family and fellowship activities as Christians more inspiring. We have found in recent years that there is much contemporary Christian music available that is biblically-sound, honors our Father and our Savior, yet is refreshing and lively. And even though one can certainly find "foreshadowings" of Y'shua, Jesus the Messiah, in some Jewish customs, He plays no prominent part in those customs. Rather than having to somehow graft references to our Lord and Savior onto music and customs, we are free to make Him an integral part as we develop our own.

Although we have appreciated what we have learned from Jewish sources, and have enjoyed learning about many of their customs and traditions, we have come to see that we **don't** have "Jewish roots." Although our Savior did live His life on earth in the Jewish community, and no doubt participated in variations of some of the customs that we studied and tried out, our connection with Him is **not** as Jews. Our roots go back much farther than first century Judaism. Our real "roots" are in the faith of Abraham—not an ethnic or cultural faith, but a supernatural faith. We have come to see that the most important thing is that we are not descendants of Abraham in the flesh, but in the spirit.

Concerns

It is the position of this **Field Guide** that any ministry or group which identifies itself with Hebrew Roots interests, and which promotes any of the following ideas, is undermining the basic elements of the Gospel of salvation through Jesus.

✓ Any claim that insists that adopting customs or traditions of Judaism is necessary to "get closer to God" or "understand the deep things of God."

✓ Any claim that such a ministry or group is revealing astounding information, unavailable to the average Bible reader, that will "transform your spiritual life." (Only Jesus truly transforms lives.)

✓ Any claim that insists that Christians must study the writings of the historical Jewish rabbis, such as those in the Talmud, in order to understand the Bible and live Godly lives.

✓ Any subtle hint, or overt claim, that the New Testament is inferior to the Old Testament as inspired by God.

✓ Any subtle hint, or overt claim, that Jesus of Nazareth was just a pious first century rabbi.

✓ Any subtle hint, or overt claim, that the Apostle Paul attempted to undermine the teachings of Jesus.

✓ Any unbalanced emphasis that takes the focus of participants from daily walking in the Spirit and truth, and shifts them to a constant search for more and more merely intellectual knowledge that is not applicable to their walk.

When understanding about the Hebrew Roots of Jesus and of the New Testament becomes not just an understanding but a definition of one's Faith, when it becomes not just a helpful perspective on the Bible but an elaborate "alternative lifestyle," then there is a legitimate concern that it may have become not just a tool but an obsession.

Nuggets of Truth

A number of principles emphasized by many Hebrew Roots ministries are absolutely true. To the extent that these principles have been ignored by mainstream Christianity, their re-introduction into the consciousness of Christians is valuable.

> Jesus was, indeed, born as a physical Jew, into a Jewish society. In fact, the twelve Apostles, the 120 original disciples who received the Holy Spirit on Pentecost in Acts 2, and the first 3000 converts that day were likely all Jews too (whether born physically as Jews, or Jewish converts). Thus the audiences who listened to Jesus preach most of the time were Jewish, and sometimes His teachings reflected their particular beliefs and culture. To the extent that those beliefs and that culture are different from our own, it is helpful to understand those differences to get the full meaning at times of what Jesus was saying, or the full implication of events surrounding His ministry.

> The Old Testament was, indeed, a Hebrew document, written in the Hebrew language. To the extent that someone unfamiliar with the nuances of that language (as it reflected the ancient Hebrew/Israelite and later Jewish culture) might misunderstand certain figures of speech, styles of writing, and types of literature common among the Hebrews, it is helpful to have information about these matters.

> The Church—the Body of Christ—founded by Jesus, which He promised to build, and which He promised to never leave or forsake, was indeed an outgrowth not of pagan religion, but of the religion of the Old Testament. The moral guidelines by which Christians understand the will of God for their behavior are, for instance, based on the principles found in the Law given to Moses on Mt. Sinai. Jesus and the writers of the New Testament quoted the Old Testament extensively as authoritative when seeking to establish the basis for many of their teachings. Some facets of the historical religious system that eventually came to be called Christianity have, indeed, been affected over the centuries by the influence of Gentile, pagan beliefs and customs. The careful student of the Bible should be able to identify those elements of his own belief system and observances which are based clearly on the scriptures of the

103

Old and New Testament, and those elements which are man-made additions. What he chooses to do with this understanding is certainly between him and his Lord. But he can only make informed decisions if he has accurate information.

Examination

The current Hebrew Roots movement does not have a central focal point. It is made up of a wide variety of ministries that do not have a common history. A number of them appear to have been started by just one person, or a small group of people, as a result of their own independent Bible study. Most have a history of twenty years or less.

Although there are some Messianic Jewish ministries that have a Hebrew Roots emphasis, they do not dominate the Hebrew Roots movement. The general Messianic Jewish movement tends to have more of an emphasis on reaching non-Messianic Jews with the claims of Jesus as the Messiah. Thus, while the Jews involved in certain branches of Messianic Judaism do maintain their Jewish traditions and customs, they may have little interest in persuading non-Jews to adopt those traditions and customs. In fact, the typical Messianic Jewish rabbi may well insist that Gentiles have no need to keep the weekly Sabbath or the annual Holy Days, observe any portion of the biblical dietary restrictions, or follow any other physical guidelines. They view all of these things as being just part of a specific covenant between God and the Jews, not as laws or even principles which non-Jews need adopt as Christians.

Those Jewish or non-Jewish representatives of much of the Hebrew Roots movement, on the other hand, are persuaded that Gentiles need to understand, and in many cases participate in, Jewish customs and traditions.

This is in distinction from the approach of various Christian Sabbatarian groups, including those that observe certain dietary restrictions and may celebrate the biblical Holy Days of Leviticus 23. This applies to offshoots of the Worldwide Church of God, the Seventh Day Adventists, and several smaller Sabbatarian groups. These groups do not make reference to Judaism in their theology, but rather claim to get their choice of observances directly from the Bible. Nor do they pay any attention to the teachings of such Jewish writings as the Talmud. Therefore, they have not historically had a perspective that they were "restoring the Hebrew Roots" of the Christian faith, but have been merely trying to follow what they perceive as the biblical roots of that faith.

One Christian Sabbatarian group that has not taken that approach is the Church of God, Jerusalem Acres (COGJA), with headquarters in Cleveland, Tennessee. The group is an outgrowth of a denomination called the Church of God which has Pentecostal roots and which formed around the turn of the last century. The founder of the COGJA off-shoot introduced the observance of the weekly Sabbath and the annual Holy Days to his followers in the 1950s. Records seem to indicate this was not a result of accepting the teachings of any other Sabbatarian group, but rather from his own Bible study.

The group has come to call its particular theology *New Testament Judaism*. Unlike the Seventh Day Adventists, and the Worldwide Church of God during the lifetime of founder Herbert Armstrong, the COGJA does incorporate some specific Jewish elements in its worship, including using the Star of David as a religious symbol. And the denomination does view itself as having a mission to persuade other Christian groups to adopt the same Jewish perspective. One of the top leaders in the denomination formed a separate outreach ministry a few years ago with the specific mission to spread a Hebrew Roots type of message via literature, conferences, speaking engagements, and so on. The COGJA continues to maintain the Pentecostal emphasis in its ministry also, and thus "speaking in tongues" is a part of its theology. This may give it an opportunity to witness for the Hebrew Roots message more effectively in Charismatic circles than Hebrew Roots ministries that do not share this doctrine.

Evaluation

As noted in the **Concerns** section above, it is the approach of this **Field Guide** that certain branches of the Hebrew Roots movement can be spiritually harmful to Christians. Those that insist that outward, man-made rituals are necessary in some way to promote spiritual growth can ensnare Christians in a bondage to attempting to get close to God by works of the flesh. And those that downplay the New Testament, as if it is merely a poor and inferior addendum to the Old Testament—rather than the revelation of the Good News of salvation available through the blood of Jesus Christ—can lead Christians away from the true Gospel into the same sort of legalism condemned by Christ in the Pharisees of the first century.

Because the Hebrew Roots Movement has so many facets, it is particularly important that believers realize that the label Hebrew Roots can be very misleading. There are some ministries which identify themselves as Hebrew Roots groups which merely wish to help Bible students understand the social setting in which Jesus taught, that they might learn more clearly the lessons of the Gospels. If someone is first exposed to the general Hebrew Roots Movement through such a ministry, they may assume that all Hebrew Roots groups have the same perspective. If another Hebrew Roots group comes along with similar teachings on the surface, but with a hidden agenda of undermining belief in Jesus Christ, the unwary may find themselves swept along into accepting error before they have a chance to closely examine the claims.

There are a number of Hebrew Roots groups which do not present the problem of rejection of Jesus, but which still may be misleading, as they place undue emphasis on Judaism of the present and its customs and traditions. Judaism is not "the religion of the Bible," as some would like to represent it. It is a human creation that has evolved over the centuries. Just as the Catholic Church has done through the centuries, Judaism has taken the very limited information in the scriptures, and encrusted it with layer upon layer of speculation and man-made traditions. There is no indication in the teachings of Jesus or the Apostles that any of this is necessary for a relationship with God. Jesus told the woman at the well that the day was coming—and in fact, already had arrived—when people who wished to worship God would no longer need to go to Jerusalem to do so, using even the God-ordained rituals of the temple. True worshippers would worship God "in spirit and in truth." Paul made it very clear in his writings that there was no need for Christians to "become Jewish" and observe Jewish customs and traditions in order to accept Jesus as Lord and Savior and become part of the family of God, part of the Body of Christ. Those Hebrew Roots groups that attempt to Judaize the lives of Christians are not following the admonitions of scripture, but their own theories about what pleases God.

A Caution to moderate Hebrew Roots ministries

Those ministries which identify themselves as part of the Hebrew Roots movement, but who sincerely wish to avoid any of the excesses and deceptions of some of the others in the movement, need to perhaps consider carefully any joint efforts with other Hebrew Roots ministries whose agenda is not totally clear. If they are not careful, they could find themselves unwittingly promoting anti-Christian speakers. And they also need to consider carefully joint projects with other groups that may show interest in Hebrew Roots concepts. It would appear from a number of conference speaking lists across America that Hebrew Roots interests are making strange religious bedfellows. Some within the Hyper-Charismatic movement, for instance, are arranging conferences that include Hebrew Roots speakers on the same schedule with representatives of the most radical edges of the Charismatic movement. As humorist Ashley Brilliant once noted, "How can I trust you if I can't trust those you trust?"

The easy availability of specific anti-Christian writings on the Internet seems to have influenced an increasing number of former Christians to abandon their faith in Jesus of Nazareth in recent years. Here are two short excerpts from an email, posted in February 1998 on a Christian Internet forum by one former member of the Worldwide Church of God, whose reading of material by various anti-Christian authors led her quickly down this path in less than two years.

> One day about two years ago, I had been down praying and had asked YHWH to help me to better understand HIS ways and His truth, because of all the mass of confusion with WCG and all the splinter groups etc. When I got up from that prayer, a thought came to my mind: "What if Christianity is the greatest fraud that Satan has deceived the world with?" I immediately repented of that thought. But it was at that time that I resolved to prove to myself whether Christianity was true or not, and so began a two year research on the subject.

> … Having weighed all the evidence and declared my verdict, I hereby publicly renounce and repent of my idolatry committed against the great Creator. I reject Christianity totally and will make all efforts to serve the Elohim of the fathers, Abraham, Isaac and Jacob and all the other faithful servants of YHWH the only Deity of Israel.

LINK

Elements of Hebrew Roots teachings can be seen these days even in the teachings of various Charismatic televangelists, such as John Hagee and Pat Robertson. And one of the most popular attractions at the Holy Land Experience theme park near Walt Disney World in Florida is a lecture about the Christian symbolism and prophetic implications of the observance of the annual biblical Holy Days, such as Passover and the Feast of Tabernacles. But the Hebrew Roots elements in these arenas is a secondary area of interest. It is the groups and teachers that define themselves as part of the Hebrew Roots Movement which are the focus of the concern in this profile.

The following website has one of the most extensive investigative reports on the Web regarding a number of popular Hebrew Roots teachers. Although some readers may not agree with all of the conclusions of the website author on specific doctrinal matters, the documentation and reporting is solid and comprehensive. Those considering affiliation with or support of one or more of the Hebrew Roots teachers profiled on the site would do well to very carefully consider the information provided before making such a decision.

www.seekgod.ca/topichr.htm

Chapter 15

Religious Lingo Lexicon

The following lexicon is a collection of terms which may be unfamiliar to many who do not have exposure to much contemporary religious debate. The definitions provided are brief and relatively value-neutral.

Within definitions, words or phrases which themselves have a separate entry in this Lexicon are indicated in *italics*. Personal names that are in *italics* indicate that the individual is identified in the **Who's Who Digest** chapter of this **Field Guide**.

Biblical passages quoted below are from the King James Version (KJV) unless otherwise noted.

Anglo-Israelism

See: *British-Israelism* definition.

"Beasts of the field"

A number of passages in the KJV Old Testament refer to the "beasts of the field." Most Bible scholars assume this is just another name for either four-footed animals of any kind, or for wild animals. However, certain racist Bible teachers allege that this term is actually a reference to all races other than Caucasians in general or Northern European "whites" in particular. All other races are alleged to have been created prior to the creation of Adam, and to not be made "in the image of God" ... with the exception that some also have a special explanation for the origin of the modern Jewish people. See: *Identity* definition.

Bible Codes

It is alleged by some writers that the Old Testament, in the original Hebrew manuscripts, contains "hidden messages." The theory is that these can be discerned by a process of starting with a given letter and going forward or backward to the next letter in the hidden message by skipping a prescribed number of letters each time. Some Jewish researchers have thus claimed to have found the names of many of the famous Jewish sages of centuries past "encoded" in the first five books of the Bible, what they would refer to as the Torah (thus the alternate name for this process, Torah Codes.)

More recently, some Christian authors have claimed to be able to use the same system on both the Torah and the prophetic books of the Old Testament. And they thus have found, they claim, "amazing" groupings of words and phrases which intersect, and tell a "word picture" of some event in the distant or recent past. The implication of all of this is that such secret, encoded wordings could only have been caused by God, and therefore substantiate the validity of the Bible as a supernatural document.

Most legitimate Bible scholars and mathematicians are highly skeptical of the validity of these claims. There are many sites on the Internet that examine the claims. Here's one:

> http://web.archive.org/web/20071010001859/http://www.nsli.com/.../torah/

British-Israelism

British-Israelism is the belief that the Anglo-Saxon inhabitants of Great Britain, as well as those who migrated from there to other parts of the British Commonwealth and to the United States, are the direct descendants of the ancient Israelite tribes of Ephraim and Manasseh. The term "Anglo-Israelism" is sometimes used as an alternative designation of this belief. The importance of this identification to those who believe in it, is that these peoples would thus be the legitimate inheritors of the promises by God to the patriarch Abraham that his descendants would have great physical blessings, including "possessing the gates of their enemies."

Brownsville Outpouring

Also called the Pensacola Outpouring. This was a *Hyper-Charismatic* "revival," a clone of the *Toronto Blessing* movement and with similar roots, begun in 1995 at the Brownsville Assembly of God Church in Pensacola, Florida and continuing for several years. BAOG Pastor *John Kilpatrick* invited evangelist *Steve Hill* to speak at the church on Father's Day that year, and the service turned to pandemonium when such manifestations as people weeping, falling to the ground, and shaking violently occurred. These were believed to be evidence of an "outpouring" of the Holy Spirit.

Here is a telling comment from one webpage which examines the Outpouring, and provides some very poignant quotes.

> www.deceptioninthechurch.com/brownsvi.htm

At the district conference referred to earlier, Kilpatrick admitted to the assembled pastors that he has been so "drunk in the spirit" that he actually struck his youth pastor's car with his own. He said that while driving he had hit many garbage cans sitting at the curb on several occasions because he was so "drunk." He added that his wife (a visitor to Toronto, by the way) has been so drunk she couldn't cook. Sometimes, his drunken stupors are so severe that he has to be taken from the service in a wheel chair, Kilpatrick said.

It is not just "outsiders" who have questioned the Brownsville Outpouring. The following is a short excerpt from a 1997 article titled *Scriptural and Theological Concerns about the Revival at Brownsville A/G—and other churches like it* by an Assemblies of God minister who had serious concerns about his denomination's acceptance of these manifestations.

http://op.50megs.com/ditc/SCRIPTUR.HTM

I myself was a polio victim 45 years ago and use a wheel chair. I've had to struggle firsthand with the doctrine of divine healing. I have come to what I feel is a balanced faith message. But some in my own denomination would disagree with me. The same is true with signs and wonders. Every Assemblies of God church did not have manifestations like "slaying in the Spirit" or "jerking and shaking in the Spirit." But since "Pensacola," more churches want the success and the numbers they've attracted.

...I am convinced that most of what is happening at Pensacola that I saw and what I have observed firsthand at [our] Church is a by-product of psychological-conditioning, the power of suggestion and mass-hysteria. Most of the people are innocently participating and desperately wanting something visible and tangible from God. Their lives are hurting and humdrum and in need of a life-changing experience. They might feel excited and refreshed now but eventually having to seek an emotional and physical experience continually, will get old and routine.

God's physical touch is offered as a quick fix. Getting into "the River of the Spirit" or asking God for "His fire to fall" in your life is said to change you drastically.

What used to come from in-depth, intensive Bible study, scripture memorization and disciplined living can now be achieved from an experience with God. "Let God knock you over and do spiritual surgery on you while you are lying on the ground. You'll be changed, made new, happier and more joyful if you come up to the altar and receive this experience. Just come forward and drink of this River and you'll never be the same." This is the song of the "Pensacola Revival." I only wish it were that easy for every Christian.

... I have felt it necessary to resign my pastoral position at [our] Church. I see this "revival" in a different way than the others. I really feel very uncomfortable around the atmosphere caused by people falling over backwards, shaking, jerking, jumping up and down, and other manifestations.

I love to teach and preach God's Word. In fact it's my personal opinion that a greater, longer-lasting change, comes more from sound Scriptural, stirring, solid Bible preaching and teaching, than supposed physical manifestations.

I only hope and pray there is still room in the Assemblies of God for me and others like me. Only time will tell. I had to leave a church I pastored for ten years because of the hyper-faith controversy. Many in the church thought I should be healed from my disability. It became such a big issue I felt it best to resign. When you have a severe physical deformity that causes daily pain and frustration, it makes it very difficult to be in a place where miracles and God's power to heal are constantly promoted. Being only human, there are deep hurts of frustration at the place of feeling terrible, that you've done all you think you can to get a miracle and still nothing happens.

You can come to a place of resolve and accept God's sovereign will, then only to be told "it is God's will you be healed if you have enough faith," or "get in on the real move of God, if you want a miracle. " etc.... A disabled person can only take so much.

Now at [our] Church I am so uncomfortable, because of the "revival controversy," I must resign.

Charismatic

The word charismatic comes from the Greek word *charisma*, which is usually translated in the KJV as "gift." Paul uses charisma in 1 Corinthians 12 to designate the supernatural "gifts" made available by the Holy Spirit. The term Charismatic when applied to religious groups, teachers or customs usually implies that the participants believe that the spiritual gifts described in the New Testament are all available to Christians in modern times and should be expected as a natural part of each Christian's life. This would include the more "supernatural" gifts such as healing and "speaking in tongues." See: *Pentecostal* definition for the connection between the terms Charismatic and Pentecostal. Also See: the ***Pentecostal and Charismatic—What's the Difference?*** chapter of this ***Field Guide*** for further discussion.

Conspiracy Theories

A number of religious ministries and secular groups promote a view of world history which is based on the theory that there are one or more networks of extremely powerful individuals behind the scenes of world events, conspiring together to manipulate either western civilization or the whole world for their own nefarious purposes. These Conspiracy Theories take many forms. Some postulate a Communist overthrow of America from within. Others insist that the United Nations is poised to impose external domination on the US, putting protestors into internment camps. Still others focus on an alleged long-term international conspiracy of financial masterminds, often called "The Illuminati," who have been allegedly plotting for over 100 years to establish a New World Order which will be the fulfillment of the prophecies of Revelation.

Cult

The word cult has historically had no particularly negative connotation. It could be used by historians and sociologists to refer to any "system of religious worship or ritual" of the past, such as the "cult of Diana of the Ephesians." Some writers have used it as an alternative to the word "sect" to indicate a religious group that has broken away from a larger religious denomination.

In addition, the term cult is used in a more contemporary sense to indicate "devoted attachment to, or extravagant admiration for a person, principle, etc." In this context one could even refer to the "cult of Elvis fans" or the "cult of strict vegetarianism."

But in the past 25 years or so the term cult has taken on more negative connotations in media reports and religious literature. Some writers and speakers use it specifically to indicate a small religious group believed to be dangerous to themselves or others. Other writers use it to indicate a group which has beliefs contrary to the standard, historically-accepted theological positions of a particular religion such as Christianity or Judaism.

Since there is no standard definition for the term cult when used in these ways, it is important when using the term in discussions about contemporary religion to carefully define how the word is being used. For more clarification on the term cult, and for a description on how it is used in this *Field Guide*, see the chapter *Cult, Occult, New Age—What's the Difference?*

Deliverance

The term deliverance in religious use describes the process by which a person believed to be under the control of an evil supernatural entity called a demon is delivered from the control of that demon. In the New Testament, Jesus and some of His disciples are described as "casting out demons" from individuals, and thus "delivering" them from "demon possession."

Certain religious groups, such as the Roman Catholic Church, have a specific ritual which they use in attempts to deliver people from what is perceived as demonic possession. Such a ritual is usually performed by a specific religious official such as a priest, and is referred to as an exorcism. In modern times, some teachers use the term demon *possession* to indicate that someone is totally under the control of the evil entity, and demon *influence* to indicate that some portion of the person's life is affected externally by one or more demons. See: *Deliverance Ministry* definition.

Deliverance Ministry

Someone who has a deliverance ministry believes they have the ability to discern demon influence or possession in the lives of others, and power to "deliver" others from this influence or possession. See: *Deliverance* definition.

Dominion theology

See: *Kingdom Now* definition.

Ecumenical

An adjective indicating the efforts to promote unity or cooperation among religious groups, particularly among the various denominations which refer to themselves as "Christian." It can range from aggressive attempts to merge denominations, to less threatening plans to just hold joint public ecumenical worship services for special occasions such as Thanksgiving.

Ecumenism

A movement of deliberate efforts to diminish concern about the differences among religious denominations, and thus to promote unity among them. This term is used in many conservative religious groups as a hostile, critical label to put on those from their own background whom they believe to be "watering down" the doctrinal distinctives of the group in efforts to break down barriers between their group and others. A charge that someone in their ranks is promoting *ecumenical* ideas is taken very seriously by those who have strong concerns about the doctrines of other groups. Broad-based movements such as Promise Keepers do seem to be built on the theory that ecumenism is good … thus they can appeal to such widely divergent groups as Catholics and Methodists.

Eisegesis

The word eisegesis is a theological term used to describe an approach to interpreting a passage in the Bible by "reading into" the passage a meaning that is not evident at all by the passage itself or the context in which it appears in the Bible. Thus eisegesis is usually perceived as a negative term, and indicates that the person using the method of eisegesis is not being intellectually honest. They are, rather, coming to the passage with a pre-conceived notion on a particular doctrinal matter, and wishing to force the passage to fit that preconceived notion. The opposite of eisegesis is *exegesis*. See: *Exegesis* definition and *Hermeneutics* definition.

Eschatology

Eschatology is the branch of Theology dealing with the ultimate outcome of history. It includes doctrines related to such topics as death, resurrection, the "afterlife," and future prophetic events such as the those surrounding the return of Christ.

Exegesis

The word exegesis is a theological term used to describe an approach to interpreting a passage in the Bible by critical analysis. It includes using the context around the passage, comparison with other parts of the Bible, an understanding of the language and customs of the time of the writing, and other factors in an attempt to clearly understand what the original writer intended to convey. In other words, it is trying to "pull out" of the passage the meaning inherent in it. The opposite of exegesis is *eisegesis*. See: *Eisegesis* definition and *Hermeneutics* definition.

Five-fold Ministry

The term five-fold ministry is a catch-phrase in certain Charismatic circles to indicate a belief that something was missing in the leadership—the ministry—of institutional Christian churches until recently. This concern was based on the following scripture:

Ephesians 4:11-13

> It was he [Christ] who gave some to be apostles, some to be prophets, some to be evangelists, and some to be pastors and teachers, to prepare God's people for works of service, so that the body of Christ may be built up until we all reach unity in the faith and in the knowledge of the Son of God and become mature, attaining to the whole measure of the fullness of Christ. (NIV)

Both the Catholic and most Protestant groups have always had the three "roles" of evangelist, pastor, and teacher as part of their systems. But it was typical for them to consider that the roles of Apostles and Prophets ceased in the first century. The usual reasoning was that these roles were necessary for the establishment of the Church, but once it was established they were no longer needed.

There have been a number of movements in the past 100+ years which have insisted that this assumption is incorrect, and that to fully function as the Body of Christ, "the Church" at large needs active, contemporary Apostles and Prophets, restoring the "five-fold" nature of leadership in the Church. In recent decades, this notion has become very prominent in some Charismatic circles, and there are a number of individuals who identify themselves as an Apostle or a Prophet and/or are recognized by others in their own circle as fulfilling that role—even though "outsiders" may find the claims spurious or even, in some cases, laughable.

Fourth Wave

Some recent writers are beginning to refer to the Hebrew Roots movement (See: *Hebrew Roots* definition) as the Fourth Wave of a series of four movements they consider necessary elements to the restoration of the Full Gospel. See: *Third Wave* definition for an explanation of the first three of these waves/movements.

Gematria

Gematria is a Jewish system of mystical rules for Biblical interpretation which relies on calculating the "numerical value" of various words and passages and then comparing these numerical values to other words and passages. Each letter of the Hebrew alphabet has a corresponding number. The numerical equivalent of each of the letters in a word is combined, and the total noted. Then an elaborate system of juggling these numbers is used to find "hidden meaning" in the words. Gematria is an integral part of the teachings of the Kabbalah. See: *Kabbalah* definition.

Generational Curse

Some teachers involved in *deliverance ministries* believe that individuals can "inherit" misfortune and a tendency to specific types of moral weaknesses and sins from their ancestors by what is referred to as a generational curse. Some view this as a demon who is given power to harass succeeding generations of individuals who were particularly given to certain kinds of sins. Others view it as more of a "genetic inheritance." It is not believed to have any connection with actual physical or chemical causes, such as a genetic tendency to alcoholism. It is rather viewed as a completely spiritual issue.

Under this theory, therefore, some people are "predestined" to commit certain kinds of sins or have certain moral weaknesses. The solution offered is to have a deliverance ministry "discern"

116

what generational curses may be involved in the life of the individual seeking help, and then to renounce the curses specifically. For those who believe the cause is an actual demon, the deliverance ministry will attempt to "cast it out." See: *Deliverance* definition, *Deliverance ministry* definition, *Spiritual Warfare* definition.

Hebrew Name

See: *Sacred Name* definition.

Hebrew Roots

Hebrew Roots is a broad term for ministries which emphasize the need for studying the scriptures from a perspective of the ancient Hebrew, Middle Eastern context they were written in, rather than trying to fit what is read into a modern Western worldview. Such ministries particularly allege that the teachings and life of Jesus can only be understood correctly by realizing that He was a Jewish rabbi living in a Jewish society. And thus one needs to understand the first century customs, traditions, teachings, and beliefs of the Jews in order to understand the Gospel.

Some such ministries also teach that not only should Christians study these things, but they should personally adopt many of the customs and beliefs of modern Judaism. Still others reject modern Judaism as a role model and attempt to reconstruct a life-style they believe to reflect the beliefs, customs and practices of ancient Israel before the time of Christ. See: the **Hebrew Roots Movement** chapter of this **Field Guide** for more details on the various branches of this movement.

Heretic, Heresy

Although the word heretic is commonly used by religious groups to indicate someone who teaches a belief contrary to the group's doctrinal understanding, the Greek word that is translated heretic in the King James Bible actually means someone who **causes division**. The New Testament condemns those who are heretics by this definition.

But this does not necessarily mean that it condemns people whose understanding on a variety of Biblical matters differs from some central "doctrinal statement" endorsed by any particular group. It rather indicates that those who hold differing views should not **use** those **differences** as a crowbar to separate the Christian fellowship of which he is a part.

Thus a heresy as defined Biblically is not just an **understanding on some doctrine** that differs from an officially-accepted interpretation, but an **understanding that is used to divide** brethren. In Romans 14, the Apostle Paul notes that it is acceptable for people in a fellowship to have different beliefs about disputable matters, but not to allow these differences to cause irreparable divisions in the group.

The information noted above about heresy and heretics is intended to clarify the implication of the Greek underlying the words in the King James Bible. However, in the English language, the words do, indeed, carry a different connotation. In most religious groups, if someone is called a heretic, it means to those in authority that that person has rejected one or more beliefs that are considered fundamental to the doctrinal understanding of the group.

Hermeneutics

Hermeneutics is a theological term for the science of careful, analytical interpretation of the meaning of passages in the Bible. The Bible is not just one document, a narrative written by one writer at one point in history. It is a collection of writings by numerous writers, created over a period of over 1000 years. And these writings include history, narrative description, poetry, revelation, symbolic dreams and visions, and more. In order to clearly understand what a Biblical writer was attempting to convey to the reader, a number of factors must be considered.

Is the passage intended to be a literal description of events, or a symbolic representation of something? Is the passage declaring a principle applicable for all time for all people, or was it intended to be relevant to just a certain group of people at a certain time and place? These and many other considerations need to be incorporated in the effort to understand how the passage may apply to the Bible student of the 21st century. See: *Exegesis* definition, *Eisegesis* definition.

Hierarchy/Hierarchical

A hierarchy is "a **system** of church government by priests or other clergy in **graded ranks**." The church is viewed as being divided sharply into two spiritual "classes" of believers. The superior class is the clergy, who are in charge of worship, who do all of the teaching and counseling, and who make and enforce the rules within Christian fellowships. And the inferior class is made up of the laity, or laymen, who obey the clergy in all matters, and whose main function within the Body is to provide the tithes and offerings by which the clergy are supported. In a hierarchical system, each rank of the clergy is in subjection to all of those in any of the ranks above them.

In some church organizations, this hierarchical system of "graded ranks" can be extremely elaborate. The 1911 edition of the *Encyclopedia Britannica* lists the ranks which were already established in the Catholic Church as early as the third century A.D. They included the primary ranks of bishops, presbyters, deacons, subdeacons, acolytes, exorcists, readers, and doorkeepers. In addition, there were a number of "minor ranks" below those which included the *copiatae* (grave-diggers), the *psalmistae* (chanters), and the *parabolani* who had the extremely risky job of visiting the sick in times of plague.

The Protestant churches have not customarily had as many ranks in their governmental systems as those listed above. And many religious groups limit the ranks to pastors, elders, and deacons. However, no matter how many ranks are involved, most of these hierarchical systems do tend to be based on the premise that an individual will "work their way up" through these ranks in order to reach the levels of most authority, power and control over those ranks of clergy below them, and the laity below all of the clergy.

Some Bible students and teachers are convinced that this whole notion of dividing the Body of Christ, the Church, into two "classes" of believers, and developing a system of graded ranks of power for the clergy class, is not found in the New Testament, but is rather an imitation of secular or pagan systems of government. Jesus said, "He who would be greatest among you shall be the servant of all." And He also said that those in positions of responsibility in the Body should not "lord it over" the rest of the members. Thus it is suggested that authority in the Body was intended by Jesus to be an **authority of example and influence** of older, more spiritually mature Christians, and developing maturity in everyone else toward that level of spiritual growth. From this perspective, the words "elder" or "deacon" or "evangelist" are not titles of an **office** of power, but descriptions of **function** within the Body.

Holy Ghost Glue

After people are "*slain in the spirit*" at some Charismatic meetings, they sometimes feel inexplicably "stuck to the floor" and unable to rise for some time. This is believed by those involved to be a manifestation of the power of God, and is often referred to as "Holy Ghost glue."

Holy Laughter

Holy Laughter is a phenomenon that occurs at certain Charismatic gatherings. Some participants (from a handful to almost the whole audience at times) find themselves laughing uncontrollably for no particular reason, sometimes even to the point of falling out of their chairs and rolling on the floor in convulsions of laughter. This can occur no matter the topic being addressed by the current speaker from the pulpit—even when the speaker is expounding on such matters as Eternal Judgment and Hell. It is taught in such settings that this is a "supernatural manifestation" that indicates a special infilling of the individual by the Holy Spirit.

Although this phenomenon has been reported in isolated instances for the past 100 years or so, it first attracted wide-spread attention in the early 1990s as one of the typical manifestations involved with the "*Toronto Blessing*" movement. The most prominent individual connected with the Holy Laughter phenomenon is South African evangelist *Rodney Howard-Browne*, who styles himself "Joel's Bartender." This is a reference to the prophecy in Joel 2 regarding the pouring out of the Holy Spirit. Those who are overcome with Holy Laughter at Howard-Browne's meetings are viewed as being "drunk with the Holy Spirit," and in some cases literally do behave as if physically intoxicated, to the point where some are unable to drive home from meetings.

Hundred-fold Blessing

Within the *Word Faith* movement, a number of preachers use a gimmick called the Hundred-fold Blessing in order to increase donations from their live audience at an evangelistic campaign or from called-in pledges for religious fund drives. The preacher will indicate that God has told him expressly, by direct revelation, that for a very limited time He will bless anyone who gives sacrificially with a miraculous return on their contribution in the near future that will be one hundred times the amount of that contribution. The audience or viewers are urged to not "miss their blessing," and to hurry and put money in the offering plate or call in their offering pledge. Anecdotal stories are shared by the preacher of people who have accepted the hundred-fold challenge in past evangelistic campaigns or religious television pledge drives and who have miraculously received unexpected monetary windfalls or gifts of cars or other expensive items. See: the **Word Faith Movement** chapter of this **Field Guide.**

Hyper-Charismatic

The term Hyper-Charismatic is often used to designate those *Charismatic* teachers and groups in recent decades which attribute extremely unusual, non-biblical manifestations in their meetings to the action of the Holy Spirit. This would include individuals being "glued to the floor" for a period by a supernatural force for no apparent reason, people uncontrollably making animal sounds such as crowing like a rooster or barking like a dog in the midst of a worship service, and other such phenomena. Hyper-Charismatic is often also used to designate those teachings which make vaunted claims that the average Christian can control with absolute certainty his circumstances, including his health and physical prosperity, through the power that he can obtain by mastering certain "keys" allegedly found in the Bible..

Identity

Identity is a term used to designate a racist religious movement whose fundamental tenet is that Northern European whites are the true descendants of the tribes of ancient Israel. They further teach that only these peoples have full access to a covenant relationship with the Creator God. Thus they declare that they need to reach these peoples with the "truth of their **identity**" as "True Israel." This is sometimes connected with an insistence that all non-whites are not descendants of Adam, are not actually made in the image of God, but were created by God in a separate creation event before the description in Genesis of the creation of Adam and Eve. Some in the Identity movement would also insist that modern Jews are not really descendants of the patriarch Jacob (Israel) at all, but are imposters. Instead, they are the descendants of a sexual encounter between Eve and the Devil in the Garden of Eden. (See: *Satan's Seed* definition.)

Jewish Roots

See: *Hebrew Roots* definition.

Kabbalah

The Kabbalah is a Jewish system of philosophy which is based on mystical methods of Biblical interpretation and finding "hidden meanings" in the passages of the Bible, such as *gematria*. Developed particularly by certain Jewish rabbis of the Middle Ages, it includes extensive occultic elements. The word itself is a Hebrew word meaning "received lore or tradition." In English it is spelled in various ways, including Cabala, Kabala, Qabbalah and Kabbala, See: *Gematria* definition, *Occult* definition.

Kansas City Prophets

The Kansas City Prophets is a designation of a group of men believed by some to be modern Prophets, who are affiliated with the Metro *Vineyard* Church in Kansas City. This church was known as the Kansas City Fellowship (KCF) under Pastor *Mike Bickle* in the 1980s when Bickle received what he believed to be a revelation from God that his ministry was to be the center of a modern "prophetic and apostolic" movement that would be part of the restoration of the *Five-Fold Ministry* to the Church at large. Bickle surrounded himself with a number of men who claimed prophetic abilities, including *Paul Cain*, John Paul Jackson and *Bob Jones* (not the same Bob Jones of Bob Jones University).

These men conducted many prophetic gatherings, offering prophetic pronouncements to individuals (*personal prophecy*), to groups (predictions about future "moves of God" the group could expect, for instance) and to the public at large about events that might affect many people, such as earthquakes. This gathered the Kansas City Prophets a wide following and support in some Charismatic circles.

This enthusiasm waned a bit in the early 1990s when it became obvious that quite a large percentage of the alleged prophecies failed. Around the same time, "Prophet" Bob Jones was exposed for immorality and stepped out of the limelight. A pastor in the Kansas City area wrote a scathing indictment of the movement which led to widespread negative publicity.

At this point, Vineyard founder *John Wimber* stepped in and offered to bring the prophetic ministry under the "covering" of his ministry and oversee a dampening of the "excesses" that had been evident in the ministry. The KCF thus became an official Vineyard congregation, and the ministry continued unabated. All of these men, including Jones, who has been pronounced "restored," still function in what they believe to be the role of Prophet, and their pronouncements are still accepted by many as being inspired by God.

Kingdom Now

Kingdom Now is the designation of a religious movement that teaches that Christians do not need to wait for the Return of Christ to the earth to set up His millennial kingdom—they can expect a powerful manifestation of that Kingdom right now … or at least in the near future. They believe that Christians will soon come, through the power of God, to have dominion over earthly society, and only then will Jesus return. This dominion will not be limited to spiritual influence, but actual social, political, and economic control. The ideas behind this movement are sometimes referred to as Dominion Theology and Reconstructionism.

Latter Rain

The term Latter Rain is used by a variety of *Pentecostal* and *Charismatic* writers to indicate a major outpouring of the Holy Spirit, evidenced by supernatural manifestations, to come before the Return of Christ. The term comes from the Biblical references to the "early" (or "former") season of rainfall and "latter" season of rainfall necessary in Palestine to create a bountiful harvest. Thus in metaphor, the "early rain" of the Holy Spirit would have been the manifestations in the first century described in the Book of Acts. And the Latter Rain would be a modern repetition of this.

Legalism

The term legalism is used by many authors to describe any belief system which implies that a Christian receives salvation and right standing with God by carefully following a list of expected behaviors which has been constructed by the creators of the system. Some teachers have used the term to describe those who accept various Old Testament Biblical laws and principles, such as tithing, as being applicable in some way to Christians. But if acceptance of those laws or principles are not being viewed as a method to "earn" or "preserve" salvation, this is not really related to the specific concept of legalism. It is entirely possible for a religious group to reject any or all of the Ten Commandments, but to substitute for them a list of forbidden activities such as card-playing or dancing, and still be proponents of a legalistic system.

Manifest Sons of God

One of the doctrines promoted by the more radical members of the Latter Rain movement (See: *Latter Rain* definition) of the 1940s was that there would come a time, before the return of Christ, when a certain group of humans called the Manifest Sons of God would achieve physical immortality and be capable of great supernatural feats.

Messianic Jew

The term Messianic Jew refers to a person who is Jewish by either birth or conversion, who has come to believe that Jesus of Nazareth is the Messiah—Anointed One—predicted in the Old Testament scriptures to come as Savior of Israel. Many Christians mistakenly assume that all "Messianic Jewish" groups are part of a specific religious movement that has a common theology.

This is not so. There are a wide variety of theological perspectives among groups which identify themselves as Messianic Jewish. Some keep almost all their distinctively "Jewish" beliefs and customs—including Sabbath observance, avoiding pork and other "unclean meats," wearing prayer shawls with fringe and the like—and merely add the belief in Jesus as Messiah. Others adopt most of the beliefs and customs of standard Protestant theology, including observance of Sunday as the primary day of worship, celebrating such traditional holidays as Christmas and Easter, and eating pork and shellfish.

Modern Apostles and Prophets

Those groups, particularly in the *Charismatic* movement, which teach of the need for restoration of the *five-fold ministry* have in recent decades come to endorse groups of individuals who are believed to be actual apostles and prophets, with the authority and prestige such titles imply.

New Age

New Age is an adjective that describes the collection of beliefs and practices that are based on the idea that Mankind is about to enter into a "new age" of peace, prosperity, and spiritual enlightenment brought about by Man's own efforts to change himself. Many New Age teachers believe Man will be able to do this as a result of contact with "higher spiritual beings" who will teach him to be "at one" with the universe. Examples of New Age beliefs and activities include reincarnation and Transcendental Meditation. See: the *Cult, Occult, New Age—What's the Difference?* chapter of this *Field Guide*.

Occult

The Occult is the collection of beliefs and practices that are based on the idea that there is a supernatural world that Man can tap into in order to control the environment, or other people, through secret, special knowledge and rituals. Occultic activities include such things as fortune-telling, astrology, and voodoo. See: the *Cult, Occult, New Age—What's the Difference?* chapter of this *Field Guide*.

Pensacola Outpouring

See: *Brownsville Outpouring*

Pentecostal

Pentecostal comes from the word Pentecost, the English word for one of the annual Biblical Holy Days outlined in Leviticus 23. The word means "fiftieth," as the proper day for the observance is determined by counting fifty days from a Sabbath during the earlier Feast of Unleavened Bread. In Acts 2 in the New Testament, the disciples of Jesus were gathered together on this annual Holy Day in Jerusalem when they first received the empowerment of the Holy Spirit after Jesus' resurrection. The most noticeable feature of this occasion was that each of the disciples "spoke with other tongues" and those in the audience, who were from many other nations, were surprised to hear them speak in their own native languages.

The term Pentecostal when applied to religious groups, teachers, or customs usually implies that the participants believe that all Christians should expect to experience the same empowerment of the Holy Spirit, particularly evidenced by the gift of speaking in "other tongues." This is usually conceived by such believers to be a separate event from conversion or water baptism.

Pentecostal and *Charismatic* are sometimes used interchangeably to designate the same groups, teachers and phenomena. However, most students of religious history tend to use the term Pentecostal to refer to the more "old fashioned," "unsophisticated" groups which developed out of a "Holy Spirit" movement begun around the turn of the century. And they use the term Charismatic to refer to a more sophisticated branch of this general belief system that has developed since the 1950s. See: the *Charismatic* definition, and the **Pentecostal and Charismatic—What's the Difference?** chapter of this **Field Guide**.

Personal Prophecy

In some *Charismatic* settings, certain individuals are believed to have "prophetic gifts" that allow them to receive direct, Divine "prophetic words" for other individuals. These are often in the nature of specific guidance for life choices of the individual. They are not at all the same as "counseling," in which an individual might ask for guidance from a spiritual advisor such as a pastor in order to understand what **Biblical principles** might be relevant to solving a personal or family problem. Rather, the person offering the personal prophecy often does so without a request from the individual at all, and may have never met the individual before or know anything about their personal life.

Such personal prophecies are often given in large public meetings such as "Prophetic Conventions," to complete strangers called out of the audience by one of the alleged "prophets." Such prophetic words might be about the choice of a mate, confirmation of a calling to a certain type of ministry, reassurance that a health problem such as infertility is going to be removed, or admonishment about a hidden sin the person offering the personal prophecy believes that God has revealed to them.

Some observers of the Charismatic scene in recent decades have issued strong warnings that the highly subjective nature of such prophecies and the total lack of any accountability of the one offering such prophecies, has led to extreme instances of spiritual abuse. Lives have been wrecked when people have ignored their own common sense and leading of the Holy Spirit and followed instead the pronouncements of alleged "prophets" in order to make serious life choices. Others have been devastated by totally erroneous personal prophecies given about them in public regarding an alleged secret sin, such as an addiction to pornography.

Petra

Petra was an ancient city in what is now Jordan. The city itself is now in ruins and uninhabited except by tourists—and roaming

Bedouin tribesmen who may pitch their tents there on occasion. But it was a significant trading center in Roman times. Many of the city's magnificent buildings, including palaces and temples, were literally carved out of the beautiful rose limestone cliffs of the area. Petra was used as the location for the filming of the end of the movie *Indiana Jones and the Last Crusade* … the "Holy Grail" was found by Indiana in one of the buildings carved into the cliffs of Petra.

Some obscure Bible passages are interpreted by a number of prophecy commentators as indicating that some group of Christians will be transported supernaturally to Petra during the "End Times" as a place of safety. (See: *"Place of Safety"* definition.) *Herbert Armstrong*, founder of the Worldwide Church of God, for instance, strongly hinted for many years that 144,000 members of that Church, which he taught was the only True Church on earth, would be whisked to Petra in 1972 to escape what he believed would be a 3 1/2 year period of the Great Tribulation. See: *Tribulation* definition.

"Place of Safety"

Some prophecy commentators believe that "the Church" will be snatched up (raptured) to heaven (See: *Rapture* definition) to escape harm while the rest of the earth endures the Great *Tribulation*. Some others, however, who do not accept this rapture doctrine, believe that some Christians will be protected during this time by being supernaturally gathered to a Place of Safety somewhere on earth. Even some who do believe in the rapture teach that a remnant of Jewish believers, converted after the rapture, will be taken to such a place at some point during the Tribulation period. One common speculation regarding the location of such a place is Petra. See: *Petra* definition.

Positive Confession

Positive confession is a term used by teachers of the *Word Faith* movement to indicate what they believe is a prerequisite to receiving the blessings of God. They admonish their audience that there is both positive and negative power actually in the words of a Christian. Whatever the Christian "confesses" or affirms determines the result he will get. According to the principle of Positive Confession, if he is sick, and speaks about his condition in a negative way, admitting with his mouth his feelings, he will hinder healing from coming to him. If instead he "confesses" positively that he is healed already, even though the symptoms are still present, then his body will manifest that healing. If he speaks negatively—has a "negative confession"—about his financial problems, he will stay in poverty. If he has a "positive confession" that declares he is financially prosperous, even though he is still deeply in debt, that prosperity will be manifested in his life. See: the **Word Faith Movement** chapter of this **Field Guide**.

Power Evangelism

Power evangelism is a term used to indicate evangelistic efforts in public settings which depend as much or more on alleged "supernatural manifestations" as on preaching from the Bible. Such manifestations would include claims of supernatural healing and delivering people from demonic possession, people falling over *"slain in the spirit,"* and other related physical and psychic phenomena.

Preterism

Preterism is the belief that most of the prophecies in the New Testament, including most of those in the Book of Revelation, were fulfilled by climactic events in the first century, primarily at the time of the destruction of the Jerusalem Temple in 70 AD. This includes the *Tribulation*, the Battle of Armageddon, and the resurrection of the saints.

Prooftext, Prooftexting

A prooftext is a verse or short passage from the Bible used by someone as part of their proof for a doctrinal belief they wish to substantiate to others. However, since verses and passages may rely extensively on the context in which they appear for correct interpretation, pulling these out of their context and having them stand alone in a "proof" can at times be very misleading. In addition, a set of such prooftexts can completely ignore other passages which, if added to the mix, might well lead to an entirely different conclusion. Thus someone who relies strongly only on a list of prooftexts in order to make a doctrinal argument may have a very weak case for their argument. Noting that a religious teacher relies heavily just on prooftexting is viewed in theological circles as a very negative evaluation. See: *Hermeneutics* definition.

Prosperity Gospel

Teachers in the *Word Faith* movement promote an idea often called the Prosperity Gospel, which indicates that not only did Jesus' death and resurrection provide spiritual salvation, but included a promise of physical health and prosperity to those who believe. Certain New Testament passages are taken as absolute guarantees that God's will for every Christian is to be permanently healthy and prosperous, and that poverty and sickness are attempts by the Devil to steal these guaranteed blessings. Believers are encouraged to use the Word of Faith to rebuke this attempt and to claim the rightful blessings. See: the **Word Faith Movement** chapter of this *Field Guide*.

Rapture, Secret Rapture

Rapture is an English word that means "snatched up" or "caught up." It comes from the same Latin root as "raptor," the kind of bird such as eagles who "snatch up" their prey. Although the word rapture is not used in the KJV Bible, or any common modern English translation, the idea is present in the following passage:

> 1Thessalonians 4

> 16 For the Lord himself will come down from heaven, with a loud command, with the voice of the archangel and with the trumpet call of God, and the dead in Christ will rise first.

> 17 After that, we who are still alive and are left will be caught up together with them in the clouds to meet the Lord in the air. And so we will be with the Lord forever.

Thus this "catching up" is called by many Bible teachers "The Rapture of the Church." Some teach that this will occur only at the return of Christ to set up a Millennial kingdom. But those who teach the doctrine of the Secret Rapture are convinced He will come secretly to snatch away all true believers and take them to heaven to wait there while the rest of mankind suffers through the Great *Tribulation*. Many teach they will then return with Him when He comes to put an end to the Battle of Armageddon, and reign with Him on earth during the Millennium.

Reconstructionism

See: *Kingdom Now* definition.

Rhema

Rhema is a Greek term that is often translated "word" in English versions of the New Testament. In many *Charismatic/Pentecostal* circles, however, it takes on a special meaning. The Greek word logos is also translated "word" in many English translations. These Charismatic folks insist that there is a very special difference between these two types of "words."

The logos kind of word is viewed as being the Biblical "written word." But a rhema word is a special, modern "revelation" to someone. It may be in the form of a flash of insight into some spiritual matter that is not clearly covered in scripture. Or it may be an intuitive understanding that a particular scripture verse or passage has immediate application to a current circumstance, even though in context in the Bible it may have nothing at all to do with the topic of the circumstance. Such rhema words are sought after to give daily guidance to the life of the Christian.

There is, however, no real linguistic validity to this theory that the Bible deliberately makes such a distinction between these two Greek words. And much of what passes for rhema words in many Charismatic circles appears to be extremely idiosyncratic, unsubstantiated, highly fanciful inventions of the subconscious of the person claiming to have the rhema word. Yet many of these "modern revelations" are collected and posted on Internet sites as being amazing evidence of a Great Move of God.

Sabbatarian Christian

A Sabbatarian Christian is an individual who believes that the fourth commandment, "Remember the Sabbath Day to keep it holy," has not been changed by the New Covenant and is applicable to Christians as well as Jews. They also believe that this day, the Sabbath that Jesus and the apostles observed, was historically the day known on modern calendars as Saturday, and was kept from sundown to sundown. Thus most Sabbatarians rest from their regular work from sundown on Friday until sundown on Saturday. Most also set aside the Saturday Sabbath as the day they meet with others of like belief for regular weekly worship services.

Sacred Name

Sacred Name is a term used by some Bible students to designate the Hebrew name of the Creator by which He identified Himself to Moses at the "burning bush." Those who hold the Sacred Name doctrine do not use the common words "God" or "Lord" when speaking of Him, but rather use what they believe to be the correct pronunciation of His name given in the original Hebrew manuscripts of the Old Testament. In the manuscripts, only the letters for the four consonant sounds (YHWH) are used to indicate this name. Scholars disagree what vowel sounds were inserted between these letters. So there is considerable disagreement among Sacred Name groups on just what version of the Name should be used. The most common choice is "Yahweh," but variants include "Yahveh," "Yahowah," "Yehovah," "YodHayVovHay," and more.

Satan's Seed

The doctrine of Satan's Seed alleges that Cain was not the son of Adam, but rather the offspring ("seed") of a sexual encounter between Eve and Satan the Devil in the form of the "serpent" in the Garden of Eden. (Thus the doctrine is sometimes referred to as "Serpent's Seed.") This theory further states that the descendants of Cain are, therefore, the descendants of the Devil himself, not just "spiritually" in terms of attitude, but literally in terms of their physical bodies.

The primary aim of this doctrine is to account for certain races of people on earth in our time—primarily those who are called, by most people, "Jews." The proponents of the Satan's Seed theory allege that the modern Jews are imposters, not descended from Abraham at all but rather from the genealogical line of Cain. Since the biblical account seems to indicate that all mankind today is descended from Noah, as only Noah's family survived the flood, there is a need to account for how the Satanic line of Cain passed through the flood. This is usually accomplished by postulating that the Noachian flood did not actually cover the whole planet, but rather was localized in the Middle East. Thus descendants of Cain survived elsewhere.

Seed Faith

Several decades ago, television evangelist *Oral Roberts* pioneered and popularized teaching of a principle he called Seed Faith that is now used by many *Word Faith* teachers. Roberts alleged that God purposes to return to the Believer blessings in direct proportion to the amount of monetary giving ("planting seed") he does to religious causes. Thus if a Christian is in financial distress and wishes to pray for help from God to escape his financial problems, he needs to "plant an amount of seed" that is in proportion to his need.

The effect of this teaching was that people with the least money available to give were encouraged to give the most to the Oral Roberts ministry. People were even encouraged to make pledges for giving for the upcoming year that were beyond their current ability to meet, "stepping out in faith" that God would honor their seed with such a great blessing that they would be able to meet the pledge and still have abundance. This teaching was very effective in increasing donations to the Roberts ministry, and thus has been adopted by many current television ministries for their money-raising projects. (See: the **Word Faith Movement** chapter of this **Field Guide**.)

Shepherding

The Shepherding movement was a particular style of church organization that was extremely popular in some *Charismatic/Pentecostal* settings in the 1960s and 1970s. The term denotes the concept that every believer needs to be under the direct supervision of a shepherd (sometimes referred to as a "covering") to assist them in their spiritual growth. In a complete shepherding setting, a local congregation would be arranged in a pyramid form. At the bottom were the regular congregation members.

The congregation would be divided up into small "house groups" (sometimes called cell groups), each group having small group sessions during the week. Each member was directly accountable to a house group leader or person with a similar role. The house group leaders were each accountable to church elders over them. The elders were accountable to a group of pastors. The pastors were accountable to the apostles. And the apostles, who were at the top of the pyramid and presumed to be the "most spiritual" fellows in the church group, were accountable to one another.

If shepherding had been merely a wholesome "mentoring"-style arrangement in which spiritually mature Christians accepted the responsibility for encouraging and discipling and being a role model for new converts and the spiritually immature, it might have had a positive influence. But as practiced in many groups it became an incredibly authoritarian, arbitrary, oppressive system which dictated the every move of all those in the lower ranks. Even details of such personal matters as accepting a new job, choosing a mate, or buying a car were dictated by those in positions of "covering" the choices of those under them.

So many abuses proliferated around the country that the whole movement came under extreme criticism by outsiders. Even one of the most influential early advocates of the system, *Bob Mumford*, finally renounced much of the fruit of the Shepherding movement and it faded as an organized movement by the early 1980s. To this day, however, certain authoritarian sub-groups within the Charismatic movement, and even some ministries that are not overtly Charismatic, still adhere to the concept of "covering" relationships, and some of the abuses of the past can be seen in their midst.

Signs and wonders

Those within the *Charismatic* movement who believe in the necessity of *power evangelism* refer to the manifestations that they expect to see and experience at such power evangelism events as "signs and wonders." These are often unusual physical phenomena such as people being "*slain in the spirit*," glued to the floor by "*Holy Ghost glue*," the "*word of knowledge*," and prophecy.

Slain in the Spirit

People are said to be slain in the Spirit at certain *Pentecostal* or *Charismatic* meetings when they fall over backwards unconscious after being touched in some way (either directly, or perhaps with the wave of a hand or blowing of the breath) by someone ministering at the meeting. The implication is that they have been "overwhelmed" by the power of the Holy Spirit and thus their bodies have been "short circuited" and they cannot remain conscious.

Speaking in Tongues

Speaking in tongues is a phenomenon within the *Pentecostal/Charismatic* movement in which individuals speak, either in their private prayers or in a public meeting, in what appears to be a language unknown to them. If they do this in private prayer, it is termed a "prayer language," and they may not have any idea during or after the prayer just what they said. It is believed that their "spirit" is in this way speaking directly to God's Spirit without use of their conscious faculties. If they offer a message in one of these "unknown languages" publicly in a religious meeting, it is viewed as a communication directly from the Holy Spirit to the group. And it is expected that someone there will be given an "interpretation" of what the one speaking in tongues has said.

It is not usually claimed that such languages are specific human languages that are spoken somewhere on earth. A typical explanation is that they are "heavenly languages," perhaps spoken by angels. Nor is the "interpretation" that is given perceived as a "translation," but rather as a loose explanation of the intent of the message, given directly by the Holy Spirit to the interpreter.

"Spirit of Prophecy"

During her lifetime, Seventh Day Adventist (SDA) prophetess *Ellen G. White* was said to have the Spirit of Prophecy. She had many alleged visions and revelations, including what she portrayed as direct conversations with God, and her writings about these were considered inspired by the Holy Spirit in the same way as the writings of the Old and New Testament writers. One of the "proofs" offered to the world that the SDA denomination was the Remnant Church, the only true representative of God on earth, was that they had a living Prophetess. When Ellen White died in 1915, they had to adjust this explanation. Since that time it is common for Adventists to refer to **the collected writings** of Ellen as The Spirit of Prophecy.

Spiritual Warfare

The term Spiritual Warfare is used in certain *Charismatic* circles to denote activities they believe to be directly challenging evil supernatural entities. This has nothing to do with the kind of scriptural concept spoken of by Paul in which he admonished individual believers to "put on the whole armor of God" so that they may resist the wiles of the Devil. Paul does indeed use the symbolism of warfare in a number of places.

But modern Charismatic Spiritual Warfare is different. It does not consist of prayer and Bible study and such—it involves such things as bombastic verbal affirmations by evangelists, joined by the voices of thousands in their audience, that they have the power to "bind the Devil" and his power—or the power of his evil accomplices in the supernatural world—over cities. A common strategy of Spiritual Warfare ministries is called "spiritual mapping." One author, in a highly critical look at the movement, describes spiritual mapping:

Spiritual mapping involves researching the secular and religious history of a city to determine the names and characteristics of "ruling spirits" over the area. In spiritual warfare knowing the name of the strongman is a must. If you are really right on, you can actually determine the address; the geographical location of the spirit! According to Dick Bernal, the way to take a city is fourfold. 1. Proclaim a fast with prayer. 2. Identify the principality over the city. 3. Determine its geographical location. 4. Call him/her by name. Bernal also tells us that God revealed to him the name of the principality over his city. "In prayer, the Holy Spirit impressed upon me that the title of the ruling principality over our area is "Self." (Bill Randles, *Making War in the Heavenlies: A Different Look*, p. 13.)

Many grandiose claims have been made for the results of these efforts, but it is difficult to find any substantiation for such claims.

Third Wave

The development of the *Pentecostal/Charismatic* movement in the past 100 years is often described as happening in successive "waves" of manifestation of the power of the Holy Spirit, during which various facets of what is viewed as "first century Christianity" are alleged to have been "restored."

One common scheme defining these waves is to call the Pentecostal movement, starting in about 1910, the First Wave, in which the "gift of tongues" and eventually other supernatural manifestations such as "faith healing" were allegedly restored to the Church. However, these manifestations were mostly limited to a few small, new Pentecostal denominations.

The Charismatic movement, starting in the 1950s, is labeled the Second Wave. This was a period in which many of the Pentecostal manifestations were spread widely into mainstream denominations in America and around the world.

Since the 1980s, teachers in the Pentecostal/Charismatic movement have been declaring the move of the Holy Spirit has now led to the Third Wave, a term coined by church growth leader *C Peter Wagner* in 1983. It includes many of the characteristics of the earlier waves, but there is much more emphasis on recognizing "*Modern Apostles and Prophets*" who claim direct, divine revelation and authority, and *"Power Evangelism,"* in which the preaching of the Gospel is said to be accompanied by miraculous "signs and wonders." (See: the **Pentecostal/Charismatic** chapter of this *Field Guide*.)

Some teachers from the Third Wave movement have begun suggesting that there is now the beginnings of a Fourth Wave of restoration. (See: *Fourth Wave* definition.)

Toronto Blessing

A *Vineyard* church near the Toronto, Ontario airport began a series of revival meetings in January 1994 that were scheduled to last less than a week. The meetings have, instead, continued the present.

Unusual manifestations occurred during the initial meetings that caught the attention of those in some *Charismatic* circles around the country and eventually around the world. And people thus started arriving by the thousands to see for themselves. The manifestations included large numbers of people *"slain in the spirit"* (falling unconscious to the floor, allegedly under the power of the Holy Spirit), people shaking uncontrollably, people laughing hysterically for no obvious reason, people "glued" to the floor unable to get up for extended periods, and people making all sorts of unusual sounds such as barking like dogs and crowing like roosters. Those involved, including Toronto pastor *John Arnott*, have claimed that all of these phenomena are evidence of a powerful "move of the Holy Spirit."

The collection of phenomena have been dubbed the Toronto Blessing, and large numbers of people who have participated in the meetings in Toronto have returned to their home churches all over the world and "brought back" a similar outbreak in their own congregations. This whole movement has drawn considerable criticism even within *Pentecostal* and Charismatic circles, with many protesting that there is no proof that the manifestations are from God, and that some of them may well be even demonic.

Even the leadership of the Vineyard movement itself, which is characterized by quite a bit of similar phenomena, became so concerned that the particular outbreak at the Airport Vineyard church was indulging in excesses and was not subject to adequate spiritual oversight that they withdrew the church's affiliation with Vineyard. The Toronto group is now dubbed the Toronto Airport Fellowship.

Tribulation, Great Tribulation

The English word "tribulation" means great distress and misery. This word is used a number of times in the New Testament to describe a time of great trouble and suffering which is prophesied to come upon the earth before the Second Coming of Christ.

> Matt 24:21
>
> 21 For then shall be great tribulation, such as was not since the beginning of the world to this time, no, nor ever shall be.

> Rev 7:13-14
>
> 13 And one of the elders answered, saying unto me, What are these which are arrayed in white robes? and whence came they?
>
> 14 And I said unto him, Sir, thou knowest. And he said to me, These are they which came out of great tribulation, and have washed their robes, and made them white in the blood of the Lamb.

According to many prophecy teachers, this is not just referring to an indeterminate time period, but rather to a specific time period they call The Tribulation. The most common speculation, based on comparing prophetic passages in the Bible, is that it will last for seven years. Some of these teachers refer to the whole seven years as not just The Tribulation, but as The Great Tribulation. Others prefer to refer to the first half of the seven years as The Tribulation, and to the second half, when circumstances on earth become even more horrifying and miserable, as The Great Tribulation.

Vineyard Movement

The Vineyard Movement, represented officially by the Association of Vineyard Churches, is the current outgrowth of the work of the late *John Wimber* (1934-1997). Wimber's congregation in the late 1970s was affiliated with the Calvary Chapel churches. In the late 1970s, they left the Calvary group and affiliated with a group of seven churches called the Vineyard Fellowships under the leadership of a man named Ken Gullickson. In the early 1980s Gullickson turned the Vineyard group over to the leadership of

Wimber, and it began a climb to explosive growth throughout the 1980s and 1990s.

Wimber had at one time taught "Church Growth" classes through Fuller Theological Seminary. Impressed in the early 1980s with what he believed to be credible evidence, in some evangelistic ministries, of dramatic supernatural manifestations, he began developing his own theory of *Power Evangelism*. According to this theory, it is absolutely necessary in our time for the preaching of the Gospel to be accompanied by powerful manifestations of healing, demonic *deliverance*, *"words of knowledge,"* and other supernatural activities such as participants being *slain in the spirit*.

Thus Vineyard Churches typically include in their meetings such alleged manifestations. A gifted musician and promoter (he formed and managed the Righteous Brothers in the mid-1960s before his conversion), Wimber was also influential in the development and promotion of an extensive collection of contemporary Christian music. This continually growing music collection is now distributed through the non-profit Vineyard Music Group, one of the largest producers of tapes and song books of Praise and Worship music.

Word Faith, Word of Faith

The doctrine of Word Faith, sometimes referred to as Word *of* Faith, is a teaching promoted by some of the more radical elements of the *Charismatic/Pentecostal* movement. The term implies that Christians not only need faith "in God," but that they need to have faith in the power of the words they speak. If they use the "word of faith," according to a number of formulas which such teachers believe they have found in the Bible, they do not need to pray to God and request answers to their prayers most of the time. They need only search the Bible to find what they consider "unconditional promises" of God, and then merely "confess" with their mouth—using "the word of faith"—that the blessings they seek are theirs, and they shall have those blessings. Such blessings would include health and prosperity.

One of the typical sayings Word Faith adherents are supposed to internalize is "What I confess, I possess," or otherwise stated as "Confession brings possession." Critics sometimes refer to this as a "name it and claim it" doctrine. (See: the **Word Faith Movement** chapter of this ***Field Guide***.)

Word of Knowledge

In *Charismatic* circles, someone is said to have a "word of knowledge" when they claim to know something about another person that could not have been known through the five senses. In other words, they are believed to have been given this piece of knowledge by direct divine revelation. Someone who is believed to be able to give such words of knowledge on a regular basis is said to have the "spiritual gift" of the "word of knowledge." This manifestation is often claimed by healing evangelists when they "call out" someone from the audience whom they do not know personally and explain that God has shown them that the person has a certain ailment. Investigative reporters have exposed a number of evangelists over the past few decades as falsifying this alleged gift, by secretly gathering information about audience members. The most notorious of these exposés was regarding televangelist *Peter Popoff.*

Unless otherwise noted, all definitions within quotes are from *Webster's New World Dictionary*, Second College Edition,1984, Prentice Hall Press .

Chapter 16

Cult, Occult, New Age—What's the Difference?

"I'm really worried about my brother. I think he's getting involved with **an occult**."

"My pastor said last week in a sermon that the church my friend goes to is a cult—I'm so worried now—what if they all kill themselves?"

"I found some *New Age* books in my sister's bookcase the last time I visited her. I wonder what cult she belongs to?"

All these comments by concerned relatives and friends are based on confusion regarding the terms *cult*, *occult*, and *New Age*. Have you been confused by all the hype that surrounds these words? This chapter will help you to clear your head.

Cult: A Loaded Word

A *Cult* is a ...

Group of people ...

... who share an intense dedication to a particular individual or belief system.

This simple definition of cult, as found in many dictionaries, can be applied to almost any type of group, whether focused on a religious belief system or not. Until recent times, the word was seldom heard outside of the academic world. Historians would use it to label aspects of ancient societies, such as the "Cult (or Latin *cultus*) of the Emperor" in Rome. Sociologists would use it, sometimes interchangeably with the word "sect," to indicate a small religious group outside the mainstream of "historical Christianity." A few decades ago, one might even hear it used humorously to describe the fanatic devotion of some admirers of entertainers, such as the "Cult of Elvis."

However, all that began to change in the 1960s, when some unusual small religious groups, including the "Moonies" and David Berg's "Children of God," started targeting high school and college students in particular with aggressive recruiting tactics.

Once such a group captured the interest of a new prospective member, they would use what many considered "brain washing" techniques to get and keep their loyalty. This often included encouraging the new convert to cut off normal family ties. Some alarmed families tried engaging the services of professional "deprogrammers," who would kidnap the young person, hold them against their will in a motel or other secure site, and attempt to "talk some sense" into them by pointing out flaws in the premises they had accepted from the group.

From that point on, the public became more and more familiar with the word *cult*, as it was frequently used in the media to describe unconventional religious groups that used questionable methods to attract and keep members.

Although the original word has no specific negative connotation to it, its common use now in our society carries the negative baggage of its use in the news media to describe some notable tragedies. The Jonestown massacre of 1978 (see the ***Afterword: Personal from the Author*** chapter for more details on that story), the Waco Branch Davidian holocaust of 1993, the Heaven's Gate group suicide in 1997, and numerous other troubling incidents connected to the activities of unconventional religious groups have forever eliminated any neutral or benign connotation to the term "cult" in modern American society.

Another View

Unfortunately, many readers, secular reporters, and commentators are unaware that the term *cult* has a **very specific** and technical meaning when used in religious circles by theologians, pastors, and authors; and that meaning has nothing to do, necessarily, with brain washing or possible violence. Thus, when they read a book written by a religious author that labels some group as a *cult*, they may totally misunderstand what is being addressed.

For in theological circles, *cult* is a term used to designate a group that does not accept and teach all the points of a very specific set of doctrinal beliefs, viewed by many to be the central tenets of historical Christianity. If, for instance, a group does not adhere to the traditional *orthodox* explanation of the doctrine of the "trinity," it is labeled a cult, no matter what sort of recruiting tactics it uses, how benign its leadership, or how many other doctrines it teaches that line up with orthodox beliefs.

This can make it very confusing for the "non-religious" reader! If a prominent religious leader is interviewed by the secular press and labels a group as a ***cult,*** both the interviewer and his readers may make the erroneous assumption that this means that the group is somehow dangerous to the safety of its members and outsiders. Therefore, it is very important for readers to be aware of the *context* of information they are considering.

Three Common Uses of cult

In summary, there are three common uses of the term **cult** in popular literature today. Be sure to ask yourself "where is the author coming from?" whenever you spot the term.

1. A religious group that has one or more unorthodox beliefs.
2. A religious group that is physically dangerous to outsiders and perhaps even its own members.
3. An *exclusivist* religious group that may use deceptive, abusive, or excessively authoritarian tactics to attract and keep members.

It is this third definition that is common when the emphasis is more sociological or psychological than theological. For a group can have totally orthodox beliefs by the standards of most Protestant theologians, and yet still be dangerous to the mental, emotional, spiritual—and, at times, even physical—well-being of its members. Many commentaries on "cultish behavior" or "cultish methods" are speaking specifically of this third type of use of the term cult.

There is really no use in attempting to avoid use of the word cult, as it is so pervasive in our society now. Nor is there a need to insist that it must be completely confined to its totally neutral definition. The reality is that it is no longer a neutral word. We may as well use it, but carefully define it in the context in which we choose to communicate.

For the purposes of this book
**a modern religious cult will be defined as
a group of people established by one human leader
or a small group of human leaders,
to whom they are intensely dedicated and obedient,
and who have such a significantly unique set of beliefs
that they are cut off from religious fellowship
with all others outside their own group.**

Given this definition of modern religious cults, the following observations may be helpful when evaluating the potential for serious spiritual harm of any particular group. (These observations include reference to the words *New Age* and *occult*. Definitions and descriptions of those terms follow this list.)

Religious cults **frequently:**

- ➢ Are started by one very persuasive teacher/leader.
- ➢ Have a tightly organized and restricted membership.
- ➢ Are convinced that they have the only way of life acceptable to God, down to every minute detail of daily living.

Many religious cults do **not**:
- ➢ Have any occult or New Age connections or beliefs.
- ➢ Have radical or violent tendencies.
- ➢ Use "brain washing" to get or keep members.

Some religious cults **may**:
- ➢ Rely on fear to keep members in line.
- ➢ Rely on isolation to keep members away from outside teachings.
- ➢ Use Christian terminology, but be unbiblical in their definitions of those terms.
- ➢ Disguise their actual teachings when dealing with the public.

Cult and Occult

The Occult *is the ...*

Collection of Beliefs and Practices ...

...that are based on the idea that there is a supernatural world that Man can tap into in order to control the environment or other people through secret, special knowledge and rituals.

- ➢ An individual **can** be involved in *occult* activities **without** belonging to a *cult*.
- ➢ An individual **can** belong to a *cult* and yet **not** be involved in any *occult* activities at all.

Examples of occult activities and beliefs:

- ➢ Ouija boards
- ➢ Fortune telling
- ➢ Astrology
- ➢ Witchcraft
- ➢ Tarot cards
- ➢ Voodoo
- ➢ Palm reading

> Spiritualism/spiritism (attempting or claiming to contact the dead)
> Belief that the material world—including the bodies and minds of others—can be manipulated just by the power in magical words or gestures
> Belief that individuals can gain wealth and power through magical words or gestures

New Age

New Age *is an adjective that describes the ...*

Collection of Beliefs and Practices ...

... that are based on the idea that Mankind is about to enter into a "new age" of peace, prosperity, and spiritual enlightenment **brought about by Man's own efforts to change himself.**

Many *New Age* teachers believe Man will be able to do this as a result of contact with "higher spiritual beings" who will teach him to be "at one" with the universe.

> *New Age* as a label for this specific concept is a fairly recent term.
> The term *New Age Movement* describes a wide variety of beliefs and practices. There is no carefully organized New Age Movement that covers all the related individuals, groups, and practices.
> **Some** occult practices are used by **some** in the New Age Movement.

Examples of *New Age* ideas and practices:

> Reincarnation
> Transcendental meditation, other types of non-biblical meditation
> "Channeling" (claiming to speak messages for "ascended masters"—humans who have become exalted spirit beings)

- ➤ Astral projection (claiming that your "soul" or "spirit" can leave your body at will to travel throughout time and the universe)
- ➤ Belief that humans are not special creations in the image of God, and are of no more value than animals and plants
- ➤ Belief that there is not an "external" Creator God who made the universe—rather that "god" is within everyone already just waiting to be tapped into

Some occult and New Age practices and ideas may be counterfeits of actual biblical ideas and practices.

However—

Many serious Bible students are concerned that *occult* and *New Age* ideas and practices are creeping into television preaching that is called "Christian," and are being spread by books and recordings available in Christian Book Stores.

Many sincere Christians are worried about having loved ones involved in *cults* that resemble the Branch Davidians or the Heaven's Gate group. They can see the danger of these *cults* clearly, when the results are so violent.

But when there are new teachings being offered by "regular Christian" teachers, these same Christians may let down their guard and accept ideas and practices that are every bit as un-biblical and **spiritually** dangerous.

And when there are those who teach much sound doctrine who, at the same time, use some of the **methods** of a *cult* to get or retain members, and who may even be using subtle variations of **occultic** and *New Age* ideas masquerading as biblical Christian principles, sincere Bible students may be swept along into un-biblical bondage by involvement with such teachers.

See *Chapter 6* of this *Field Guide* for an overview of some of the "Characteristics of Potentially Harmful Religious Groups."

Chapter 17

Pentecostal and Charismatic: What's the Difference?

The origin of the word Pentecost

Pentecost is the English name for an annual religious Holy Day of the biblical calendar given to the ancient Israelites. God told Moses:

> Leviticus 23:10-11
>
> "Speak to the Israelites and say to them: 'When you enter the land I am going to give you and you reap its harvest, bring to the priest a sheaf of the first grain you harvest. He is to wave the sheaf before the LORD so it will be accepted on your behalf; the priest is to wave it on the day after the Sabbath…

This was traditionally done during the Days of Unleavened Bread, a week-long festival connected to the Passover. Many biblical commentators believe this ceremony to be a foreshadow of the resurrection of Jesus. It occurred on the "day after the Sabbath," that is, the Sunday after Passover.

> Leviticus 23:15-17, 21
>
> From the day after the Sabbath, the day you brought the sheaf of the wave offering, count off seven full weeks. Count off fifty days up to the day after the seventh Sabbath, and then present an offering of new grain to the LORD. From wherever you live, bring two loaves made of two-tenths of an ephah of fine flour, baked with yeast, as a wave offering of firstfruits to the LORD … On that same day you are to proclaim a sacred assembly and do no regular work. This is to be a lasting ordinance for the generations to come, wherever you live.

Note that this annual observance is to occur on the fiftieth day after the sheaf was waved during the Days of Unleavened Bread. By the time of Jesus' ministry on Earth, the Greek name for this feast was Pentecost, which means "fiftieth" in Greek. English has borrowed this same word to designate this particular religious observance.

After His resurrection, Jesus appeared a number of times to His disciples over a period of forty days, and then was taken up to heaven. But just before that event, the following is recorded:

Acts 1:4-8

On one occasion, while he was eating with them, he gave them this command: "Do not leave Jerusalem, but wait for the gift my Father promised, which you have heard me speak about. For John baptized with water, but in a few days you will be baptized with the Holy Spirit."

So when they met together, they asked him, "Lord, are you at this time going to restore the kingdom to Israel?" He said to them: "It is not for you to know the times or dates the Father has set by his own authority. But you will receive power when the Holy Spirit comes on you; and you will be my witnesses in Jerusalem, and in all Judea and Samaria, and to the ends of the earth.

Acts 2 describes what happened in Jerusalem fifty days after the resurrection, on the annual biblical Holy Day of Pentecost, to the Apostles and disciples of Jesus. Note that these were all Jewish men and women, and that they would thus be observing the annual day of Pentecost as they had throughout their whole lives. Also note in the passage below that there were "God-fearing Jews from every nation under heaven" in Jerusalem—because all Jews who were able to, made the pilgrimage to Jerusalem each year to worship on this day (as well as the other annual biblical holy days.)

Acts 2:1-6

When the day of Pentecost came, they were all together in one place. Suddenly a sound like the blowing of a violent wind came from heaven and filled the whole house where they were sitting. They saw what seemed to be tongues of fire that separated and came to rest on each of them. All of them were filled with the Holy Spirit and began to speak in other tongues as the Spirit enabled them.

Now there were staying in Jerusalem God-fearing Jews from every nation under heaven. When they heard this sound, a crowd came together in bewilderment, because each one heard them speaking in his own language.

Acts 2:14-18

Then Peter stood up with the Eleven, raised his voice and addressed the crowd: "Fellow Jews and all of you who live in Jerusalem, let me explain this to you; listen carefully to what I say. These men are not drunk, as you suppose. It's only nine in the morning! No, this is what was spoken by the prophet Joel: "'In the last days, God says, I will pour out mmy Spirit on all people. Your sons and daughters will prophesy, your young men will see visions, your old men will dream dreams. Even on my servants, both men and women, I will pour out my Spirit in those days, and they will prophesy.

Thus the word Pentecost is not just a Christian theological word that was invented to mean "the day on which the Holy Spirit was poured out" on the disciples who were the first Christians. Some Christians have used the phraseology "We need another Pentecost" to indicate a desire for a repetition of the events or manifestations of that particular day described in Acts. But this is a poor choice of terms. The day of Pentecost is still observed annually by Jews, by a number of Sabbatarian Christian groups that observe the annual biblical Holy Days, and it has even been "adopted" into the Catholic and some Protestant annual liturgical calendars.

What does the word Pentecostal mean in current common usage?

To the average Christian, the biblical significance of the word Pentecost has been pulled from its biblical roots, and has become a catch-phrase solely designating the events described in Acts 2. Therefore, the word Pentecostal has become an adjective to describe any supernatural manifestations that are believed to be like those described in Acts 2 and elsewhere in the Book of Acts. And it is used to refer to those individuals and groups which claim to experience those manifestations and attribute them to the power of the Holy Spirit. This would particularly include *speaking in tongues* and instantaneous healing.

What does the word charismatic mean in general?

The word charismatic is derived from the Greek word charisma, which means gift. Thus the word charismatic, even in non-religious circles, is used as an adjective to describe a certain type of person who has "a special quality of leadership that captures the popular imagination and inspires allegiance and devotion." (*Webster's New World Dictionary*, Second College Ed.) The implication is that he or she was "gifted" with this quality by an outside source, such as God or Fate. However—in religious circles the word charismatic is almost exclusively used in relationship to the following passage in the letter of Paul to the Corinthians:

1 Corinthians 12:1-11

Now about spiritual gifts [translated from *charisma*], brothers, I do not want you to be ignorant... There are different kinds of gifts, but the same Spirit. There are different kinds of service, but the same Lord. There are different kinds of working, but the same God works all of them in all men. Now to each one the manifestation of the Spirit is given for the common good. To one there is given through the Spirit the message of wisdom, to another the message of knowledge by means of the same Spirit, to another faith by the same Spirit, to another gifts of healing by that one Spirit, to another miraculous powers, to another prophecy, to another distinguishing between spirits, to another speaking in different kinds of tongues, and to still another the interpretation of tongues. All these are the work of one and the same Spirit, and he gives them to each one, just as he determines.

This same concept of "spiritual gifts" also appears in Paul's letter to the Romans:

Romans 12:4-8

Just as each of us has one body with many members, and these members do not all have the same function, so in Christ we who are many form one body, and each member belongs to all the others. We have different gifts, according to the grace given us. If a man's gift is prophesying, let him use it in proportion to his faith. If it is serving, let him serve; if it is teaching, let him teach; if it is encouraging, let him encourage; if it is contributing to the needs of others, let him give generously; if it is leadership, let him govern diligently; if it is showing mercy, let him do it cheerfully.

As is evident from the two passages above, a gift or charisma attributed to the empowerment of the Holy Spirit can include both obviously supernatural manifestations, such as prophesying and speaking in tongues, as well as less spectacular abilities, such as teaching and showing mercy. Most Christian groups would have no disagreement that many individuals among them have particular gifts—sometimes referred to as "talents."

149

These may be "natural gifts" they seem to have been born with. In addition, most groups will not dispute that some such gifts may have been enhanced by God through the power of the Holy Spirit, so that the person can use the gift more effectively to serve within fellowship groups of Christians. But many such groups believe that the more supernatural of the gifts listed in Paul's letters, such as the gift of speaking in tongues or of miraculous powers, are no longer to be expected as a natural part of the experience of Christians.

What does the word Charismatic imply in current common usage in religious circles?

The word Charismatic has come to be an adjective attached to those individuals and groups who disagree with the conclusion that the supernatural gifts of the spirit are no longer manifested in the world. Charismatics believe that all of the gifts are still available within the Christian community. In fact, the term Charismatic usually implies in particular those supernatural gifts—sometimes called *sign gifts*, as they are viewed as an outward sign of the power of the Holy Spirit—such as speaking in tongues, prophecy, and discernment of spirits.

What similarities and differences are there in the common implications of the words Pentecostal and Charismatic in current common usage?

The earliest groups in the modern resurgence of interest in the supernatural manifestations of Acts 2, which began forming in the U.S. around the turn of the last century (1900), referred to themselves as Pentecostal. Their particular emphasis was on restoration of the gift of tongues as an outward sign of what they referred to as the "baptism of the Holy Ghost." Up until the 1950s, this movement was on the fringes of religion in modern American society. The few denominations that espoused this doctrine were not part of the mainstream of religious groups.

Beginning in about 1960, interest in the biblical concept of spiritual gifts, including speaking in tongues, began spreading to individuals and congregations which had historically been in the mainstream, including the Roman Catholic Church and many Protestant denominations. Rather than align themselves with the Pentecostal groups that had been around for fifty years or more, they preferred to refer to themselves as a Charismatic *renewal* movement within their own denominations. Even when some found themselves at odds with those in their old denominations who resisted this renewal, and were forced to form new outside groups, most preferred to retain the designation Charismatic.

Specifically in the matter of speaking in tongues, a number of groups (but not all) which are historically defined as Pentecostal have made this manifestation an absolute prerequisite to salvation. They do not view it as merely one of the spiritual gifts that may be given to a Christian. They believe it to be the unmistakable **sign** of conversion. On the other hand, most Charismatic groups believe that it is the privilege of all Christians to speak in tongues, but it is a gift that is given subsequent to the conversion experience. Thus a person who has not yet spoken in tongues but who has professed Christ, and perhaps even been baptized in water, would still be considered a brother or sister in Christ.

Are there other variations on the meaning of the word Charismatic as it is used by some in general conversation?

Most Charismatic groups have a tendency to have worship services that are lively and quite interactive. Rather than just a message by one designated pastor, a variety of participants may contribute words of encouragement, prayer requests, praise reports, "prophetic words" they believe to have been inspired on the spot by God, and so on. The music that many Charismatic congregations use for praise and worship may be loud and enthusiastic, and very rhythmic at times, with an emphasis on contemporary music rather than the historical hymns of the more formal religious denominations.

Thus many people tend to use the term Charismatic to designate a religious setting in which music is lively, or in which many members of the congregation may contribute to the service. However, this is not really an accurate use of the term. Many groups which play lively contemporary music, and which have less formal services, do not emphasize the supernatural gifts at all, and would be surprised if someone interrupted their service with a "message in tongues" or a prophecy.

In this *Field Guide*, the use of the term Charismatic (with a capital C) is reserved for use in indicating those groups which emphasize what they believe to be the modern manifestation of supernatural spiritual gifts.

Chapter 18

Who's Who Digest
of the Wild World of Religion

Brief profiles of 125+ individuals that are influential in the Wild World of Religion of the 21st Century

About the Who's Who Digest

Keeping up with **all** of the activity in the Wild World of Religion would be absolutely impossible. In the interest of assisting those whose main interest is just "identifying" a variety of individuals and groups, the following collection of over 125 brief profiles of some of the most influential is offered.

Please Note: This is an "all inclusive" listing, past and present, positive and negative, of individual writers, speakers, teachers, and religious personalities related to modern religious movements. Some are included because of their negative influence on a significant number of people. Others are included because of their positive contribution to sorting through the confusion in the Wild World of Religion. And still others are included just because their names show up frequently in information about modern religious movements, and folks wonder, "Who is that?" Some profiles are just a few sentences. Some are a paragraph or two. A few are quite a bit longer. The length is totally idiosyncratic, based on how much the author felt might be interesting and/or helpful as overview information, and does not imply anything in particular about the relative "importance" of the subject of the thumbnail.

Careful effort has been made to represent as accurately as possible any biographical information and the actual teachings and policies and practices of the individuals in this collection of information. When practical, quotations from their own publications or recordings have been provided to substantiate their teachings, and documentation from public records, including news articles, has been provided to substantiate information regarding their activities. Any corrections of fact, with supporting documentation, are welcome and will be incorporated in any future editions of this book.

No effort has been made to provide a comprehensive overview of all of the teachings or activities of any one person. That is beyond the scope of the purpose of this material. Every teacher and group has positive and negative attributes. Any reader who wishes to investigate these matters in more detail is referred to the bibliography sections of the *Field Guide to the Wild World of Religion website*. They include many books and weblinks to information—pro and con—about most of the entries in this database. It is not the purpose of this book or the website to dogmatically impose opinions and evaluations on anyone—the purpose is to call attention to those areas believed to be of serious spiritual concern in the actions or words of some religious leaders. It is left to the reader to evaluate the evidence presented and come to their own conclusions. More information on how individuals and groups have been chosen for inclusion is available in the *Field Guide FAQ* on the website.

Some profiles include reference to other individuals who have their own entry in these listings. Their names will be *italicized*.

Some groups, movements, and ideas referenced in some of the profiles are identified and explained in the *Religious Lingo Lexicon* chapter of this *Field Guide*. Their names will be **bolded**.

A.A. Allen

Asa Alonzo Allen (1911-1970). Prominent, flamboyant, and controversial **Pentecostal** "healing evangelist" of the 1940s—1960s. Allen made many outrageous, unsubstantiated claims of miracles.

From *James Randi*'s book *The Faith Healers*

On June 14, 1970, listeners in the United States, the United Kingdom, and the Philippines were hearing a recorded message from A. A. Allen on his radio program saying: "This is Brother Allen in person. Numbers of friends of mine have been inquiring about reports they have heard concerning me that are not true. People as well as some preachers from pulpits are announcing that I am dead. Do I sound like a dead man? My friends, I am not even sick! Only a moment ago I made a reservation to fly into our current campaign. I'll see you there and make the devil a liar." At that moment, at the Jack Tar Hotel in San Francisco, police were removing A. A. Allen's body from a room strewn with pills and empty liquor bottles. The man who had once said that "the beer bottle and gin bucket" should have been on his family coat of arms was dead at 59 from what was said to be a heart attack but was in reality liver failure brought about by acute alcoholism. (p.88)

Carlos Annacondia

Argentinian revival leader whose massive **Hyper-Charismatic** healing/evangelistic campaigns in South America are said to have reached many millions since his first such meeting in 1982. Annacondia specializes in bombastic verbal attacks on Satan and demons as part of what is termed **spiritual warfare**. And he claims huge numbers of people attending his campaigns are healed and delivered from demons. As with most claims of such **healing ministries**, actual documentation of instantaneous healing of serious illness or injury seems to be totally lacking.

Garner Ted Armstrong

(1930-2003) Radio and television evangelist, son of *Herbert W Armstrong*. Garner Ted Armstrong was former chief spokesman, during the 1960s and 1970s, on the *World Tomorrow* television and radio programs, which were media outreaches of the Worldwide

Church of God (WCG), a denomination founded by his father. The younger Armstrong founded his own denomination, the Church of God, International (CGI), and the Garner Ted Armstrong Evangelistic Association after being expelled from the WCG in 1978 during a leadership power struggle in that organization. He later founded the Intercontinental Church of God (ICG) after being expelled from the CGI in 1998 as a result of a highly-publicized sex scandal. Armstrong was the self-proclaimed "Ezekiel Watchman" … a Bible analogy he used to indicate the main prophetic spokesman for God on earth today.

Herbert W Armstrong

(1892-1986) Founder of the Worldwide Church of God (originally the Radio Church of God), the *Plain Truth* magazine and the *World Tomorrow* radio and TV programs. During his lifetime, Armstrong was the self-proclaimed "Apostle" of the "only true church on earth today." Herbert Armstrong was father of television and radio evangelist *Garner Ted Armstrong*.

John Arnott , Carol Arnott

John Arnott was pastor of the **Charismatic** Toronto Airport **Vineyard Church**, now called the Toronto Airport Christian Fellowship (TACF), in 1993 when the so-called "**Toronto Blessing**" revival broke out in that congregation. The Association of Vineyard Churches expelled the congregation in 1996 over the strange **Hyper-Charismatic** excesses going on in the revival, and Arnott (along with his wife Carol Arnott) now pastors the TACF as an independent fellowship.

A detailed overview of the Toronto manifestations and the Arnotts' ministry can be found in the free online version of the book *Weighed and Found Wanting* by Bill Randles at the URL below.

http://web.archive.org/web/20040703040810/http://www.geocities.com/Bob_Hunter/1.htm

John Avanzini

Word Faith_teacher and author, frequent guest on *Paul and Jan Crouch*'s Trinity Broadcasting Network (TBN). Avanzini specializes in grandiose promises of financial prosperity. He is well-known for promoting the "**hundred-fold blessing**" gimmick for fund-raising.

Here is a vignette from a typical Avanzini appearance, part of a longer 2009 blog entry titled "John Avanzini and His Talking Stones" at the URL below.

http://web.archive.org/web/20090625035643/http://www.sliceoflaodicea.com/false-teaching/john-avanzini-and-his-talking-stones

"After a rambling, free-ranging talk about the worsening economy and the price of gas, John Avanzini told us that he would give us all two things to help us get through perilous times. The first was a list of 7 Bible promises, as he called them, that he had printed up on a card. The mixture of truth and error was very evident here.

The list... gave the following "seven anchors for these perilous times". Note that the word prosperity as he uses it is referring to material wealth. Spiritual wealth was never mentioned that night.

1. God has already made plans for your prosperity. Jeremiah 29:11

2. Everything you will need and want has already been provided for you by your great God. 2 Peter 1:3

3. God has already given you his best so there is no need to worry about him denying you anything else. Romans 8:32

4. God wants you to live with limitless supply. Judges 18:10

5. Your wealthy place is always on the other side of the perilous times you are facing.

6. It gives God great pleasure to prosper you in good times...in bad times...at all times. Psalms 35:27

7. In good times or in bad times, God is willing to make you rich. Proverbs 10:22

...All of those Scripture verses given do talk about the prospering of God's people. The idea that this is always referring to physical wealth is patently absurd. Avanzini

156

and all of his huckster compatriots only use Scripture as proof texts for their own ridiculous claims that God wants everyone wearing Brioni suits and Rolex watches.

Avanzini told a story of how his grandchildren sometimes sit and watch him count money at the table. He described his stacks of 100's, 50's, 20's and so on. He mocked at how his daughter told them, "Don't ask for anything, children." He told us that she should have been teaching them to ask for money. He again mocked how she taught the children to say, "thank you" when he would give them money. He claimed that what they should have said instead was, "Can I have some more?" Avanzini apparently believes in training children early to be greedy and ungrateful.

The next thing Avanzini said he would give us to help us through "perilous times" was a stone. He went through several Bible references where stones "talked" in the Old Testament. Here Avanzini introduces the stone idea. He strolled down the aisles, his ring winking in the lights, and held out a shiny stone for a woman to hold. Avanzini told the assembled crowd of about 650 people that these stones should be rubbed whenever people faced rising prices or higher prices at the pump. The ushers went down the aisles with buckets of shiny, smooth stones and handed them out. …

…He began transitioning to his real message by telling the story of Gideon's sacrifice as recorded in the book of Judges. Repeatedly, Avanzini described the poverty of Gideon and how his offering of a goat was such a sacrifice for someone who lived in a cave. He described how the angel of the Lord IGNITED the offering on the rock. We, who were in possession of the lucky rubbing stones, would need to ignite ours. I'll give you a guess how that should be done.

At this point, Avanzini turned to the pastor in the white suit, sitting in the audience and asks innocently, "Do I have a few more moments?" Well, not surprisingly, the pastor agreed. It's a good thing, because as it turns out, Avanzini had a whole new doctrinal revelation to tell us about: the doctrine of reverse entrapment. If you've never heard of that before, that's because God just showed it to

157

him right there. Reverse entrapment is when you put a gift to Avanzoni on a credit card and outsmart the lenders who are trying to get rich off your debt. When you put a gift on a credit card, I quote, "Something happens in the spirit world." Here he tells everyone how to have a credit card breakthrough. Turns out Avanzini has a way for you to get rid of your mortgage debt. All you have to do is to give him a gift the size of your house payment and God will see that your mortgage gets paid off right away. If you don't have a house, $500 will do nicely for future debt. Avanzini assured us that it worked for him.

Perhaps the man sensed a few hostile vibes from the audience (from our row in particular) because he warned us not to let the devil keep us back from getting free from debt by putting a gift for his ministry on our credit card. The credit card "invitation" began as the keyboardist began to noodle around with some mood music. Then Avazini warned everyone again not to let the devil keep us away. The people streamed down to the stage area and wrote out their credit card numbers and house payment gifts and left them at the expensively shod feet of the speaker. While the people came down to the front to divest themselves of their money, Avanzini appropriately chose to tell an Al Capone joke. I doubt if one other person in the house recognized the irony.

Avanzini then prayed an igniting prayer over the stones everyone was clutching. Presumably, we still have to ignite our own with a credit card gift, but maybe his igniting prayer was considered the first step."

Don Basham

(1926-1989) One of the founders of the controversial so-called **"Shepherding Movement"** branch of the **Charismatic** renewal of the 1970s, along with *Bob Mumford, Charles Simpson,* Derek Prince, and *Ern Baxter.*

Their Christian Growth Ministries, headquartered in Ft. Lauderdale, Florida, published a monthly magazine called *New Wine,* with Basham as editor.

A detailed overview of the Shepherding Movement and these five men is available on the Seek God website at the URL below.

http://www.seekgod.ca/shepherding.htm

Ern Baxter

One of the founders of the controversial so-called "**Shepherding Movement**" of the Charismatic renewal of the 1970s, along with *Bob Mumford, Charles Simpson*, Derek Prince, and *Don Basham.*

A detailed overview of the Shepherding Movement and these five men is available on the Seek God website at the URL below.

http://www.seekgod.ca/shepherding.htm

Mike Bickle

Pastor of the former Kansas City Fellowship—now Metro **Vineyard** of Kansas City—home of the "**Kansas City Prophets**" group. Bickle has been considered by many to hold the office of "modern prophet" and thus regularly receive direct revelations from God, along with *Paul Cain,* John Paul Jackson and Bob Jones (not the same Bob Jones that founded conservative Bob Jones University.)

An overview of Bickle's ministry and the Kansas City Prophets titled "The Kansas City Prophets: Inside a Prophetic Service" is available at the URL below.

http://www.deceptioninthechurch.com/8.htm

Reinhard Bonnke

German healing evangelist who specializes in huge outdoor mass campaigns in Africa, sometimes preaching to audiences of one million or more. Bonnke is founder of the Christ for All Nations ministry. He makes spectacular but usually unsubstantiated claims for astounding healings at his meetings.

An extremely conflicting account of one of these healings is available on the Net at the URL below.

http://www.letusreason.org/popteac13.htm

William Branham

(1909-1965) One of the most influential "healing evangelists" in history. Branham's healing crusade career from 1946 until his death in 1965 was marked by grandiose claims by his supporters and considerable skepticism from his detractors. A number of prominent modern **Pentecostal** and **Charismatic** leaders still praise his ministry, and a number of doctrinal perspectives and methods in such circles can be traced to his influence.

Branham claimed, and his devoted followers believed (and still do), that God spoke primarily with one man in each "era" of the Church, who was then the "messenger" to that Church era. These eras were believed to be sequential time periods from the first century to the twentieth century. Each of the "Seven Churches of Asia" in the Book of Revelation was believed to represent one of these time periods. The messengers of the final three eras, Sardis, Philadelphia and Laodicea, were believed to be Martin Luther, John Wesley, and finally William Branham.

Many of the claims for Branham's prophetic role are based on alleged "miraculous signs" which were captured on film. It is admitted by Branham's promoters that the phenomena in the pictures were not noticed by the people present at the time, but showed up only when the film was developed. It is further claimed that none of the negatives or prints were tampered with (although it would be impossible to establish that double exposure, faulty chemicals in the photography process, or other factors had not affected the outcome of the photo printing process.) Two of the most famous photos are one showing what could be described as a "halo" above his head, and another showing some smeared areas of glowing red, allegedly a "fiery altar" around Branham at the lectern.

Branham taught a version of a doctrine called "Serpent's Seed" (or **"Satan's Seed"**) common in many racist groups in the 21st century. He claimed that God revealed to him that Eve's sin in the Garden of Eden was not eating a piece of fruit. That was only a metaphor for the fact that she had sexual relations with the Devil himself in the form of the serpent, and became pregnant with Cain. The physical line descended from Cain was thus literally the "seed of Satan." Thus when Jesus told Jews of His day that they were "of their father the Devil," He meant that literally, not figuratively.

Branham claimed to be able to "call things into existence" out of nothing. This included a claim at one point that a number of one dollar bills in his pocket were miraculously changed into twenty dollar bills. One would have to wonder why Branham would have then ever needed to accept offerings from followers—He could have just made "spiritual counterfeit" money any time he needed it!

When Branham died in 1965 from injuries received in an automobile accident, many of his followers expected him to be resurrected within three days. He was not.

A fascinating behind-the-scenes look at Branham at work is available in a 1990 interview with one of his associates from a crusade in Saskatchewan that was held back at the height of his career, which can be read at the URL below.

www.wayoflife.org/files/00507af4db4acc1e1e3149466afb 28b8-667.html

Even over forty years after his death, a large number of people around the world still revere Branham's memory and teachings, believe implicitly in his grandiose claims, and consider themselves "Branhamites." The most comprehensive source of detailed information on Branham on the Web is available at the URL below, on a site created by a former Branhamite who became disillusioned with the claims made for Branham.

http://people.delphiforums.com/JohnK63/home.htm

Paul Cain

One of the **"Kansas City Prophets"** group. Cain has been considered by many to hold the office of "modern prophet" and thus regularly receive direct revelations from God, along with *Mike Bickle*, John Paul Jackson and Bob Jones (not the same Bob Jones that founded conservative Bob Jones University.)

Harold Camping

In May 2011, Harold Camping's name became a household word in the US and many countries throughout the world. Up until then, he had been an obscure religious radio broadcaster and founder of a network of approximately 150 small, conservative religious radio stations named Family Radio Network (now officially called Family Stations, Inc.)

Although he had started out on his *Open Forum* radio show clear back in 1961 preaching a pretty standard "Reformed Church" theology, in recent decades his Bible interpretations had become increasingly idiosyncratic and increasingly controversial in some church circles. Although he had developed a loyal following among many in the Family Radio audience, his speculations and his personal theology were ignored at best and criticized vociferously at worst by many outside religious commentators.

Those who pay attention to fringe elements of the Wild World of Religion had been aware of Harold for quite some time. Up until 2011, he was most famous in religious circles for two things: (1) A failed dogmatic teaching, promoted through his radio ministry and through his book *1994?*, that Christ would return in 1994. (2) His teaching, promoted bombastically by him since about 2002, that every single local church congregation on earth has been abandoned by God, and that thus all true believers need to remove themselves from any church affiliation at all, as well as abandon any thought of taking part in baptisms or communion activities. At one point he recommended that they form "home fellowship groups" with likeminded believers, with no leadership of any kind (such as pastors, deacons, or elders) recognized. (While, of course, he strongly suggested that they continue to look to his teachings and broadcasts on Family Radio as authoritative.) But by 2011 he was recommending even against that. Individuals were to just worship privately at home—while, of course, still continuing to look to his teachings and broadcasts as their source of spiritual understanding.

After his bombastic claims for the Return of Christ in 1994 failed miserably, few expected him to stick his neck out as far as he did in early 2011! For a few years he had softened his rhetoric. But by 2011, rather than continuing to tone down his dogmatism, he ramped it up to the ultimate degree… launching a multi-million-dollar campaign to trumpet the announcement that Judgment Day, the resurrection of true Christians, and the Return of Christ to Rapture His Church to be with him in heaven were all going to occur Saturday, May 21, 2011.

The scenario was described something like this:

As sundown at the end of May 21 arrived at the International Date Line in the South Pacific, a giant earthquake would occur there. As the sun continued to set around the world in each time zone, the "rolling earthquake" would arrive also. This earthquake would herald the resurrection of the dead Christians of all ages. They would rise out of their graves, and join the living true Christians (mostly Harold's followers, evidently) who would have their bodies "changed" as described in the Bible. Christ would return and catch

162

them all up ("rapture" them) into the air to go to be with him in heaven.

By the time the sun set in the last time zone for May 21, all true Christians would be gone from the earth, and every nation would be in devastation. This would trigger five months of terrifying conditions on the earth, including more earthquakes, along with famines and disease epidemics. At the end of the five months, on October 21, God would then destroy the whole earth, along with every living thing on it, and the "heavens" as well. Camping does not believe in an ever-burning hell, so this would be the ultimate annihilation of all humans who were not true Christians. For some reason, his estimate of how many this would be out of all the billions of people who ever lived was 200 million. This would include all the true Christians since the first century.

Since Camping believes in total predestination… that is, that God just arbitrarily has chosen who will be saved and who will be lost even before they were born, the purpose of his advertising campaign was not to get anyone to "repent" of their sins so that they could be saved. It wasn't a warning. It was just an "announcement."

This announcement was spread by voice over the airwaves, by individuals passing out tracts in public places all over the world, by about 1200 large billboards across the US and 2000 more in selected countries overseas … and most famously by a fleet of RaptureMobiles, vehicles from cars to RVs decked out as rolling billboards that criss-crossed the U.S. in the closing weeks before the Big Date. Family Radio itself reportedly invested over a million dollars in this publicity blitz. But that was augmented by many followers who "stepped out in faith" and gave up jobs, and sometimes homes–and even families–to dedicate their "final days" to being part of the volunteer publicity brigade.

Some liquidated their savings to pay for advertising materials–including one 60-year-old New Yorker who invested his entire life savings of $140,000 to pay for advertising materials, including placards to plaster on the subways and bus shelters of New York City.

As the date got closer, the advertising blitz eventually caught the attention and fascination of much of the world's media. Stories about the situation became daily fodder for major newspapers in the US and around the world, all the main US broadcast networks and Cable news networks, and magazines such as *Time*.

On May 7 an NPR radio show included an interview with Camping.

> The interviewer asked, "So you're not planning for May 22?"
>
> "Absolutely not," Camping says. "It is going to happen. There is no Plan B."
>
> I've asked a dozen of Camping's followers the same question. Everyone said even entertaining the possibility that May 21 would come and go without event is an offense to God. They all hope they'll be raptured. Some worry about being left behind.
>
> "If I'm here on May 22, and I wake up, I'm going to be in hell," says Brown. "And that's where I don't want to be. So there is going to be a May 22, and we don't want to be here."

But of course Harold Camping was "here" on Sunday, May 22, bewildered for a short while about the failure of his prophecy. That didn't last long, though. Monday night, he was back on his *Open Forum* radio show, explaining to bewildered callers eager to hear the answer to "what happened??" that he had it all figured out now. Judgment really **had** come on May 21. It was just "spiritual," rather than something that could be seen with the eyes. God had just "closed the door" of salvation on that day. Everyone not already a Christian on that day would remain that way until October 21, and then be annihilated.

What about the earthquake predicted? That was a metaphor. What about Christ coming and rapturing the saints? Another metaphor. And the resurrection of the dead? Yes, another metaphor.

This wasn't much comfort to those now without jobs and homes and savings, and with their families totally alienated from them because of their involvement with this strangeness. Even if they believed the "new" understanding that the Real End wouldn't come for another five months, many were desperate for advice from their guru on how to put their lives back together so they could survive those five months!

164

So what advice did he give them on the *Open Forum*?

> When confronted with the question of how to address his followers who spent their life savings thinking that the world would end on May 21... he says, "The fact is that just as I'm talking very candidly to you... please understand we don't advise anybody what to do... we're not in the business of financial advice. We had a great recession... there are lots of people that lost their jobs... their houses. Lots of people had this and that... and somehow they all survived. Maybe a cousin helped them or the city... some cases were very severe... I'll tell ya, what has happened to the average person listening to Family Radio isn't nearly as grievous. People cope. "

That was his solution for the man who gave up his $140,000 life savings. "People cope."

Reports at the time of the failed May 21 prophecy indicated that perhaps up to 80% of the employees of the network actually didn't believe his predictions, but merely stayed with the organization because it was their source of income. For two weeks after the failure of that date, nothing seemed to have changed. Camping's 90-minute *Open Forum* program was still broadcast every weeknight, and he seemed to be as much in charge as ever.

But on June 9, 2011, Camping, age 89 at the time, suffered a stroke which affected his verbal communication. At first Family Radio played repeats of old *Open Forum* shows at the regular time. But on June 23 the Associated Press reported that Family Radio had announced that the show would be replaced with new programming at the end of June. Harold had survived the stroke, and was at the time in a "nursing facility" receiving rehabilitation. But he was evidently not expected to be able to return to his microphone.

But there was no indication on the Family Radio website that the management of the network intended to recant Camping's October 21 prediction, nor revise the intent to not "preach the gospel" any longer because ... no one can be saved any longer, so why bother? The plan was just to "encourage the flock" of people who were already Christian with uplifting music and messages about the goodness of God and such, to help them be patient until October.

Harold's date for the Final Destruction has now passed. As with many such groups throughout history, a significant portion of his followers who had pinned their hopes on that date are now just busily re-calculating, and convinced that if they just be patient, the End will come. Soon. Very soon. (See the **When Prophecy Fails** chapter of this **Field Guide** for insight into why so many don't give up even after such devastatingly obvious failures.)

Charles Capps

Long-time, prolific **Word Faith** ("**positive confession**," "health, wealth and prosperity") writer and speaker. Capps' books and pamphlets and taped messages on the fundamentals of the Word Faith doctrines are extensively imitated—almost to the point of plagiarism—by many younger Word Faith writers, teachers, and preachers.

Morris Cerullo

Pentecostal evangelist active since the 1950s. Cerullo is part of the **Healing Ministries** movement and the **Word Faith** movement.

Mahesh Chavda

Part of the **Modern Apostles and Prophets** movement, viewed by many as one of the modern Apostles. Chavda is active in the **Toronto Blessing** movement and other manifestations of the so-called **Third Wave** of the **Charismatic** renewal. Originally from India, he is now an American citizen.

(Paul) David Yonggi Cho

Pastor of "the world's largest church" that is a single congregation, not a denomination. Korean Yonggi Cho (who changed his name to David in recent years for some obscure reason) heads the **Charismatic** Yoido Full Gospel Church in Seoul that claims to have over 1 million people in regular attendance. Cho teaches an extreme occultic form of **Word Faith** doctrines, including the concept that if someone has an adequate "positive confession," their words literally enter into the "Heavenly Holy of Holies" and can emerge manifested as tangible objects that the believer is "naming and claiming."

J. R. Church

Popular prophecy pundit of the End Times Prophecy movement. Church spreads his theories via his *Prophecy in the News* TV show and numerous books. He is most famous for his 1986 book *Hidden Prophecies in the Psalms*, which alleged that the Psalms contain a hidden prophetic guide to the Twentieth Century. In other words, something in Psalm 1 applied to the events of 1901, Psalm 86 applied to 1986 and so on. Using utterly speculative and fanciful interpretations of vague passages, he strongly hinted in the first edition of his book that 1988 would be the year of the pre-tribulation rapture, followed by the Tribulation for 1989-1994, and the return of Christ in 1995. When none of this panned out, it didn't stop him, he just re-interpreted the vague passages to imply what did happen in those years. And he still continues to this day using his Nostradamus-style gimmick to sell books, gather and keep a TV audience, and garner invitations to speak at prophecy seminars and conventions. There's no accounting for the gullibility of folks who are desperate for someone to tell them "secret things."

Randy Clark

Senior Pastor of the **Vineyard** Christian Fellowship of St. Louis, Missouri. Clark started a "**holy laughter**" revival at his home church after attending a 1993 meeting featuring *Rodney Howard-Browne* at *Kenneth Hagin*'s Rhema Bible Church in Tulsa, Oklahoma. He was invited by *John Arnott*, pastor of the Toronto Airport Vineyard Church to conduct a four day conference at the Toronto church starting January 20,1994. Clark's appearance triggered the beginning of what came to be known as the "**Toronto Blessing**" revival. As a result, Clark and his Global Awakening team are regularly invited to conduct or participate in revivals and revival training sessions all over the world to promote the same kind of activity as that in Toronto.

Jack Coe

(1918-1957) One of the most well-known "healing evangelists" of the 1950s. Coe was part of the **Healing Ministries** movement. He was described in the book *The Century of the Holy Spirit* by *Vinson Synan* as "bold and flamboyant" and as having "pushed claims of divine healing to the uttermost boundaries."

Raymond Cole

(d. 2001) Founder of the Church of God, the Eternal (COGTE), a split-off group from the Worldwide Church of God under *Herbert Armstrong*. Cole's family had been supporters of Armstrong since the 1930s, and he was one of the first students at Armstrong's Ambassador College in 1947. At one time an influential player in the leadership of the WCG, Cole left the group in 1975 and started the COGTE over what he believed to be "watering down true doctrine" by Armstrong. The doctrines in question were particularly the issue of divorce and remarriage, and the setting of the proper date for the church to observe the Holy Day of Pentecost.

Strangely enough, for the next 25 years, until his death, Cole preached that Armstrong was divinely chosen by God to restore truth to the Church that had been lost since the first century. And he taught that all the doctrines Armstrong had taught in his early years were absolutely binding on members of the COGTE, because they had been divinely inspired by God to Armstrong. Yet he did not believe that Armstrong had any authority to change his mind on any doctrine, and thus no one had the right to accept any later changes to earlier church doctrine.

Kenneth Copeland, Gloria Copeland

Pentecostal/Charismatic televangelists and authors. The Copelands are the most currently influential protégés of the teachings of **Word Faith** Movement pioneer _Kenneth Hagin_. Kenneth Copeland studied at Oral Roberts' Oral Roberts University (ORU). And he and wife Gloria spread their "name it and claim it" doctrines via their _Believer's Voice of Victory_ program,

Paul and Jan Crouch

Husband and wife founders of the Trinity Broadcast Network (TBN), which is the primary media outlet for most of the preachers, teachers, and evangelists of the **Word Faith** Movement. The programs on the network primarily promote **Hyper-Charismatic** and Word Faith teachings along with prophetic speculations. It is reported to currently air on 2500 television stations, 17 satellites, and thousands of cable systems around the world.

William F (Bill) Dankenbring

Former member of the Worldwide Church of God (WCG) under _Herbert W Armstrong_, writer at one time for Armstrong's ministry. Dankenbring was disfellowshipped from the WCG in the 1980s, and began Triumph Prophetic Ministries (now referred to on the Triumph website as Triumph Prophetic Ministries Church of God) in 1987. The ministry produces _Prophecy Flash_ newsletter/magazine. Dankenbring has a small following of enthusiastic regular supporters, primarily drawn from ex-members of the WCG or its

168

offshoots, who look to him as their religious leader/guru. Here is a sample from a 2000 *Prophecy Flash* letter to the editor:

> "Thank you for the PF and the TAPES!! I am so greedy, it took me only 3 days to listen to your 12 Tapes! As you may have noticed -- I get very nervous when your material is DELAYED, and if by a very BAD CHANCE --- I don't get it AT ALL -- I go mad!! It's the price you have to pay for being so VITALLY INDISPENSABLE in our life, Dear Bill!! So, please make a careful note in your computer of my new order if you please . . . .

> "Your impatient sister in Yeshua! God Bless you!

> "P.S. . . . I stick closely to your narrow path!

> -- France

Guru Bill spreads his teachings primarily through the magazine, articles, and sermon/teaching recordings, as well as the Triumph website. He accepts a certain amount of Hebrew Roots/ Jewish custom emphasis, including wearing a Jewish-style prayer shawl. He is particularly famous for frequently using a bombastic, aggressive, dogmatic, condescending style even when dealing with his own supporters.

Dankenbring specializes particularly in prophetic End Times speculations and in promoting his own idiosyncratic take on obscure Bible points. In February 1999 he speculated in *Prophecy Flash* that Bill Clinton was the Beast of Revelation. In April 2001 he speculated that Ariel Sharon was the fulfillment of Biblical prophecies of a latter-day "Zerubbabel," who would oversee the rebuilding of the Temple. After 2001 he speculated that the seven year Tribulation started that year, and would end in 2007 with the Return of Christ.

It didn't, of course. He is now speculating that the Tribulation has started in 2011:

> It is very possible the final 3 1/2 year ministry of the two witnesses will begin around the Feast of Trumpets in the year 2014, about three years from now! Of course, we don't know the exact date or hour. However, many indications give us reason to believe that the coming of the Messiah may be about 70 years from the founding of the state of Israel in 1948 – which would be spring of

2018, perhaps around Passover or Pentecost! Counting back 3 ½ years from then would bring us to fall of 2014.

The time of Great Tribulation has indeed opened its voracious, yawning, gaping, devouring Mouth, with gleaming, wicked teeth, to consume the raw material of this wicked, self-destructive world. Its destruction rushes onward like a thundering freight train in the night.

It's not quite clear why anyone pays attention to Bill's speculations on this matter since he's been equally bombastic about the same thing numerous times in the past twenty years and has failed miserably every time.

Bill made it very clear in 2008 where he believes his ministry fits in the greater Plan of God on Earth when he announced on his website,

TRIUMPH PROPHETIC MINISTRIES CHURCH OF GOD is the 'only' remnant body in the World, of "Jesus Christ," the Church He said He would "BUILD" which preaches what He, the twelve apostles, and the apostle Paul, all faithfully taught.

A loyal supporter writing to the *Prophecy Flash* in the mid-1990s noted that he had no one else in his local area who adhered closely to Dankenbring's teachings. He wondered if it would be OK to look for Christian fellowship with others who at least held similar beliefs, particularly observance of the seventh-day Sabbath and the biblical Holy Days. Dankenbring's answer was NO. It would be best not to risk being tainted by those who didn't understand what the reader understood from studying under him. So for fellowship on the Sabbath, he literally suggested such folks ought to "fellowship" with Dankenbring tapes! This is surprisingly reminiscent of Herbert Armstrong. When asked a similar question in the 1960s, Armstrong forbade his followers from either gathering in informal fellowship and Bible Study without a minister, or attending any other kind of church. He rather recommended that those who could not fellowship with an official Radio Church of God congregation endorsed by Armstrong in their own area for Sabbath worship services should sit quietly and respectfully in front of their radio on the Sabbath and listen to the *World Tomorrow* Broadcast.

John Nelson Darby

(1800-1882) Key leader in the "Brethren" movement of the 1800s. Darby was a prolific writer whose views on a number of doctrinal issues and prophetic speculations had a wide impact outside the Brethren groups. For details on that influence, see the Wikipedia article at the URL below.

http://en.wikipedia.org/wiki/John_Nelson_Darby

Jack Deere

Writer and conference speaker who extensively promotes the **Modern Apostles and Prophets** movement. Deere was a professor in the Department of Old Testament Exegesis and Semitic Studies at Dallas Theological Seminary from 1976-1988. He was Associate Pastor at the **Vineyard** Christian Fellowship in Anaheim, California, 1988-1992. He is currently the Senior Pastor at Trinity Fellowship Church, Amarillo, Texas. As well as the Executive Director of Covenant Ministries International (CMI). CMI is "an organization that connects apostolic church networks and provides resources and training for the apostolic churches." ("Apostolic churches" seems to be a term for those groups that recognize a circle of alleged modern apostles and prophets.) Deere is also head of Evangelical Foundation Ministries, Inc., and conducts a conference ministry with *Paul Cain, Mike Bickle* and *Rick Joyner.* Two significant books he has authored: *Surprised by the Power of the Spirit* and *Surprised by the Voice of God.*

C O Dodd

Author of a 1930s book called *History of the True Church*, along with co-author *Andrew Dugger.* Both were affiliated with the Church of God, Seventh Day (COG7) at the time, and the book was an attempt to create an unbroken historical record of Sabbatarians backward in time to the first century. The Worldwide Church of God under *Herbert Armstrong* (called the Radio Church of God at the time) used the material in the book as the primary source for their own booklet with a similar goal, titled *A True History of the True Church*. More recent investigation into the material in the Dugger and Dodd book has shown much of the "historical research" to be very shoddy, and their conclusions to be poorly reasoned.

Dodd began his own ministry in 1937 with publication of a magazine called *The Faith* at Salem, W. Virginia. The original purpose of the magazine was to promote observance of the annual

Biblical Holy Days among those affiliated with the Church of God, Seventh Day. In 1938 he organized the *Faith Bible and Tract Society*. Dodd eventually accepted the so-called **Sacred Name** doctrine, the requirement of believers to use the Hebrew names of deity rather than the English words God and Jesus. He left the Church of God movement and was instrumental in the development of a loose association of independent Sacred Name groups which usually adopted the name Assemblies of Yahweh. After his death, publication of the magazine was continued by various Sacred Name assemblies. It has been published since 1969 by a group in Eaton Rapids, Michigan, which has been meeting continuously as a Sacred Name group since 1939. The Faith Bible and Tract Society was continued by Dodd's family.

John Alexander Dowie

(1847-1907) Early forerunner of the **Healing Ministries** movement. Born in Scotland, Dowie lived as a youth and young adult in Australia, and eventually moved to America. He began a ministry in Australia in1875 based on the "guaranteed healing in the atonement" theory. He moved to the U.S. in 1888 and set up healing meetings in 1890 across the street from the site being prepared for the 1893 Chicago World's Fair, to draw attention to his ministry.

Dowie insisted his followers totally reject medical treatment of any kind, considering drugs and doctors to be of the Devil. His own daughter died as a result of untreated severe burns—Dowie had even forbidden anyone to try to soothe the pain of her injuries with Vaseline. He founded the Christian Catholic Church in Chicago and produced a magazine called *Leaves of Healing* that had a wide influence. He created his own closed society in 1900 of over 6000 residents called City of Zion on the lakefront near Chicago, that he ruled with dictatorial authority. Although not a **Pentecostal** himself, many men and women who were later very influential in the Pentecostal and **Charismatic** movements were at one time a part of Zion City, including several of the founders of the Assemblies of God denomination. Dowie claimed in 1901 to be "Elijah the Restorer," and in 1904 to be the "divinely commissioned first apostle of a renewed End Times Church." Many supporters did not accept this new revelation, and his ministry went downhill from that point, with the City of Zion leaders eventually voting him out of his leadership role there. Dowie was accused of sexual improprieties late in life, suffered a stroke, his City went bankrupt, and he spent his final months of life nearly totally despondent. The city did eventually recover, and is now just a regular small suburb of Chicago, with population of about 20,000.

Andrew Dugger

Author of a 1930s book called *History of the True Church*, along with co-author *C. O. Dodd*. Both were affiliated with the Church of God, Seventh Day (COG7) at the time, and the book was an attempt to create an unbroken historical record of Sabbatarians backward in time to the first century. The Worldwide Church of God under *Herbert Armstrong* (called the Radio Church of God at the time) used the material in the book as the primary source for their own booklet with a similar goal, titled *A True History of the True Church*. More recent investigation into the material in the Dugger and Dodd book has shown much of the "historical research" to be very shoddy, and their conclusions to be poorly reasoned.

Dugger was an elder in the COG7. Although he agreed in principle with some of the same doctrinal positions of C.O. Dodd, including observance of the annual Holy Days and use of the Sacred Name, Dugger did not leave the COG7 in the 1930s as did Dodd. However, he later split with the organization over non-doctrinal issues, and because of his particular view of prophetic speculation. In the 1950s he established his own ministry with headquarters in Jerusalem, and began publication of *The Mount Zion Reporter* in 1953. After his death in 1975, some of the members of his family continued his ministry, which goes under various names, including Church of God (Jerusalem), Congregation of Elohim, and Family of Elohim.

Jesse DuPlantis

Word Faith television preacher and conference speaker. Founder of Jesse DuPlantis Ministries with a weekly television show of his own on *Jan and Paul Crouch's* Trinity Broadcasting Network. DuPlantis has guest speaking spots on many TBN specials, especially the fund raising telethons. He is best known for his almost non-stop huge grin and hyperactivity in delivery, using corny jokes to make his points. The topic of his messages seldom strays from the "prosperity gospel."

Gary Ezzo, AnneMarie Ezzo

173

Founders of the controversial Growing Kids God's Way ministry, which includes special programs for teaching parents of infants to teens the Ezzo's own idiosyncratic childrearing methods. Particularly of concern to their critics are their recommendations for feeding infants. They insist that even the tiniest breast-feeding infants should be put on a rigid schedule of four-hour feedings or the like. There are numerous reports giving evidence that this regimen has led to both breastfeeding failure on the part of some mothers, and serious nutritional deficiencies in some infants. Critics also claim that the Ezzos have refused to address legitimate concerns brought to their attention regarding various aspects of their training materials. Information and extensive details on areas of concern regarding their ministry is at the URL below.

www.ezzo.info/

Gerald Flurry

Former member of the Worldwide Church of God under *Herbert W Armstrong*. Flurry was founder, after Armstrong's death, of a rival organization to the WCG called the Philadelphia Church of God (PCG). He claims to be the spiritual successor to Herbert Armstrong as head of the Only True Church of God on Earth. And he has gathered a fairly large following from among those former WCG members who believed that Armstrong was used by God to "restore the Truth" to the "Church in the End Time." Many such individuals seem to believe that the PCG adheres most closely of all the major exWCG splits to the original doctrines and practices of Herbert Armstrong. This perception is disputed by followers from other WCG split-off groups, who believe their own chosen guru is more faithful to Armstrong's teachings. This is particularly true regarding the topic of prophetic speculation. Flurry has changed a number of Armstrong's teachings in this area. For instance, Armstrong had insisted that there were no actual "prophets" in the modern era of the Church, and would be none. (Armstrong had instead styled himself as an Endtime "Apostle.") According to some observers, Flurry has evidently attempted to distract his followers from this emphasis in some of Armstrong's writings by selective editing of the texts of Armstrong's writings that are reprinted by the PCG. The reason for this is that Flurry has adamantly identified himself as the one and only prophet of modern times.

Flurry publishes the full-color *Philadelphia Trumpet* magazine, a clone of Armstrong's *Plain Truth* magazine at its height of polished attractiveness in the 1970s. He has a TV program modeled after Armstrong's *World Tomorrow* program. He has even attempted to create in Tulsa a miniature version of Armstrong's Ambassador College Pasadena, California, campus, complete with a scaled-down version of Armstrong's Ambassador Auditorium and its popular concert series

The PCG for some time re-published Armstrong's major full-length book, *Mystery of the Ages*, until the WCG won a copyright infringement judgment against them. The PCG later paid the WCG 3 million dollars for the publication rights to all of Armstrong's major writings. The PCG is the most secretive, and the most worrisome of the main splits from the WCG in the eyes of people who have family members within the PCG. Flurry runs the organization in a totally dictatorial way and has implied strongly to members that they may soon leave for "a **place of safety**" if the Great **Tribulation** appears about to begin in Flurry's estimation. Flurry currently demands that his members cut themselves off totally from all family members, including parents and children, who were ever a part of the WCG or the PCG but who are not now loyal members of the PCG. This has caused great distress in many families, with even aged and dying parents separated from their loved ones.

Useful links for those looking for more detailed information about Flurry:

> www.exitsupportnetwork.com/mike_ep/pcg/pcg.htm

> A helpful overview of Flurry's ministry with links to other commentary and documentation

> www.exitsupportnetwork.com/mike_ep/letters/ltrspcg06.htm

> The most recent information about activities within Flurry's organization

Hobart Freeman

(1920-1984) Founder of the Faith Assembly in northern Indiana and its well-known meeting hall which he gave the name "Glory Barn." Freeman taught and enforced among his followers one of the most radical positions in the **Healing Ministries** movement: that healing was "guaranteed in the atonement," it is always God's will to heal, and that any acceptance of any human aid to healing would be evidence that one did not trust God. He embraced the radical healing position in the 1960s, but was, prior to that, a respected professor of Old Testament at Grace Theological Seminary, author of a widely-accepted text, *An Introduction to the Old Testament Prophets* published by the Moody Bible Institute

Freeman's radical healing position led to over 90 deaths, many of them children, in the local congregation which investigation indicated would not have occurred with proper medical attention, many from simple ailments.

John MacArthur wrote regarding Hobart's group in *Charismatic Chaos* (Chapter 9, available on the Internet at www.deceptioninthechurch.com/chaos9.htm):

> After a 15 year old girl, whose parents belonged to Faith Assembly, died of a medically treatable malady, the parents were convicted of negligent homicide and sentenced to ten years in prison. Freeman himself was charged with aiding and inducing reckless homicide in the case. Shortly afterward, on December 8, 1984, Freeman himself died, interestingly enough of pneumonia and heart failure complicated by a severely ulcerated leg.

> Hobart Freeman's theology did not allow him to acknowledge that polio had left one of his legs disfigured and lame. He said, in spite of the obvious, "I have my healing." And that is all he would say when anyone pointed out the rather conspicuous inconsistency between his physical disabilities and his theology. Ultimately, his refusal to acknowledge his infirmities cost him his life. He had dutifully, according to his own theology, refused all medical treatment for the maladies that were killing him, and medical science could easily have prolonged his life, but in the end he was a victim of his own teaching.

Claudio Friedzon

One of the primary leaders of the **Hyper-Charismatic** "Argentine Renewal/Revival." Friedzon was influenced in the early part of his public ministry by the work of fellow Argentinian *Carlos Annacondia*. He entered a new phase after exposure to *Benny Hinn's* book *Good Morning Holy Spirit*, and subsequent meetings in 1992 with Hinn during a visit to America to attend Hinn crusades. Shortly thereafter Friedzon led his Argentine congregation in experiencing the kind of extravagant displays of alleged supernatural manifestations that later became identified by name as the **Toronto Blessing**. This catapulted him to a career in large urban mass evangelism crusades where these manifestations became the norm.

It was at a Claudio Friedzon meeting in Argentina in late 1993 that Friedzon prayed over Toronto Airport **Vineyard** pastor *John Arnott* and his wife. Their reaction to the experience led directly to the initiation in January, 1994, of the "revival" in their own church back in Canada and thus the actual beginning of the Toronto Blessing Movement.

Dan Gayman

One of the earliest and most influential leaders in the white racist **Identity** movement. Gayman founded the Church of Israel in 1972, with headquarters in Missouri. He added the observance of the weekly Sabbath and the annual Holy Days of Leviticus to the church's doctrines in the 1990s. He is author of a number of books and articles on the Serpent's Seed/**Satan's Seed** doctrine which are disseminated widely in racist circles. Gayman teaches that the modern Jews are actually the descendants of a sexual liaison between Eve and "the serpent" in the Garden of Eden, in which Satan—not Adam—begat Cain. And he teaches that only genetically pure, white Caucasian people—descendants of Adam's son Seth—are made in God's image, and that thus only they can be in covenant with God, and inherit eternal spiritual salvation as His sons and daughters. All non-whites are descended from a pre-Adamic creation by God, and are referred to in the book of Genesis as "**beasts of the field**."

An overview of the history of Gayman's organization and its white extremist affiliations is available at the URL below.

www.adl.org/learn/Ext_US/gayman.asp?xpicked=2&item =gayman

Bill Gothard

Founder of the Institute for Basic Life Principles (IBLP), the Advanced Training Institute (ATI), and creator of the materials used for the Character First! (CF!) programs being used by various schools, businesses, and communities throughout the US and other countries. Through the IBLP Gothard offers seminars on child rearing and family living, including a series called "Basic Youth Conflicts" regarding parenting teenagers. ATI is a comprehensive homeschool program for families, and CF! uses character training and success motivation material from the ATI curriculum , after purging it of references to God and the Bible. This program is offered to cities, businesses, schools, and other groups as being a totally secular program, and all references to its connection to the Gothard ministries have been obscured.

Gothard's methods and teachings have come under close scrutiny and criticism in recent years. A growing number of individuals and families which formerly looked to Gothard as a spiritual guru have become disillusioned and disenchanted with him and his ministries. Some are actively seeking to publicize their concerns about the spiritual and even physical abuse suffered by many who have been involved with Gothard's programs.

The most extensive and well-documented material covering the areas of concern about Gothard's ministry is that available on the Midwest Christian Outreach (MCO) website at the following URL.

> http://web.archive.org/web/20090412192605/http://mi
> dwestoutreach.org/02-Information/02-
> OnlineReference/02-UnorthodoxyGuide/105-
> IKnowSomething/Gothard-IBLP/index.html

And the definitive book on the topic is *Bill Gothard--A Matter of Basic Principles*, an excellent investigative report by MCO affiliates Don and Joy Veinot and Ron Henzel. Ordering information is at the URL below.

> www.midwestoutreach.org/blogs/a-matter-of-basic-
> principles-bill-gothard-and-the-christian-life

John Hagee

(Born 1940) Founder and pastor of the 15,000+ member Cornerstone Church in San Antonio, Texas. Hagee is President of Global Evangelism Television, which broadcasts his daily and weekly programs on television and radio throughout the United States and around the world. He is also author of a series of popular books on End Times prophecy.

His broadcast, *John Hagee Ministries*, is seen twice daily on *Jan and Paul Crouch's* TBN (Trinity Broadcast Network) and is carried in America on 110 full power TV stations and on the Inspirational Network (INSP), and from coast to coast in Canada on the Vision Network (VN). Hagee's specific emphasis on his program and in the many books he has written for the "popular Christian market" is his own idiosyncratic take on End Times Prophecy, making him a significant player in the End Times Prophecy movement.

Often referred to on TV and in complimentary articles as "Dr. Hagee," this is evidently because he holds a 1989 "honorary" doctorate from Oral Roberts University (ORU) (1989). His theological training was from Southwestern Bible Institute near Dallas. Although he does not come across as particularly **Charismatic** in his preaching, Hagee is firmly within the Charismatic **Word Faith_**camp, and associates and cooperates freely with such **Hyper-Charismatic** personalities as Benny Hinn and the other TBN regulars.

Below are excerpts from one highly critical webpage called "The Other Gospel of John Hagee" at

www.pfo.org/jonhagee.htm

Most people who see and hear the Rev. John C. Hagee are impressed. He is rotund, strident, authoritative (and could well pass for Rush Limbaugh's older and more serious brother). His delivery alone gives the impression of one who really knows what he is talking about. However, careful evaluation of the teachings of Hagee, pastor at the San Antonio-based Cornerstone Church, reveals false teaching and a defective view of a basic and essential issue regarding salvation and the Gospel. Hagee preaches another way of salvation for the Jew, which is in direct violation of Paul's warnings in Galatians 1:6-9.

This theological concept, which has many forms, is primarily referred to as the "Two Covenant" or "Dual Covenant" theory.

Hagee's web site tells us that his "vision is for world evangelism. The burning passion of his heart is to win the lost to Jesus Christ in America and around the world." That statement is not altogether true since he will not

179

evangelize Jews and teaches salvation on another basis than the Gospel for the Jewish people.

Hagee has become extremely popular since the 1987 dedication of his Cornerstone Church (an event that featured an appearance and a blessing from W.A. Criswell, then pastor of First Baptist Church of Dallas) and because of the daily programs from Global Evangelism Television of which he is president. His best-selling books have also made him a celebrity. He associates with the likes of Benny Hinn and appears with him from time to time at crusades and other Charismatic congresses.

...That there are moral and ethical concerns with Hagee and a serious question as to his being biblically qualified as a pastor and teacher are not the main issues of this article. However, one very important factor should be noted. The Liberty Flame reported in May 1994 that during the time when Hagee was serving the Charismatic congregation at Trinity Church (1976) in San Antonio, he divorced his wife, resigned and married a young woman in the congregation, Diana Castro. Custody of Hagee's two children by his ex-wife, Martha, went to her.

In a letter to the church, Hagee admitted immorality, which later became part of the court records in the custody battle. Martha later also remarried and started another family. Not surprisingly, there is a hiatus from 1976 to 1987 left out of Hagee's web site biography.

...The Christian Research Institute panned Hagee's 1996 book, Beginning of the End, not only for its premise that Yitzhak Rabin's assassination triggered prophetic events and set the prophetic clock ticking somehow but because he falsely predicted that Shimon Peres would succeed Rabin. The later elections brought Benyamin Netanyahu to power.

...While most of Hagee's prophetic books become instant best-sellers, they do not always receive the best of reviews. As noted above, CRI faulted his Beginning of the End and the normally courteous CBA Marketplace Magazine gave a "thumbs down" to his book, Final Dawn Over Jerusalem, saying:

"In his long list of Jewish people who have blessed the world, Hagee makes no distinction between individuals who simply have a Jewish background and those who truly fear and seek God. He lists Goldie Hawn, Dustin Hoffman, and Barbara Streisand, among others, as Jews who have proven the Scripture 'in thee shall all the nations of the earth be blessed.' The contributions of these entertainers can hardly be seen as a fulfillment of God's promise to Abraham in Genesis. Hagee also goes as far as branding anti-Semitic those who don't agree with his enthusiastic support of Israel."

Despite its criticisms, CBA Marketplace Magazine in June 1998 listed Final Dawn Over Jerusalem as the No. 1 clothbound nonfiction book.

Christian author and conspiracy debunker Gregory Camp also is critical of Hagee's writings:

"The Texas-based minister has recently published a book dealing with the end times in which he predicts the end of Israeli independence as a result of giving up the Golan Heights and then signing a treaty with the Antichrist. Titled Beginning of the End, this Thomas Nelson publication will doubtless sell by the hundreds of thousands. It rehashes old pre-millennial prophecy themes and like an increasing number of such ministries, throws conspiracy theory into the mix. The book unfortunately is just one more of a series of tired conspiracy-tainted prophecy monographs so common these days; there is scarcely an original idea to be found between its covers. The reader is 'treated' to sensationalistic predictions about the Israeli State and the nearness of Christ's return based on conspiracy and closet date-setting."

...Yet, of additional and more serious concern is that Hagee reported to the Houston Chronicle that he believes that Jews already have a covenant with God and a relationship to God and do not need to come to the cross. Hearing this is startling. Hagee told the newspaper:

181

"I believe that every Jewish person who lives in the light of the Torah, which is the word of God, has a relationship with God and will come to redemption."

This certainly is a shocking statement in the light of Jesus' words that "no man comes to the Father but through me" (John 14:6). John further writes, in his first Epistle: "He who does not have the Son of God does not have life" (1 John 5:12).

The Apostle Paul, as well, would say the opposite of Hagee: "I do not set aside the grace of God: for if righteousness comes through the law, then Christ died in vain" (Galatians 2:21). Paul is affirming that nothing that the Old Testament offered could avail apart from the death of Jesus.

The Houston Chronicle article further reported:

"John Hagee, fundamentalist pastor from San Antonio and friend of Israel, is truly a strange fish. ... The man has a mission. He's out to attack anti-Semitism. He also believes that Jews can come to God without going through Jesus Christ."

The Houston newspaper then quoted Hagee's own shocking words: "I'm not trying to convert the Jewish people to the Christian faith."

And further revealed:

"In fact, trying to convert Jews is a 'waste of time,' he said. 'The Jewish person who has his roots in Judaism is not going to convert to Christianity. There is no form of Christian evangelism that has failed so miserably as evangelizing the Jewish people. They (already) have a faith structure.' Everyone else, whether Buddhist or Baha'i, needs to believe in Jesus, he says. But not Jews. Jews already have a covenant with God that has never been replaced by Christianity, he says."

182

(See the website referenced above for much more commentary on Hagee and his teachings.)

Kenneth Hagin

Most influential pioneer of the **Word Faith** Movement. Hagin is the founder of Rhema Bible School, alma mater of a number of well-known televangelists. He is also author of many books, booklets, articles, and magazines that provide the doctrinal basis for standard Word Faith teachings. Documentation has shown that he blatantly plagiarized some of his writings directly from material written by earlier mystic evangelist *EW Kenyon*. An extensive investigation and documentation of Kenyon's formative years and influence on the Word Faith movement, including documentation on Hagin's plagiarism of Kenyon, is available in D.R. McConnell's 225-page book *A Different Gospel* (c. 1988, updated 1995), Hendrickson Publishers Inc. The chapter about Hagin's plagiarism is available for free download online at the URL below.

www.mtio.com/articles/bissar51.htm

Hank Hanegraaff

Controversial successor to the late Walter Martin as the head of Martin's Christian Research Institute. Hanegraaff hosts the *Bible Answer Man* national radio program. He is author of a number of books of research on modern religious movements, and a member of *Chuck Smith*'s Calvary Chapel. Although the documentation in his books is usually solid, his credentials as a legitimate researcher have been challenged by admission of incidents of plagiarism, and by charges of former CRI employees that he took credit for research done by others. Martin's widow and family have challenged Hanegraaff's claims to have been Martin's hand-picked successor, and disagree with some of his decisions involving the ministry. Details on this matter can be seen at the URL below:

www.apologeticsindex.org/c174aa.html

Yisrayl Hawkins

Founder and dictatorial leader of the House of Yahweh (Yahweh is one possible pronunciation of the Hebrew name of God as seen in the Old Testament writings) in Abilene, Texas. The HOY is an exclusivist religious group that adheres to an extreme form of pseudo-Biblical "legalism" based heavily on Hawkins' interpretations of the Old Testament (unrelated to any connection with orthodox Judaism). The belief system, including polygamy introduced in the group in 1993—and the teaching that "Satan" is female—is a totally idiosyncratic creation of the founder. Although claiming to believe in "Yeshua" (one possible pronunciation for the Hebrew version of Jesus' name) as Messiah, His role in the religious system is almost negligible. It is taught that He had no pre-existence prior to His birth, and that His primary purpose in His ministry was to reinforce the need to keep the "613 Laws" of the Old Testament. Hawkins proclaims himself to be the only leader of the only true Work of the Almighty on earth now, and requires total obedience of all supporters to his every edict.

Hawkins' name was originally Buffalo Bill Hawkins. Hawkins' late brother Jacob first founded a House of Yahweh in Odessa, Texas, in 1975. Bill, who changed his name to Yisrayl (his choice of how he believes the name Israel would have been pronounced in Bible times) in 1982, established his own independent congregation in 1980. For a time Bill billed himself and Jacob as the Two Witnesses of the Book of Revelation. But the fact that Jacob didn't believe this, and had nothing to do with his brother's ministry, made this revelation difficult to sustain, and it became even harder after Jacob died in 1991.

Followers from all over the country have left their homes in the past decade and cast their lot in with Hawkins, moving to live in his trailer compound outside Abilene. Others travel there three times a year for conventions held to observe the Levitical Holy Days.

By 1997, things were getting stranger in the group ... one of the few that this **Field Guide** has no qualms about labeling a severely spiritually abusive cult. Reportedly, over 300 of the members of the group legally changed their last names to "Hawkins," and Yisrayl was dogmatically prophesying that the Messiah was going to return in October, 2000 and that "80% of the world's population would be killed by mid-2001."

This didn't happen, of course. So he shifted his dates. Wikipedia entry "House of Yahweh":

> September 12, 2006- Hawkins announced in the "House of Yahweh" newsletter (February 2006) that nuclear war would start September 12, 2006. He claimed it is a part of the HoY's commission to warn the nations and the people of the world. Hawkins was interviewed on the Channel 4

web show "thisisaknife" about his apocalyptic predictions. Among other things, he claimed that Abilene, Texas would be saved from the impending destruction and invited the show's presenter to join him there so he would be safe.

June 12, 2007- Hawkins amended his prediction to state that a nuclear war was only conceived on September 12, 2006, and that it would follow the natural birth cycle of a woman, finally being "born" nine months later on June 12, 2007. On May 7, 2007 a new counter was put up on his website, counting down to the June 12 date when supposedly, the "Nuclear Baby" (conceived September 12) would be born.

Whether the entire nuclear event was to take place on that date, or in the months leading up to was never made clear. He also stated that by four months after June 12, October 13, 2007, four-fifths or 80% of the human race would be dead from nuclear war.

June 12, 2008- Most recently, he has stated the nuclear war would begin on Thursday June 12, 2008. Since the passing of this date without incident, Hawkins has yet to predict another date for a nuclear war.

The "Religioustolerance.org" website, which is extremely conservative in its approach to labeling groups as cults notes that it finds Hawkins' group to fit ten out of ten of their list of "ten indicators of a destructive cult."

For more details on Hawkins ministry, see the following URL for a collection of articles about the House of Yahweh:

www.rickross.com/groups/yahweh.html

Norvel Hayes

Hard-core **Word Faith** teacher and conference speaker and prolific writer. Founder of Norvel Hayes Ministries and New Life Bible College. Author of such full-length books and small booklets as *Confession Brings Possession, How to Cast Out Devils, Putting Your Angels to Work,* and *Why You Should Speak in Tongues.*

Jack Hayford

Founder of the Church on the Way, First Foursquare Church of Van Nuys, CA. Head of Jack Hayford Ministries which produces and broadcasts Hayford's *Living Way* radio program and *Spirit Formed* TV program. His calm and almost conservative speaking style belies the fact that his doctrinal background is hard-core **Hyper-Charismatic Word Faith**. He is a regular on *Jan and Paul Crouch*'s Trinity Broadcasting Network. And he supports, cooperates with, and appears on speaking schedules regularly with more flamboyant ministers such as *Benny Hinn*.

Marilyn Hickey, Sarah Hickey Bowling

Marilyn Hickey is a popular **Hyper-Charismatic Word Faith** televangelist. Husband Wallace is the pastor of Orchard Road Christian Center in Greenwood Village, Colorado. Marilyn Hickey Ministries produces and distributes the TV program *Today With Marilyn and Sarah*, hosted by Hickey and her daughter Sarah Bowling, and publishes Hickey's magazine, *Outpouring*.

The most notorious aspect of Marilyn Hickey's ministry is her shameless fundraising techniques. She sends out letters to her supporters regularly which include small token objects, which she instructs them to use in various ritual ways, then send back with a "seed" offering to her ministry, in order to get prayer requests answered. These have included mustard seeds, "Stop the Devil" stickers (to put on the bottom of your right shoe—evidently to symbolically "tread the Devil under foot"), two pieces of red string, a packet of cornmeal, and much more. These gimmicks have often imitated those of earlier faith-healing ministers such as *Robert Tilton* and *Oral Roberts*.

A number of examples are given in the 1999 article from *The Christian Sentinel*, "Marily Hickey, Fairy Godmother of the Word Faith Movement?" available on the Web at

> http://web.archive.org/web/20080305075909/http://www w.cultlink.com/sentinel/hickey.htm

Excerpt:

In analyzing these mailings there are two tricks of the trade that she puts into practice consistently: 1) send the people something that has to be returned in order to be effective; and 2) give a strict deadline for the readers to comply with. And of course, all of the gimmickry stands on the theory that Hickey's faith is more anointed and powerful than the readers' so they have the illusion they're tapping into a direct pipeline from Hickey to God. Almost every mailing promotes the false teaching called "seed faith" that has been popularized for years by the false teacher, Oral Roberts. Basically, the seed faith concept fits neatly within the Word-faith camp. It states that if you want more riches, simply give to God's ministries financially, and these gifts become "seeds" that can grow into more wealth later for those who contribute. Thus the motive behind giving to God, in direct contradiction to Scripture, becomes giving to God's ministries **in order to get from God.** Hickey's fundraising letters have this idea reduced to a science. They repeatedly say that none of her formulas for miracles can work unless money is sent in to seal the deal with God. After all, you can't reap unless you sow something first, they'll say.

Her latest mailing received by the Christian Sentinel in January 1999 focused directly on poor widows and women struggling with financial troubles. She mailed us two pennies stuck to the return card with an invitation to join in on her "prayer tunnel." The two pennies represented the two coins the poor widow woman put in the temple offering in the 21st chapter of Luke.2

The appeal reads in part: "THIS IS WHAT I WANT YOU TO DO: #1) TAKE your Personal Prayer Sheet, place the palm of your right hand over the two copper pennies. We are going to use them as our miracle point-of-contact together... #2) NOW, write down today's date in the box marked TODAY. #3) BE SPECIFIC and write in the miracle amount of money that you need... #4) WRITE DOWN any other personal areas of lack and need for which you are desperately desiring a miracle—and want me to release my faith for... #5) FINALLY. . . Search your heart, and write a check. Whatever you give, make it the BEST gift to Him that you possibly can!"

Then the appeal concludes with: "HERE'S WHAT WE'RE GOING TO DO: FIRST: . . .I'm instructing every one of my prayer warriors who come in contact with your prayer request sheet to make sure that they touch it, lay their hands on it, touch the same 2 coins you've

187

touched... NEXT: we're going to form a 'Prayer Tunnel' of financial faith for you... it's a powerful thing! . . . I'm believing as your request sheet passes through my 'Prayer Tunnel' of faith—you'll pass through your dark tunnel of financial pressure... I really want you to hear my heart: THIS IS A VERY SERIOUS MATTER and we are not playing games with the devil...this is WAR!... Like the little widow, sow a seed out of your need!"

See the website linked above for numerous other examples of this bizarre type of fundraising.

Below are just two samples of the goofy, unbiblical concepts in Marilyn's teaching materials and fundraising letters.

From "Claim your Miracles," audiotape #186:

"What do you need? Start creating it. Start speaking about it. Start speaking it into being. Speak to your billfold. Say, 'You big, thick billfold full of money.' Speak to your checkbook. Say, 'You, checkbook, you. You've never been so prosperous since I owned you. You're just jammed full of money.'

"Say to your body, 'You're whole, body! Why, you just function so beautifully and so well. Why, body, you never have any problems. You're a strong, healthy body.' Or speak to your leg, or speak to your foot, or speak to your neck, or speak to your back; and once you have spoken and believe that you have received, and don't go back on it. Speak to your wife, speak to your husband, speak to your circumstances; and speak faith to them to create in them and God will create what you are speaking."

Outpouring magazine, special edition 2001

"God put it in my heart to call Oral Roberts and his son Richard to ask them if they would join Sarah and me to form a 'next-generation' prayer circle of faith, believing God for Him to place a 'miracle-overflow Next Generation anointing' on some oil."

"During a particularly powerful prayer time, we fervently laid our hands on some SPECIAL anointing oil...and together, we released our faith for God to impart a

MIRACLE-OVERFLOW Next Generation Anointing upon that oil. Now we want to pass it along to YOU, your children, and your grandchildren...as we invite you to become Faith Covenant Partners with us and this ministry of 'Covering the Earth with the Word.'"

"We've taken this oil and blended and prepared it for you to carry with you in a beautiful, gold- colored metal locket..allowing you to bring a MIRACLE-OVERFLOW Next Generation Anointing to everyone you touch...whenever and wherever the need arises." "When you become PARTNERS with a ministry, you ACTIVATE A POWERFUL SPIRITUAL PRINCIPLE in your life: the same power of God that is available to that ministry...becomes available to YOU!...You can literally walk in the same anointing they walk in!"

Hickey is also an avid supporter of the **Holy Laughter** movement and other **Toronto Blessing**-style manifestations. Notice these comments from her, quoted in the *Christian Sentinel* article above:

"I have watched the Holy Spirit minister joy from one side of the auditorium to the other," she writes in her *Outpouring* magazine, "...very prim and proper Christians rolling on the floor, people glued to the floor until released by the Holy Spirit; people so drunk on the Holy Spirit that they staggered, unable to walk, and people frozen in trances for hours. It is way too late to convince me that this outpouring of the Holy Spirit is anything but God."

Steve Hill

Evangelist who initiated the **"Pensacola/Brownsville Outpouring"** revival, a clone of the **Toronto Blessing** movement. This "revival" began at the Brownsville Assembly of God Church in Pensacola, Florida, in 1995, when Brownsville pastor *John Kilpatrick* invited Hill to speak there. .

The following description of Hill's role in the Revival is excerpted from a website promoting this type of movement at

www.pastornet.net.au/renewal/journal10/e-hill.html

In 1995, Hill read an article in Time magazine about the move of God in an Anglican Church in London. He arranged for a meeting at three o'clock on January 19 with Pastor Sandy Miller of the Holy Brompton Anglican Church to see what was going on. Over 500 people were shaking and laying on the floor under the power of God when Hill arrived. Instead of having the appointment, Hill asked Miller to lay hands on him. He received a new impartation from Miller's prayer.

On Father's Day, June 18, 1995 Hill was invited by John Kilpatrick, the Pastor of Brownsville Assembly of God, to speak at the Sunday morning service. Kilpatrick had just lost his mother to cancer was emotionally and physically weary, so he requested his longtime friend Hill to speak in his place. Hill issued an altar call and a thousand people responded. Kilpatrick says that he felt the sensation of a wind blowing in the church. Various manifestations occurred such as falling to the ground, weeping and violent shaking. The morning service was scheduled to finish at noon but continued till 4 p.m. Likewise the night service was extended and became a five-hour long service. The Pensacola Revival had begun.

Congregation members asked Hill to stay a several more days. This he did and began to cancelling appointments, including a trip to Russia. He decided to stay and moved his family to be near the revival. It is estimated that over 100,000 people have been saved and over 1 million people from all over the world have visited Pensacola since 1995. Hill continues to minister in the revival services Wednesday to Saturday nights at Brownsville Assembly of God to this day. Steve Hill is a leader in current revival. [See below for his latest activities.]

And here are a few quotations from a website opposing this revival at

www.cephasministry.com/steve_hill.html

Steve Hill quotations are in italics

Steve Hill said, "*If you must analyze, then look at me, look at the musicians and singers, look at the congregation, look at the person to the left of you and to the right of you, and just analyze, analyze,*

analyze get it out of your system. Now let yourselves go: don't even think about what you are doing, forget about those around you and what they are doing. Release your mind release your spirit and let the mighty river of the "Holy Ghost" take you wherever He wants you to go." ("Revival ... or Satanic Counterfeit?", Jimmy Robbins, 1996)

"In these latter days preaching and simply teaching the word is no longer sufficient, the Spirit has to get involved, through signs and wonders due to much sin that abounds." ("What We Saw," Robert C. Gray, 12/14/96)

"When you ridicule those whose bodies are twitching or shaking under the influence of God's glory, beware! Have you forgotten that God's Word and the annals of Church history are filled with the supernatural dealings of our supernatural God?" God does deal with his creatures supernaturally, but God's Word is silent about God ever sending His Holy Spirit to produce these types of manifestations, except in judgment, and certainly not as a blessing or by laying on of hands. Church history is full of stories of these manifestations which have been roundly dismissed as unbiblical and demonic by former church leaders such as Edwards, Spurgeon, Tozer and many others. (Stephen Hill, *The God Mockers*, chapter 1, 1997 with comment by Sandy Simpson)

See more at the link above. Below is another description of the Brownsville events from *Religion Today* 6/22/2000 as reported at

www.deceptioninthechurch.com/hill.html

An evangelist who intended to preach just one sermon has left after 5 years of continuous revival meetings. Steve Hill is moving his ministry to Dallas after preaching hundreds of times at Brownsville Assembly of God, a Pensacola, Fla., church that has been the center of an international charismatic revival movement. About 3 million people have visited the church during that time, pastor John Kilpatrick said, according to the *Pensacola News Journal.*

...The revival fervor "didn't happen because of Steve and I know it sure did not happen because of me," Kilpatrick said. "God came down and kissed this place." Hill's final service June 18 turned raucous. "For almost 20 minutes people raced through the aisles, danced, laughed uncontrollably, jumped, jerked, and collapsed," the newspaper reported.

> ... "If somebody who is not Christian dropped in this morning, they would look at us and think we went bonkers," Kilpatrick said, according to the *Journal*. "Well, we have gone bonkers. People go bonkers over football and baseball. Why can't we go bonkers over Jesus?" He said he hoped that, even though crowds have diminished to about half what they were a few years ago, the revival will not stop, but go to "a different level."

It would seem that the following scripture might apply to this situation. Paul is talking about everyone in a congregation "speaking in tongues" at the same time. How much more applicable might his point be to people "going bonkers" via laughing uncontrollably, jumping, jerking, and collapsing?

> 1Corinthians 14:23 If therefore the whole church be assembled together and all speak with tongues, and there come in men unlearned or unbelieving, will they not say that ye are mad? :24 But if all prophesy, and there come in one unbelieving or unlearned, he is reproved by all, he is judged by all; :25 the secrets of his heart are made manifest; and so he will fall down on his face and worship God, declaring that God is among you indeed.

After the Brownsville Revival faded, Hill and his wife Jeri founded Heartland World Ministries Church in Dallas, Texas. Hill and the Church evangelistic team hold crusades around the world. Hill also has a separate ministry, Steve Hill Ministries, that emphasizes Internet outreaches.

Benny Hinn

Premier "healing evangelist" in the **Hyper-Charismatic** world of the present, part of the **Healing Ministries** movement. Although he regularly speaks to packed crowds of many thousands at his "Miracle Crusades" at sports stadiums and other venues in the U.S., it is the crowds at his overseas Crusades that are particularly astonishing. One three-day outdoor crusade in India in 2004 boasted a combined attendance of over 5 million, with a crowd of over 2 million the final night, the largest such "healing service" in history.

Hinn's outrageous onstage antics are proverbial … he can be seen in clips on Youtube performing such stunts as removing his white suitcoat and slinging it violently back and forth around in the air toward people on stage with him. He may even beat them over the head with it. They then fall over backwards, allegedly under the power of the Holy Spirit which he is "dispensing" with his coat-flinging. See a sample at

www.youtube.com/watch?v=c9U_lWmAsYM)

It is impossible to present a "succinct" overview of Hinn's ministry. But the satirical *Wittenburg Door Magazine* tried in an article from their 5/20/2008 edition. A sample excerpt is below. See the whole article at the URL below.

> www.wittenburgdoor.com/why-benny-hinn-became-our-wacky-neighbor
>
> … Hinn's TV show, "This Is Your Day!," originates in studios in Orange County, California, and airs in 192 countries, making it one of the most widely disseminated programs in the world. Hinn is so ubiquitous on religious TV, in fact, that you would assume by this point—35 years into his preaching ministry—that he would have become one of those household names, like Billy Graham, who's expected to lead the invocation at the Super Bowl and counsel the President and appear on The Today Show in times of national crisis.
>
> But the opposite is true. Aside from his twice-monthly appearances at his own choreographed "crusades," held in the largest sports arenas on the planet, Hinn is a virtual recluse, surrounded by armies of bodyguards, ensconced in an $12 million oceanfront hacienda in southern California, traveling by private jet for "snorkeling vacations" in the Cayman Islands, staying in $10,800 per night presidential suites in Italy, a $15,000 per night suite in Greece, and claiming a level of financial secrecy and paranoid internal security that's more often associated with drug dealers than men of the cloth. By surrounding himself with yes-men and stage-managing every detail of his public image—even to the point of stiff-arming the occasional paparazzo who tries to photograph him—he has more in common with Michael Jackson than Jerry Falwell. He may, in fact, be the first Christian rock star.

The analogy is not Paul McCartney, though--Benny's career is more like Cher, as he makes it up as he goes along, re-inventing himself whenever necessary.

...Hinn runs the largest evangelistic organization in the world that is not a member of the Evangelical Council for Financial Accountability. That means his finances are private, his salary is secret, and his income is anybody's guess. Royalties from his books alone are estimated at $500,000 per year, but he essentially has carte blanche to take anything out of the till he wants. "He lives the lifestyle of a billionaire," says Ole Anthony, "all on the backs of false promises and selling false hope."

As Hinn put it himself, in a moment of rare revelatory candor, "I don't need gold in heaven, I gotta have it now."

Rodney Howard-Browne

Hyper-Charismatic evangelist primarily responsible for the introduction of the "**Holy Laughter**" movement and boosting the **Toronto Blessing** movement to international prominence.

A detailed overview of the Toronto manifestations such as Holy Laughter, including commentary on Howard-Browne's ministry, can be found in the free online version of the book *Weighed and Found Wanting* by *Bill Randles*.

> http://web.archive.org/web/20040703040810/http://www.geocities.com/Bob_Hunter/1.htm

Charles and Frances Hunter, Joan Hunter

(Frances Hunter, 1916-2009, Charles Hunter 1920-2010) Charles and Frances were a husband and wife team of "healing evangelists" known in **Charismatic** circles as the "Happy Hunters." They are perhaps best known for holding "Healing Explosion" revivals, which often included seminars in which they purported to teach others "how to heal". The Hunters were part of both the **Word Faith** movement and the **Healing Ministries** movement, and wrote many books with typical themes for those movements.

David Cloud, in an 11/18/2002 article called "Beware the Happy Hunters" published by the Fundamental Baptist Information Service provided several samples from the writings of the Hunters:

"Spinal Stenosis: A narrowing of the spinal column around the spinal cord. ... Recommended Prayer: Command the spirit of arthritis to come out in the name of Jesus, command the spurs to dissolve with no problem to the spinal cord and command the spinal cord to open up in the name of Jesus. Then command the spirit of pain to leave in Jesus' name. Schizophrenia: A doctor had done research on Schizophrenia and discovered an inadequate blood supply to the thalamus gland, in the brain, when the patient is asked to think. Recommended Prayer: Command an adequate supply of blood to the thalamus gland so the patient will be able to think. Command the spirit to come out in the name of Jesus."

It would seem that Jesus and Paul and Peter didn't understand this principle, for this sort of "healing technique" is nowhere to be found in the scriptures. Nor are there any documented cases of the Hunters actually healing anyone of these afflictions by this technique.

Cloud notes:

In the book *How to Heal the Sick*, the Hunters give instructions on how to heal baldness. This is interesting—because Charles Hunter is bald! They give instructions on how to heal eye problems—but Frances Hunter wears glasses to correct her eye problems!

After the death of Charles and Frances, their daughter Joan Hunter has continued their legacy. Her Joan Hunter Ministries website notes that she even "flows in a greater anointing than her parents." Her ministry offers, among many other things, a three day program leading immediately to Ordination. Here's an example ad for the "Fall Ordination 2011" program.

Ordination

IMPARTATION and ACTIVATION CONFERENCE - Fall Ordination

Thank you for your interest in being Ordained through Joan Hunter Ministries/Hunter Ministries. Our Fall Ordination will be October 20-22, 2011 in the Houston, Texas area.

195

Ordination Fee: $295 Ordination registration includes the following: Bible College on Healing that will be mailed to you, 3-day anointed Holy Ghost power-packed Ordination weekend, your lunch each day, Ordination Ceremony DVD, group Ordination picture, and your individual picture with Joan.

The books are required reading and will be used during Ordination (and the rest of your life). You will need to bring them with you to Ordination.

Power to Heal

Healing The Whole Man Handbook

Healing Starts Now! Instructional Manual

Healing The Heart

Healing The Whole Man 8 hour teaching on CD or DVD

Got Guilt? Get Free! – DVD

Close the Door on Stress and Trauma – DVD

The requirements and steps for Ordination are:

Have a call of God on your life to take the healing power of God to the 4 corners of the earth, make disciples, and set the captives free.

Complete an application form and mail it to JHM, P O Box 777, Pinehurst, TX 77362 with the non-refundable $130 processing fee and two current photos (head and shoulders only).

Provide two recommendations (neither of which are from family members), one from ministry and one personal, which must be sent directly to JHM (address above) or emailed to ord@joanhunter.org . If no email capability, please fax recommendation to 281-789-7497. Recommendations must be returned to us by the one supplying the recommendation, and are not to be sent to us with your application. Note: Ministerial References will be checked.

196

Attendance at all nine classes of the conference.

Required to read all 4 of Joan's books listed above prior to Ordination.

Approval of application by Joan Hunter Ministries.

The Bible? No, there appears to be no requirement that you have read *any* of the Bible in order to qualify for Ordination by Joan Hunter Ministries.

Noah Hutchings

(Born 1922) President of the Southwest Radio Church, spokesman of the *Watchman on the Wall* radio broadcast. Part of the End Times Prophecy movement, Hutchings has for many years been one of the more prolific "speculators" about the connection between current events and Bible prophecy. As with most other such speculators, his batting average is close to zero, but that doesn't prevent him from continuing to be viewed by many as an "expert on prophecy."

One listing of failed prophecies noted this about Hutchings:

A little different twist on 1988 was offered by David Webber and Noah Hutchings in their 1974 book *Prophecy in Stone*. They proposed that the Tribulation would end about 1988-1992. A later book by these same authors (*New Light on the Great Pyramid*, 1985) pushed the schedule back a hair. Now the Tribulation was to begin in 1988. Other books and newsletters produced by the Southwest Radio Church (currently headed by Hutchings) have proposed a wide variety of other dates for various events associated with the return of Christ and the end of the present age.

T. D. Jakes

One of the most influential African-American **Word Faith** televangelists. Jakes is founder and pastor of the 28,000+ Potter's House church in Dallas, Texas, cited by some as the fastest-growing church in America. He is author of many popular inspirational books on topics from family relationships to "charismatic gifts." And he is the host of the *Potter's Touch* daily TV show broadcast by TBN. Jakes' website notes ...

In January, 1999, the *New York Times* named Bishop T.D. Jakes as "one of the top five evangelists most frequently cited by scholars, theologians, and evangelical leaders to step up the international pulpit behind the Rev. Billy Graham" while *Time* magazine featured Bishop Jakes on a September 2001 cover and named him "America's Best Preacher."

Although many might agree with this evaluation of Jakes' popularity and even preaching skills, opinions of the Biblical soundness of his teachings vary widely. The Personal Freedom Outreach (PFO) has a 1996 article on its website titled "Get Ready for T.D. Jakes, the Velcro Bishop with Another Gospel." Although this article is now 15 years old, nothing has changed in Jakes' ministry that would in any way alter the perspective of this article—other than that he has written many more books and has an even bigger income. He still appears with and endorses the same Word Faith teachers noted below, in these excerpts from the PFO article.

> Jakes gives deference to the ministries of Marilyn Hickey and Joyce Meyer. Both these "celebrated ministers" are heretical and promote Word-Faith doctrine without apology. How many erroneous camps can you occupy and still be considered a good example? In 2 John 9-11, we are commanded not to endorse heretical teachers in any way.

> Jakes has also shared the platform at a September 1996 conference with Roberts Liardon. Any discerning Christian should want to stay as far away as possible from Liardon who claims he was transported to heaven and there met Jesus face to face and that he and Jesus had a water fight in the River of Life! Liardon further claims he was shown a building filled with unclaimed body parts (hair, eyes, skin, legs, etc.). This heavenly warehouse of unclaimed body parts is overstocked, according to Liardon, simply because here on earth believers have failed to appropriate them by faith. Liardon's charade is either lunacy or sheer deception and should be given public rebuke, not public relations.

> Jakes patronizes and clearly finds himself among the celebrities of the Charismatic camps. A full-color advertisement on the inside cover of the January *Charisma* announced that Jakes would appear at the August "Victory

Word Explosion" in Tulsa, Oklahoma with Benny Hinn, Richard Roberts, Rod Parsley, Joyce Meyer and Jerry Savelle. With this roster, it might better be called "Heresy Explosion."

... The *Dallas Observer* goes on to report:

"He says he is not embarrassed by this, even though his extravagant lifestyle has caused controversy in his hometown that will likely follow him to Dallas. His suits are tailored. He drives a brand new Mercedes. Both he and his wife Serita are routinely decked out in stunning jewelry. His West Virginia residence — two homes side by side — includes an indoor swimming pool and a bowling alley. These homes particularly caused the ire of the local folks. One paper wrote at length about the purchase and made much of their unusual features. A columnist dubbed Jakes 'a huckster.'"

Yet, what is most disturbing about Jakes' prosperity is not the wealth itself, but his false teaching about Jesus to justify his fortune. The Dallas Observer shares further:

"Besides, Jakes says — during an interview and in his sermons — Jesus was a rich man. He had to have been, in order to have supported his disciples and their families during his ministry."

To add to his false and mythical Christ, Jakes brazenly says:

"The myth of the poor Jesus needs to be destroyed, because it's holding people back."

Jakes obviously perverts the true biblical picture of Jesus in an effort to advocate his own lifestyle. The *Fort Worth Star Telegram* reports:

"Jakes, who drives a Mercedes, has moved with his wife and their five children to a luxurious seven-bedroom home with swimming pool in the White Rock Lake area of Dallas. He said the home cost more than $1 million. 'I do think we need some Christians who are in first class as well as coach,' Jakes said."

Sadly, in the case of so many prosperity teachers, they are the ones flying in "first class" by way of the donations of their impoverished flock while the latter fly in "coach" — or miss the flight altogether because they lack the money to even buy a ticket.

For more details regarding aspects of Jakes' ministry which cause many religious commentators concern, see the PFO link below.

www.pfo.org/jakes.html

Grant Jeffrey

Popular prophecy pundit, part of the End Times Prophecy movement. Jeffrey's 1988 book *Armageddon: Appointment with Destiny* was based on his personal theories regarding the Jubilee cycles of ancient Israel, and strongly suggested 10/9/2000 as the probable date for the Return of Christ. This of course didn't pan out.

His later prophetic speculations have emphasized the importance of the hotly debated— and now debunked—Bible Codes, starting with his 1996 book *The Signature of God*. In spite of virtually no verifiable positive record of speculating in advance anything of significance, and in spite of the miserable failure of the theories put forth in his 1988 book, he is still a "recognized prophetic scholar" in many circles. He appears regularly on *Jan and Paul Crouch*'s Trinity Broadcasting Network, and is a coveted speaker at prophecy seminars and such.

Why is he still viewed as a guru? That is as mysterious as his mysterious prophetic theories.

Bob Jones

One of the **"Kansas City Prophets"** group. Jones been considered by many to hold the office of "modern prophet" and thus regularly receive direct revelations from God, along with *Paul Cain*, John Paul Jackson, and *Mike Bickle* .(**This** Bob Jones is not the same Bob Jones that founded conservative Bob Jones University.)

Rick Joyner

Prolific **Charismatic** speaker and writer viewed by many in the **"Modern Apostles and Prophets"** movement as among the most significant "modern Prophets." Joyner is founder of Morningstar Minstries, which publishes the *Morningstar Journal* and the *Morningstar Prophetic Bulletin.*

The ministry also hosts numerous "Prophetic and Apostolic" Conferences and Councils. Both Joyner's own "prophetic" pretensions and those of other individuals he promotes and is affiliated with are hotly contested by many critics. Joyner has charged in many books, articles, and recordings that other Christian ministries and teachers who question the validity of the current **Hyper-Charismatic** "revival movements" such as the **Toronto Blessing** and other "signs and wonders" movements are fighting against a true "move of God" and thus may incur the wrath of God.

For more commentary on Joyner's ministries see the articles at the URLs below

> "The Higher Life of Rick Joyner: Chasing the Illusion of Power and Dominion"

> www.pfo.org/r-joyner.htm

> Some of Joyner's latest activities

> > http://barthsnotes.wordpress.com/2011/03/17/ rick-joyner-predicts-earthquake-in-us-economic-collapse/

Monte Judah

Judah is founder of Lion and Lamb Ministries and editor of *Yavoh, He Is Coming* newsletter. He is a popular speaker on the "End Times Prophecy" circuit. Although his repertoire of teachings does include a distinctive element of **Hebrew Roots** concepts, including promoting observance of the weekly Sabbath and annual Biblical Holy Days, that is not really the emphasis of much of his teaching materials and lectures. Rather, he emphasizes his speculations about the imminency of the **Great Tribulation**.

Judah is viewed by a growing number of prophecy students, particularly in Hebrew Roots circles, as having great insight into the correlation between contemporary world events and Bible prophecy. He is quoted on a number of websites as an authority on such matters, and has been a guest speaker at conventions and on widely popular radio programs such as *The Prophecy Club.*

The two most significant factors of Monte Judah's continuing teaching on prophetic matters is his record of making strong claims for specific time frames for End Time events, and his insistence that Prince Charles of England will be the one to fulfill the prophecies in the book of Revelation regarding "the Beast" whose mark is imposed on all mankind.

Monte Judah's Lion and Lamb Ministries, begun in 1995, seems to have grown quickly primarily based on the enthusiasm surrounding Judah's dogmatic prophetic claims. These same claims evidently also quickly became controversial. Consider this challenge by him in the February, 1996 *Yavoh* newsletter. (Underlining added to emphasize main points.)

> <u>After the Lord instructed me to do so</u>, I declared that the Middle East Peace Accord of 1993 started the 70th week of Israel. Therefore, I am warning others to look for specific events to occur in 1996 and 1997 consistent with the timeline and the center event of the 7-year period, the Abomination of Desolation. To that end, I am preparing and warning others that the Great Tribulation spoken of by Daniel and Yeshua <u>will begin</u> Feb/Mar of 1997. <u>These dates were set by God when He started the 70th week</u>.
>
> Because I teach people to look for specific things, I am criticized as a "datesetter." But in defense of the argument, I remind people that I didn't make the Middle East Peace Accord of 1993 happen, nor did I select the Feast of Booths by the mouth of Zechariah. I am drawing a conclusion based on a Scriptural understanding. Further, I have openly called all men to examine my words and scrutinize them. If what I say does not happen, <u>then brand me as a false prophet, listen to me no more, and heap the ridicule on to prevent others from making the same mistake.</u> But I would remind you in accordance with the Scripture not to despise a prophetic utterance until it has been proven false.
>
> The irony of this whole situation is stunning. <u>I call for the testing of all prophets</u>. I have made my message and its measurement clear. If the altar is not stopped in Feb/Mar of 1997 in Jerusalem, then <u>throw me on the trash heap</u>. But if the altar service is stopped 3 1/2 years after the

peace agreement, will you then trust God to deliver you? <u>Will you believe the other prophecies that follow?</u>

Obviously, this dogmatic prophetic proclamation failed miserably. And initially Monte Judah "apologized" for that failure and indicated he might be thinking of ending his ministry. However, like many other prophetic teachers whose dogmatic scenarios have failed, he quickly reevaluated his position. He noted that so many of his loyal supporters encouraged him to continue, and was later to claim that <u>God told him to get back up</u>. This, of course, was the <u>same God</u> that he claimed had "instructed him" to declare the failed prophetic scenario quoted above.

The problem in all of this is not just that Judah made a mistake in his "Bible interpretations," but that he claimed that his understanding wasn't just from his own studies, but from God directly "instructing" him.

He labeled himself with the term "prophet."

We have only three basic choices here. Either:

1. Judah mistook the "instruction" of some other being for the instruction of God.

2. He was not really instructed by anyone but spoke from his own heart and misled his followers to believe that he was being instructed by God; or …

3. He was totally confused about how to receive instruction from God and mistook the imaginations of his own mind for instructions from God.

No matter which of these possibilities are what actually happened, the reality is that the supporters of Monte Judah had no rational reason, at the point his dogmatic declarations were proven wrong, to believe that he had any more true insight from God about prophetic matters than anyone else. But people desperately eager to know "what will happen next" are not usually driven by rational thought.

E. W. Kenyon

(1867-1948) Early pioneer of the **Word Faith** movement, whose writings were extensively plagiarized by *Kenneth Hagin* … word for word … in numerous Hagin publications.

Common sayings in the Word Faith movement such as "What I confess, I possess" were originated by Kenyon. The following bold and controversial statement which appears in Hagin's "The Incarnation," (*The Word of Faith*, December 1980) was originally published in Kenyon's, *The Father and His Family* : "Every man who has been 'born again' is an Incarnation, and Christianity is a miracle. The believer is as much an Incarnation as was Jesus of Nazareth."

Kenyon's own religious roots were not in the **Pentecostal** movement of his time, but in the teachings of various "metaphysical" groups such as Christian Science. An extensive investigation and documentation of Kenyon's formative years and influence on the Word Faith movement, including documentation on Hagin's plagiarism of Kenyon, is available in D.R. McConnell's 225-page book *A Different Gospel* (c. 1988, updated 1995), Hendrickson Publishers Inc. The chapter about Hagin's plagiarism is available for free download online at the URL below.

www.mtio.com/articles/bissar51.htm

John Kilpatrick

Pastor of the Brownsville Assembly of God Church in Pensacola, Florida, who invited *Steve Hill* to speak there in 1995 and thus ignited the "**Brownsville/Pensacola Outpouring**", a clone of the **Toronto Blessing** movement.

Kathryn Kuhlman

(1907-1976) One of the most famous female evangelists of the Healing Ministries movement. Kuhlman modeled her preaching style and flamboyant personal appearance on earlier woman evangelist *Aimee Semple McPherson*. Beginning her preaching career as a "tent evangelist" in the 1920's, by the late 1940s Kuhlman had inaugurated her "miracle healing" crusades which she took to some of the largest meeting halls in the country and finally on to TV. She claimed huge numbers of people were miraculously healed at her meetings over the years, although, as with almost all such healing ministries, no hard documentation of any specific healings of organic conditions seems to be available anywhere.

Contemporary healing evangelist *Benny Hinn* considers Kuhlman his primary mentor, and he obviously models his stage presence and appearance (he consistently wears all-white suits at his meetings, she typically wore long white dresses) and other aspects of his ministry on her example. For instance, old-time healing evangelists such as *Oral Roberts* typically encouraged people who needed healing to come forward so that he might lay hands on them with the expectation that at that point the healing would come. Kuhlman instead used the same method now employed by Hinn: People in the audience decide from where they sit that they **have** been healed as a result of their attendance at the meeting. And Kuhlman and Hinn would ask any who were convinced that they had experienced such a healing to come forward and declare it, explaining their affliction and its symptoms, and what has now convinced them that it is gone. After their declaration Kuhlman, as Hinn does now, would reach her hand toward them and most would fall backwards in what is termed being "**slain in the spirit**."

In fact, Hinn is so enamored of the memory of Kuhlman that he has mentioned visiting her gravesite (as well as that of Aimee Semple McPherson) and believing that he received more of the "anointing" for his own allegedly miraculous manifestations there.

Tim La Haye

Co-author of the hugely-successful *Left Behind* series of books, which fictionalize LaHaye's speculations regarding End Time prophecy. Since La Haye was a well-known author and speaker before publication of this series, many readers may be unaware that his role in production of the books has not been one of "writer," but merely "consultant." Jerry B. Jenkins, listed on the book jackets as co-author, has really done the actual nuts and bolts of the creative process that resulted in the series. As the FAQ on Jenkins' own website puts it:

> How do Jerry Jenkins and Tim LaHaye work together? Who writes what?
>
> The book series was Dr. Tim LaHaye's idea. He asked Jerry Jenkins to write a series of novels to fit his view of the End Times. And that's exactly what Jerry did. Dr. LaHaye is the biblical expert and prophetic scholar and Jerry Jenkins is the author who writes the books.

Prior to involvement with the *Left Behind* series La Haye was most famous as a Christian motivational author and speaker on family living and emotional and psychological well-being topics, frequently collaborating in books and speaking engagements with his wife Beverly. Beverly La Haye, an individual author of a number of books in her own right, has also had her own outreach ministries which have included anti-abortion advocacy, promoting various pro-family causes, and hosting an award-winning talk show in the 1990s. Tim La Haye has also authored a number of non-fiction books emphasizing his own prophetic speculations.

Many of La Haye's teachings in all of these areas, as well as the theological and Biblical foundation of the *Left Behind* series of books and movies, have been controversial for a long time. The book series is based on a conviction regarding what is called the Pre-Tribulation **Rapture**, which is not accepted by many Bible students and teachers. And many of his writings regarding psychological topics, such as his 1966 book *Spirit Controlled Temperament*, are viewed by some critics as attempts to wed unproven secular psychological theories with Biblical concepts in ways that are not theologically sound.

 A detailed overview of the history of La Haye's career, with an examination of some of the controversial areas of his teachings can be seen at the Biblical Discernment (BDM) website at the URL below.

> www.rapidnet.com/~jbeard/bdm/exposes/lahaye/genera l.htm

Paul LaLonde, Peter LaLonde

Brothers who originally became notable in the End Times Prophecy movement as hosts of their television show, *This Week in Bible Prophecy*, on *Jan and Paul Crouch*'s Trinity Broadcasting Network. They were also authors of a number of books on prophetic themes. They left behind their TV career to branch out into motion picture production. Their "Cloud Ten Productions" studio has now made several "Christian" movies, including bringing the first of the *Left Behind* (Tim La Haye and Jerry Jenkins) books to the big screen.

Larry Lea

Pentecostal/Charismatic evangelist and author specializing in the topic of prayer and "**spiritual warfare**." Lea is the founder and former pastor of the Church on the Rock of Rockwall, Texas and former dean of the school of theology at *Oral Roberts* University in Tulsa, Oklahoma. He first came to national prominence in the

1980s via publicity in the media regarding his evangelistic crusades emphasizing "coming against territorial spirits" in metropolitan areas.

In October 1990, Lea organized a crusade in San Francisco, sponsored by Jubilee Christian Center of San Jose and its pastor Dick Bernal, to be held beginning Halloween evening. Plans at first included a march by up to 10,000 Christians through the streets of San Francisco, in a show of resistance to what they believed to be the rulership of the supernatural demonic "strongman" over the area. Warned by local authorities and other Christian organizations that this might lead to unpleasant or dangerous physical confrontations with other groups marching in the area that night, the plans were changed to hold all rally activities completely indoors at the San Francisco Civic Auditorium. A news interview at the time noted:

> "Larry and I are beginning to look like a couple of wackos," says Bernal. "The misconception is that we're a bunch of narrow-minded goody-two-shoes. San Francisco's a city where everybody has parades; I wanted our people to be a presence, too. We weren't going to call down fire on anybody; it was not going to be a confrontation, just a little show of force.

> "But the war on Satan will go on - inside the auditorium. There won't be any pussy-footing around," Bernal promises. "There'll be singing, preaching and speaking in tongues. It'll be wall-to-wall spiritual warfare."

> Bernal, a former ironworker and self-described hell-raiser who says he was born-again a dozen years ago, has gained some fame himself as a televangelist and spiritual warrior.

> After the Tiananmen Square massacre in 1989, Bernal traveled to Beijing and in a much-publicized ceremony, anointed the stones of the square with oil to drive the devil out. He also has prayed to cast the devil out of several sites in the South Bay, including the *San Jose Mercury News*.

There are no records to show that this "spiritual warfare rally" had any lasting affect at all on the San Francisco area. But there was one significant result from the crusade—the alleged conversion of a man named Eric Pryor, who claimed at the time to be a witch and an influential force within the **occult** movements of America. Pryor had come to public attention just before the crusade by claiming to be organizing a counter-demonstration to Lea's efforts. Yet within days, he became a member of Bernal's congregation. For the next few years, Lea used Pryor's amazing conversion story as part of his ministry efforts. And Pryor went on to become a regular speaker on the Spiritual Warfare circuit within the Charismatic movement.

Lea continued his efforts during the following year, which included more crusades and his own regular television show. Then on November 21, 1991, the ABC show *PrimeTime with Diane Sawyer* ran an investigative reporting piece on several televangelists, including Larry Lea.

Here's how one article about televangelism in 1994 summed up the show and its aftermath for Lea:

> Lea's most embarrassing moment may have been when ABC ran videotape of the televangelist persuading viewers that when his house burned to the ground he was left virtually homeless, losing everything he and his family had but the clothes on their backs. When *Prime Time* cut to Lea's other, unmentioned home -- a mansion filled with furniture and other valuables -- his fate was sealed. Donations dropped off, churches canceled his appearances, and for many Lea became persona non grata.

> His ministry crippled and floundering in up to $800,000 in debt, Lea left Tulsa and in February [1994] assumed the pastorate of friend Jerry Barnard's Christian Faith Center in La Mesa, California. According to staffers at Barnard's office, Lea's organization -- now called "The Prayer Ministry" -- is on the rebound and looking like "the old Larry Lea."

> In an April appeal letter, the unrepentant evangelist reminds his followers of "the horror of the 'Prime Time' television program that ABC-TV aired nationwide" and "the lies and distortions about me and about our ministry that they spoon-fed to an unsuspecting American public." Lea describes a prophecy in which Pentecostal leader Jack Hayford compared him to the biblical Joseph, condemned to languish in "a prison of disbelief" in North America for two years.

For Lea, the predicted release came in February at the "National Conference on Prayer & Spiritual Warfare" in Anaheim, California. At the conclusion of Lea's message, Fuller Seminary church growth specialist C. Peter Wagner unexpectedly approached Lea on the platform and, "as a representative of the Body of Christ," asked the stunned televangelist to forgive the church for believing Satan and his "false reports."

In the words of the appeal letter, "IT'S A NEW DAY....the headline over our ministry is now the same as the headline over Joseph's life: FALSELY ACCUSED, FULLY EXONERATED....We've been set free from the chains of disbelief and confusion that have sought to bind our ministry here in North America!" Lea then summons his "worldwide Prayer Army" to give to "Operation Goliath," his debt-reduction campaign, urging them to "obey the Lord" even if He impresses them to give "an amount that seems impossible."

(See full story at the URL below.)

www.iclnet.org/pub/resources/text/cri/cri-jrnl/crj0188a.txt

Unfortunately, the record does not show at all that Lea's record was "fully exonerated."

Another issue brought to light by the *Prime Time* program was the conversion of Pryor. The report alleged that there were many questions about the credibility of Pryor's claims about his past, as well as the circumstances surrounding his "conversion" and his later connection to Bernal's church. Other reports from the time included details of a phony "marriage ceremony" performed at Bernal's church in which Pryor and his live-in lover were supposed to become man and wife. Yet at the time, Pryor was still legally married to a former wife. More questions involved Pryor's financial windfall from going around giving his "testimony," and the denial by those involved in such groups as Wicca that Pryor ever had any influence in any Wiccan, **occult**, or **New Age** movement in the US.

One report from that time period gives evidence of the reason for concerns about the financial matters:

The "PrimeTime Live" report also cited a Herb Caen column in the San Francisco Chronicle saying Pryor made $100,000 last year. Pryor vigorously denies it, maintaining that he's only virtually penniless. His only sources of income, he says, are "love offerings" from the church and people moved by his preaching - as well as sales of "From Pagan to Pentecost," a $25 video version of his purported transformation. He gets $3 in royalties per sale.

Pryor also says he spends one day a month passing out money to homeless people and inviting them to listen as he spreads the word. "I do this because I've been there and I care," he tells them, "and this is my way of serving the Lord I call king of my life, Jesus."

As Pryor is making his case, Bernal enters the room to offer his support. At the same time, however, the minister clearly is taken aback by Pryor's flashy attire, extravagant jewelry and Rolex watch. "You're supposed to be penniless," Bernal says with a chuckle, "and you're sitting here dressed like a riverboat gambler."

Later, Pryor explains that his watch, gold chains, and bejeweled rings - some real and some fake - are all simply more "love offerings."

Whatever the ultimate truth about the situation at the time, things went downhill for Pryor from that point on:

(From the November 1998 *Silicon Valley Metro):*

"Pryor's situation started heading south, so to speak, on October 24--just a few days after a Metro interview in which he professed to have returned to Satanism after an eight-year stint preaching at San Jose's Jubilee Christian Center. That evening Pryor and his wife had an argument in the communal home where they live in the Santa Cruz mountains. When the argument moved into the hallway and Pryor began shoving and hitting his wife, according to witnesses, tenant Barbara Abbot intervened. She says Pryor ripped her glasses off and stepped on them, and she beat a hasty retreat back to her room.

When she came out later to retrieve them, she says, Pryor threatened to kill her and kicked her in the leg and in the groin, leaving bruises. And the next morning, Abbot says, while she was making lunch in the communal kitchen, Pryor told her never to come between him and his wife and said, "I will slit your throat."

Deputy Christine Swannack responded to Abbot's call at about 2pm on Sunday afternoon and arrested Pryor on charges of battery, spousal battery, and being under the influence of narcotics--most probably heroin, according to her report, as well as alcohol.

Four years ago, while still at Jubilee, Pryor did time in the Santa Clara County jail after a violent fight with his then-wife Sarah, in which he threatened to slice her face up with an eight-inch knife so no one else would "want" her. That marriage ended, and Pryor is back with his first wife.

In spite of the enthusiasm expressed in the 1994 Larry Lea letter above, the set-backs to Lea's ministry started by the *Prime Time* expose' led to continued deterioration of the ministry and his family life. This led to a divorce from his first wife in 1999 after 26 years of marriage. He married again three years later. Lea no longer has a television program or an extensive Internet presence. The website of Larry Lea ministries seems to just offer his books for sale, without even a schedule for speaking engagements. And the website of Jerry Barnard's ministry no longer shows any direct involvement by Larry Lea.

In *Charisma* magazine, 1988, Lea was quoted making the following assertion:

> "Several years ago one of my dear pastor friends said, "Larry, when I was praying for you the other day, I had a vision. I saw you with great big 'Mickey Mouse' ears. Everything else about you looked normal except for those elephant-sized ears. When I asked the Lord to tell me what the vision meant, the Spirit of the Lord spoke back to me and said: 'Larry Lea has developed his hearing. He has developed   his   spiritual   ears."
> (Quoted from *Charismatic Chaos* by John F. MacArthur, p. 67, citing Larry Lea, *Are You A Mousekateer*, as published in *Charisma*, August 1988, 9)

It would appear that Larry Lea's friend was in error and not "hearing" from the Lord at all to arrive at his interpretation of his

211

"vision." For the fruit of Lea's ministry from that point on in time shows very little evidence that Lea had the sort of spiritual discernment that such Big Ears would indicate.

Zola Levitt

(1938-2006) Zola Levitt was the first "Messianic Jewish" teacher, author ,and TV evangelist widely accepted in Protestant circles. He had his own TV show since the 1970s, and shared lessons on such topics as "Christ in the Passover." Levitt was not a "Torah observant Messianic"—one who still adheres to the requirements of Jewish law. He took the approach of most of those Jews involved in such evangelical Protestant outreach groups as Jews for Jesus—retaining some Jewish cultural trappings and family traditions, but, for instance, observing Christmas.

Hal Lindsey

End Times Prophecy_pundit, author of the all-time best-selling prophetic speculation book *The Late Great Planet Earth* (© 1970). In spite of the fact that almost none of the specific dogmatic speculations of that book panned out (including that the "end" would come in 1988 since that was 40 years after the birth of modern Israel) as he speculated, he has written many more prophetic speculation books since then.

And in spite of the fact that almost none of the specific dogmatic speculations of **those** books have panned out as he speculated, he continues to be widely honored in many religious circles as a prophetic speculation expert, and continues to issue almost all his opinions dogmatically.

There is no accounting for why such failures at prophetic speculation are considered "credentials" for such pundits. For many years he has had his own regular prophetic speculation news show, *International Intelligence Briefing*, on Jan and Paul Crouch's Trinity Broadcasting Network. He has a website that used to have the humble URL "hallindseyoracle.com," although it is now just hallindsey.com, and is a regular guest speaker on religious TV shows and for Prophecy conventions.

Francis MacNutt

Former Roman Catholic Dominican Priest who is a well-known leader in both the Healing Ministries movement_and the **Deliverance Ministry** movement. MacNutt evidently left the priesthood some time back under a special dispensation which allowed him to marry and yet still be in good standing as a layman in the Roman Catholic Church. But his current ministry efforts are totally ecumenical, and he often appears with and endorses teachers from many Protestant **Pentecostal** and **Charismatic** healing and deliverance ministries. MacNutt has particularly noted that he considers *Kathryn Kuhlman* to have been a major mentoring influence for his own efforts.

Walter Martin

(1928-1989) Founder of the Christian Research Institute, and author of the classic *Kingdom of the Cults*, probably the most widely-read book on non-mainstream Christian religious groups. The CRI under the leadership of Martin, and now under the leadership of *Hank Hanegraaff*, has been a leading investigator and documenter of the teachings and activities of such groups.

Martin's definition of "cult" was not the same as that used in this *Field Guide*. He emphasized mostly "doctrinal orthodoxy" in evaluating religious groups. Thus even if a group used extreme methods of control, and indulged in spiritual abuse, if the leadership promoted standard historical Christian theology it would likely not be subject to scrutiny as a possibly spiritually unhealthy organization.

However, since a large proportion of those groups investigated by CRI actually have indulged in questionable tactics in attracting and keeping followers, much of the research of the organization has been helpful even to those who do not share the exact same perspective on what constitutes sound Biblical doctrine. In general, the documentation provided by CRI appears to be objective, and it is quite easy to sort out the specific facts under consideration from the subjective opinions and evaluation of the CRI authors.

Bill McCartney

Founder and CEO of the Promise Keepers Movement. McCartney was a former University of Colorado football coach, and member of *James Ryle*'s **Vineyard** congregation.

Aimee Semple McPherson

(1890-1944) Flamboyant **Pentecostal** woman evangelist who played a significant part in the history of the Healing Ministries

Movement. McPherson was founder of the Pentecostal denomination International Church of the Foursquare Gospel. She was involved in a major scandal in 1926. Here is how one website summarizes the incident, which pretty well lines up with most historical accounts:

> McPherson, a radio evangelist whose eloquence and showbiz flair drew thousands to her Los Angeles temple every week. When not giving sermons, "Sister Aimee" liked to swim. On May 18 [1926], leaving her secretary on the beach, she swam out into the ocean and didn't come back. There was a huge uproar. A massive search failed to turn up the body. The newspapers churned out extras as ten thousand followers kept vigil on the shore.
>
> Rumors swirled. Some said she hadn't drowned but had been eaten by a sea monster; others said the whole thing was a publicity stunt. She was sighted more times than Elvis—16 times in one day, in locations all over the country. The coroner refused to issue a death certificate. On June 20, McPherson's mother received a ransom note from "the Avengers" demanding $500,000.
>
> Three days later the evangelist showed up in Agua Prieta, Mexico, just across the border from Douglas, Arizona. She told a bizarre story. She had been wading in the surf when a couple lured her into their car with a story about a dying child. She was chloroformed, driven to a two-room shack in the desert, and held there by two men and a woman. A few days later the men left, then the woman announced she was going into town for supplies. McPherson cut her bonds on the jagged lid of a five-gallon syrup can. Once free, she walked across the desert for 17 hours before collapsing inside the gate of a house.
>
> But the story was fishy. The shack she'd described could not be found. Despite her supposedly lengthy trek, she was not dehydrated or sunburned, and her dress showed no signs of sweat. Her shoes weren't scuffed or worn except that she had somehow contrived to get grass stains on them in the desert. She was wearing a watch given to her by her mother that she hadn't taken to the beach, and so on. The cops searched halfheartedly for the kidnappers while hundreds of reporters tried to figure out what McPherson had really been up to. Soon it was reported

that she had spent ten days in the seaside resort town of Carmel, California, with Kenneth Ormiston, her radio engineer, with whom she was thought to be having an affair.

A grand jury hearing on the kidnapping turned into an interrogation of McPherson. A woman claimed she had been bribed by McPherson and her mother to say that she, not the evangelist, had been with Ormiston in Carmel. Despite McPherson's protestations that she was an innocent victim, she was indicted for obstruction of justice, along with Ormiston and others. The story filled the newspapers for months and became an embarrassment for Los Angeles civic leaders. Finally William Randolph Heart's Examiner reported that the district attorney was dropping the charges. The DA declared he was doing no such thing but eventually took the hint, saying the evidence was too confused to permit prosecution.

What really happened? The story doesn't make sense any way you look at it. McPherson's kidnapping yarn was silly, but if all she wanted was a tryst with Ormiston there were a dozen easier ways to have one than faking an abduction. I've yet to hear a persuasive account of the whole mess. McPherson returned to preaching but remained a controversial figure for the rest of her life, dying of a sedative overdose in 1944.

From
http://web.archive.org/web/20041018092427/http://www.straightdope.com/columns/010921.html

Roderick C Meredith

Formerly a high-ranking minister in the Worldwide Church of God (WCG) under founder *Herbert W Armstrong* (HWA). Meredith attended Armstrong's Ambassador College as a young man, was ordained as an "evangelist rank minister" by Armstrong upon graduation in 1952, and served in numerous capacities at the church's Headquarters in Pasadena for many years. These included writing extensively for the *Plain Truth* magazine and other church publications, and eventually positions of administration over other ministers. At one time he was believed by some to be in line, right after Herbert Armstrong's son *Garner Ted Armstrong*, to inherit leadership of the WCG if something happened to the elder

Armstrong. But he fell out of favor with HWA before Armstrong's death. Thus, even though Garner Ted Armstrong had been put out of the WCG several years before HWA's death, Meredith never achieved the position of top leadership to which he evidently believed he was entitled.

HWA died in 1986, and was succeeded as dictatorial leader of the WCG by *Joseph Tkach, Sr.*, who in short order began dismantling the doctrinal base of the church. In the early 1990s, Meredith left the organization and founded his own rival group, the Global Church of God (GCG), which restored all of the doctrines of HWA. Although some ministers and members who joined his group were hoping for a more "collegial" style of church leadership, Meredith obviously intended to re-create the one-man rule that was HWA's policy.

By 1998 a struggle for leadership within the GCG led Meredith to pull out and form another split, which he dubbed the "Living Church of God." Once again he was the undisputed leader. The Living Church of God, with several thousand members throughout the world, supports Meredith's evangelistic efforts through the *Tomorrow's World* magazine and television show.

Meredith was famous in the WCG for the bombastic and dogmatic way he wrote and spoke about Bible Prophecy, as well as a number of controversial areas such as race relations. Articles by Meredith in the *Plain Truth* in the mid-1960s promoted the idea that God had ordained racial segregation in the Bible.

Here are samples of Meredith's pronouncements from the 1960s, during a time when Herbert Armstrong was dogmatically declaring that Christ would return to earth in 1975, and that the WCG's members would be taken to a "**place of safety**" by 1972 where they would ride out the worst years of the "Great Tribulation."

> "Frankly, literally dozens of prophesied events indicate that this final revival of the Roman Empire in Europe-and its bestial persecution of multitudes of Bible-believing Christians-will take place within the next seven to ten years of your life!" (The *Plain Truth*, Feb. 1965, p. 48.)

> "Bible prophecy indicates that the final attack on the U.S. and Britain by this coming 'Beast' power could easily be launched perhaps as early as the spring of 1972-or earlier

216

....”
(The *Plain Truth*, May 1965, p. 45.)

> "After 1965, we are destined to run into increasing trouble with the Gentile nations. America and Britain will begin to suffer from trade embargoes imposed by the brown and oriental races.... We will begin to experience the pangs of starvation and the scarcity of goods!"
> (The *Plain Truth*, August 1957)

> "You might as well wake up and FACE FACTS! The world you live in won't be here 15 years from now!"
> (The *Plain Truth*, December 1963)

In spite of the fact that none of these predictions turned out to be true, Meredith to this day continues to make similar dogmatic predictions in his own publications and broadcasts:

> We are going to be spanked by the Great God [spanking is a recurrent theme with Rod]... World War III is coming up... I am God's servant and God's witness... I myself, Mr. Ames and others, may be killed or martyred... We are at that time now... We are entering the last generation... those under 20 years of age are undoubtedly living in the last complete generation of this world's society. (*Tomorrow's World* broadcast, 2001, "Is this the last generation.")

The doctrinal base of Meredith's organization attempts to follow the teachings and emphasis of Herbert Armstrong as closely as possible. Meredith was unable to get Armstrong's endorsement as the inheritor of his mantle, but he has created a system in which he is viewed by his supporters as the legitimate heir to Armstrong's ministry. Rather than Armstrong's "Apostle" or "Pastor General" titles, Meredith is referred to as the Presiding Evangelist of the organization.

The primary emphasis of the organization is speculative prophecy. Since the beginning of the LCG, Meredith has regularly issued warnings to his flock, and to his public audience, that the Second Coming is imminent, and that it will be preceded by the Great Tribulation.

Check out, for instance, this bombastic declaration by Meredith in a magazine article:

WHERE ARE God's true prophets today?... Listen! This work has been warning America of definite and tremendous events to come for many years! The popular, denominationally supported evangelists often... use the words 'may,' 'could,' or 'might.' They are afraid to be definite and specific! The truth of the matter is that they DARE NOT be specific about the future because they just DO NOT KNOW what the Bible says is going to happen! But on the ... broadcast and in this magazine we have dared to unlock the Bible prophecies and apply them to specific nations and events that are NOW being affected.

The problem is, this statement was made clear back in 1957 by Meredith in the *Plain Truth*. The broadcast he was referring to was Herbert Armstrong's *World Tomorrow* broadcast, not Rod Meredith's much more recent *Tomorrow's World* broadcast. At the time, Armstrong and "This work" that Meredith referred to, which he was deeply a part of, was proclaiming that Jesus would return by 1975, and that the members of their organization would be whisked to a **Place of Safety** by 1972 before the world was plunged into three and a half years of hellish famines, wars, pestilences, and more.

Not one of the "specifics" which Meredith or any of the other WCG writers or speakers proclaimed (nor any of the specifics Herbert Armstrong had proclaimed since 1934) had ever come to pass. By Meredith's own criteria, readers should have concluded he and his associates were NOT "God's true prophets." In fact, Meredith himself should have realized this.

He didn't. In 2005 he wrote in his own *Tomorrow's World* Magazine:

But, as a servant of the living God, I do know the basic outline of what God says will happen to our peoples at the time of the end. We are definitely now in the prophesied "last days!" We need to be willing to heed the direct words of the Bible in a way we have never done before!

If you are willing to genuinely listen and understand, please take seriously the warnings we give you in the pages of this magazine! For you will definitely see these events unfolding over the next several years of your life in a way that "mainstream" religions do not remotely understand—and certainly that mainstream news writers and columnists do not remotely understand, either! For, human as we are, we in this Work are true servants of the great God who is working out an awesome purpose here on earth. Are you "listening"?

Of course, according to Rod Meredith, "we" were definitely "in the prophesied last days" in 1957. And you could know that he and the Work he was part of back then were the "true servants of the great God," the "true prophets," because they were telling you the Plain Truth ... that your world would be gone within fifteen years of 1963. All you needed to do was wait and watch it happen. But it didn't happen.

In spite of all this, Rod Meredith still fancies himself the prime prophetic voice in the End Times. And enough people accept his delusions of grandeur that he has enough finances to spread his false prophecies indefinitely. Well, not indefinitely. Meredith turned 81 in 2011. There is little doubt that his time will run out before the End Times run out–and before they even begin.

Jacob O Meyer

(1934-2010) Founder (1960s) and authoritarian head of the Assemblies of Yahweh denomination. For decades Meyer was the prime public promoter of the **Sacred Name** doctrine. He published the *Sacred Name Broadcaster* magazine and used a shortwave radio tower to disseminate his *Sacred Name Broadcast* radio program around the world. The denomination and the magazine and broadcast seem to be continuing after Meyer's death in 2010 under the supervision of his son Jonathan S Meyer and other elders of the organization.

Joyce Meyer

One of the most influential women **Word Faith** teachers. Meyer offers common sense advice and her own personal inspirational approach to healing emotions and relationships, but unfortunately mixes them with hard-core Word Faith doctrinal teachings. She disseminates her teachings via the *Life in the Word* radio and TV broadcasts, public conferences, many audio recording collections, and numerous books.

Some sources of information on Meyer's ministry and teachings, including some areas of controversy, can be found at the following URLs:

"Joyce Meyer–Are You Paying Attention"

www.letusreason.org/popteac17.htm

"The Teachings of Joyce Meyer"

www.equip.org/articles/the-teachings-of-joyce-meyer

"Joyce Meyer–False Teacher?"

www.theanswerischrist.com/id35.html

Wiki Article

http://en.wikipedia.org/wiki/Joyce_Meyer

Chuck Missler

Hebrew Roots teacher with a prophetic ministry. Missler speculates extensively on various conspiracy theories. He promotes the "**Bible Codes**," and the belief that angels had sex with women before the Flood of Noah.

Bob Mumford

One of the founders of the controversial so-called "**Shepherding Movement**" of the **Charismatic** renewal of the 1970s, along with *Charles Simpson*, Derek Prince, *Don Basham*, and *Ern Baxter*.

A detailed overview of the Shepherding Movement and these five men is available at the URL below.

www.seekgod.ca/shepherding.htm

Mike Murdock

Pentecostal/Charismatic author and televangelist, part of the **Word Faith** movement, who specializes almost exclusively in fund-raising—on his own TV show and the shows of other televangelists. He learned the "**seed faith**" principle from his mentor, *Oral Roberts*, and enthusiastically promotes it throughout all of his own efforts in writing and preaching. Some religious commentators compare Murdock's money-solicitation tactics to those of discredited televangelist *Robert Tilton*. The comparison is apt. Like most popular Word Faith televangelists, Murdock lives an unabashedly lavish life-style, which has brought his ministry's non-profit status under scrutiny by the press and tax authorities. And like many of the others, although it might be difficult to pin on him charges of technically illegal actions, the ethics and Christian integrity of his ministry seem to well deserve such scrutiny and criticism.

Resources for more information on Murdock:

A three-part investigative report regarding Murdock's ministry, reprinted from the Fort Worth Star Telegram newspaper, beginning 3/2/2003 can be read at the following URLs:

www.trinityfi.org/press/murdock01.html

www.trinityfi.org/press/murdock02.html

www.trinityfi.org/press/murdock03.html

An in-depth evaluation of Murdock's teachings as they compare to the Scriptures is at the URL below.

www.letusreason.org/Popteac19.htm

Sample excerpts:

> On LeSea's telethon [Lester E Summerall Evangelistic Association's TV network] to raise the funds he appeals in unusual manners by saying the blessing is only for 120 or for 70 people. Using biblical numbers that people recognize he abuses the context they were used in explaining to them that it is the Holy Spirit that is giving him this number. He prompts a certain number of people to quickly go to the phone. He explains they need to call in now while he is on the program, don't hesitate now is the time, don't miss the opportunity (If they hesitate and think about it they may certainly change their mind). Whether they are the 5, 13, 25, 40, 70, 100 or 120; different numbers are used all the time as he says God is leading him to give them a blessing for their seed. He asked the Holy Spirit to show him 120 people who would sow a $200 seed (June 18, 2001). Another time he asks the Lord to give him twelve unusual seed sowers of $1,000 each on his program. I wonder, if more than twelve give a $1,000 seed does he say we can't accept this money and return it saying the Lord only told me 12? I don't think so, do you!

... Murdock even offers upgrades on your seed - on one Telethon "there is somebody who called in the last 24 hours ... the Holy Spirit is telling you to upgrade your seed." "The Holy Spirit is telling you come back to the telephone dial the 1-800 number... The Holy Spirit is telling you right now to upgrade your seed. When you change your seed you change your harvest." But if you don't do this quickly you will miss the opportunity. Like a sale at the shopping center people are prompted by Murdock's advertising to move on this quickly or lose their opportunity for a miracle harvest. Now there are upgrades to seed faith, but its not free. Again I ask if there such a promise in Scripture? He then tells the people "the thousand dollars you keep wouldn't make you debt free, if you kept the thousand you still owe everything you owe." Not if you're saving it to pay off a debt; but the truth is if you give Murdock the thousand dollars you're way more in debt than when you first started. Something to seriously think about.

... Murdock says "There is about 6 levels of sowing that I have had uncommon blessing, one of them was one thousand seed"

Murdock gives a powerful significance to certain amounts of the seed "There's been 5 levels of uncommon reaping in my life. One was a $58 seed I've been telling you about. One was $100, $200, $1,000 and $8,500. The thousand dollar seed broke the back of poverty in my life." Nobody can sow this thousand dollars for you, you say Mike I never sowed any seed like that. That's why you never reaped from that kind of harvest." (Keys to the Kingdom LeSea).

"In the name of Jesus I speak four supernatural uncommon miracles in your life" He then tells the listeners to plant a $1000 seed.

"There is an uncommon anointing even right now on the thousand dollar seed through this ministry." In my experience I believe there is the greatest anointing on a thousand dollar seed right now that there has ever been on any telethon on any service I've ever spoken" (Lesea fund raiser19 97 video tape).

When his convincing has not worked He resorts to manipulate his viewers by thinking it's the devil who holds them back "Whatever seed stops you, that's what Satan has purchased your future for, if Satan can stop my giving at $1,000 faith that's where Satan has found the price tag on my future."

..."I broke the back of poverty with a thousand dollar seed, its what you can walk away from you mastered. If you can walk away from a thousand dollars you've mastered greed for the rest of your life. Satan can't torment you."

Is he kidding! What kind of a promise is this? Can a thousand dollars given to Murdock or his ministry actually make one free from greed their whole life? Where does Holy Scripture ever say such a thing? I guess for these people who so earnestly give it does not have to be in Scripture but said by the mouth of a prosperity prophet. If someone has a lot of money $1,000 is a drop in the bucket how would this affect their greed? He's making this all up and the naïve and gullible believe it! Better know your Bible before you give away all your money to people like this.

Arnold Murray

Founder and spokesman for the *Shepherd's Chapel* ministry and television program. The program has been on local Public Access channels late at night for many years. In recent years it has shown up on an increasing number of commercial stations, both secular and religious. Casual viewers who don't follow the program consistently seem to view it as just a nice old gentleman helping Bible students to carefully study the Bible verse by verse. Only those who commit more diligently to listen to all the programs and send for extra recordings of "deeper studies" will finally realize that Murray's "exegesis" of Bible passages is extremely idiosyncratic, his interpretations range from fanciful to fanatical, and are laced with both racism and anti-semitism ... and much more.

Resources for more documentation and commentary on Murray's teachings:

"Who is Arnold Murray?"

http://carm.org/who-arnold-murray

"Arnold Murray and the Shepherd's Chapel"

http://carm.org/who-arnold-murray

"Profile: Shepherd's Chapel"

www.watchman.org/profile/murraypro.htm

Gary North

Prominent leader in the Reconstructionist or **"Kingdom Now"** movement. North is son-in-law of the *late R. J. Rushdoony*, who is considered the father of the Reconstructionist Movement.

North is most famous for his many failed predictions, including his prognostications regarding the "Y2K" computer bug. Here is a sample excerpt from a *Wired* article in January 1999 about his predictions:

> WASHINGTON -- For decades Gary North has made a living predicting modern society will end in panic and ruin. In 1980, he forecast rationing of housing and a nuclear war with the Soviet Union. He warned his followers to buy "gold, silver, a safe place outside the major cities." Then AIDS became the threat: "In 1992, we will run out of available hospital beds.... The world will eventually panic," he wrote in 1987. Now North has found Y2K and a skittish audience receptive to predictions of doom. A recent advertisement for his Remnant Review newsletter proclaims: "A bank run like no other will bankrupt banks all over the world in 1999." If you fork over $225 for a 24-issue subscription, North will cheerfully equip you with "the tools you need to build untouchable wealth." His advice is familiar, if unsurprising: Close your bank accounts, sell your stocks. Buy guns, gold, and grain. Move to a remote cabin where you can survive the collapse of Western civilization, safe from riots and hungry looters.

> "The code is broken. It cannot be fixed. The panic is inevitable. It's a question of when," he wrote on garynorth.com last month. "Through his Web site he can help to fan the flames of Y2K panic to create social disorder so the social systems of the world crash. It's out of the ashes of those systems that he thinks the kingdom

will rise," says Frederick Clarkson, author of the book Eternal Hostility: The Struggle Between Theocracy and Democracy. Nope. It's none other than the Kingdom of God and the return of Jesus Christ, events that North believes won't happen until a Draconian biblical law is imposed for a thousand years. For North, there's no better way to pull the plug on an ungodly society than fanning the flames of Y2K panic. "He wants to make sure the banking system crashes. It's a self-fulfilling prophecy," Clarkson says.

See the URL below for more details.

www.wired.com/news/culture/0,1284,17193,00.html

You can read comments that *Wired* made after North's Y2K predictions failed miserably at the URL below.

www.wired.com/news/technology/0,1282,33445,00.html

What might North's "Reconstructionism/Kingdom Now" theology imply? Here's a quote from his book *Political Polytheism*.

> The long-term goal of Christians in politics should be to gain exclusive control over the franchise. Those who refuse to submit publicly to the eternal sanctions of God by submitting to His Church's public marks of the covenant – baptism and holy communion – must be denied citizenship, just as they were in ancient Israel. The way to achieve this political goal is through successful mass evangelism followed by constitutional revision.

Agnes Ozman

(1870-1937) The first person to allegedly receive "the Baptism in the Holy Spirit with the initial evidence of speaking in tongues" in the **Pentecostal** movement that began in 1900. Ozman was at the Bethel Bible School led by Charles Parham in Topeka, Kansas. Parham later recorded that on December 31, 1900, he laid hands on her and prayed that she would receive "the baptism" and "**speak in tongues**." And she allegedly immediately began "speaking in the Chinese tongue."

Dave Pack

Former minister with the Worldwide Church of God. Pack founded the Restored Church of God in 1999, and considers himself to be the only mouthpiece of God on Earth today. He rules his organization with an iron hand, and demands extreme financial and other sacrifices from his small group of followers to support his megalomania. Sample quotes from a November, 2007 sermon to "the Faithful":

> Go get a big chunk out of your home. And put your money where your mouth is and send it here. And I'm not talking about one, two, three thousand either. How about ten, twenty, thirty, fifty, or one hundred thousand dollars? Go do it

> Wives, you can be independent in this. You have 1/2 the worth of whatever you have in your house. I'm officially telling you this...Wives, legally you have the 1/2 the funds. What are you going to do about it?...Husbands... 'well, my wife is not in the church'...tell her... 'you don't have a voice woman.'

> ...Let us know how much you plan to send and when you plan to send it...You must be willing to communicate...If you do need to counsel, please do that...If you are not ready to distribute what you have...you don't believe the flow of prophecy"

> This is announcing the last blast, the clarion call as it were, to finish the work...Whether it is 4,5,7, 9 years to go, God knows...This is liquidating assets...I have the authority to tell you to do it...I have the moral and spiritual, and ecclesiastical authority to tell you to do what I have also done.

> Get it now when it requires faith...when you are dead you don't need it...if you named us in your wills, it can take us months or years to get it.

J. I. Packer

Anglican teacher and prolific writer. Packer is author, contributing author, or editor of over 140 books, a number of them considered "classics" in the field of popular Christian/inspirational writing. He has been Senior Editor of *Christianity Today* magazine.

Luis Palau

International evangelist who has patterned his highly successful ministry after that of Billy Graham. Born in Argentina, Palau moved to the US as a young man, attended Multnomah School of the Bible, and began a career in public evangelism in the 1960s. Although his ministry is centered in the U.S., his evangelical efforts in South America have earned him the nick-name "the Billy Graham of South America." The main thrust of his ministry since 1999 has been what are called "Festivals," large, free evangelistic extravaganzas held in metropolitan areas, described on his website:

> Envision the biggest party you've ever attended. Multiply attendance by 100 or even 1,000. Now add two full days of live concerts by popular musicians, a children's area, a community care area, a skate park featuring professional, world-class skateboarding, BMX and FMX demos, a food court, and opportunities to see your friends and family come to Jesus Christ. That, my friend, is a Luis Palau festival. Add in a Season of Service in the weeks leading up to the festival, and a strategy for continuing, long-term community impact, and you begin to see the whole picture.

> These free, family-friendly events have drawn more than 8.5 million people since 1999 in such diverse locations as Ft. Lauderdale, Florida (300,000), Nashville, Tennessee (90,000), Houston, Texas (225,000), Manchester, England (55,000), Lima, Peru (650,000) and Buenos Aires, Argentina (850,000).

These festivals are sponsored by local churches in the area around where the festival will be held, with plans taking up to two years to put in place. As with Billy Graham, Palau's version of the Gospel is so "doctrinally neutral" that it is not uncommon to find such diverse groups as Roman Catholics, Charismatics, Methodists, Presbyterians, Lutherans, Nazarenes, and more cooperating in bringing Palau's Festival to town.

Rod Parsley

Word Faith televangelist and Pastor of independent **Charismatic** World Harvest Church in Columbus, Ohio, which supports Parsley's *Breakthrough* television show and associated Breakthrough Ministry. Parsley is particularly notable for his old-time-fire-and-brimstone, flamboyant, bombastic, dripping-sweat preaching style which is full of gratuitous theatrical posturing and gesturing and

227

lots of "oratorical devices" such as catchy phrases emphasizing alliteration of sounds.

A detailed overview of the history of Parsley and his ministry, with an evaluation of some of his specific teachings in light of the scriptures, is available in the article "Rod Parsley: The Raging Prophet–'Breaking Through' His Unorthodox Doctrine and Practice" at the URL below.

www.pfo.org/parsley.htm

Earl Paulk

(1927-2009) Referred to in his own circles as "Bishop Earl Paulk," Paulk was the foremost popular preacher in the **Kingdom Now** movement, and one of those men recognized in the **Modern Apostles and Prophets** movement as a bonafide modern prophet. He was Pastor and chief "prophet" of the independent **Charismatic** Cathedral at Chapel Hill (formerly Chapel Hill Harvester Church) in Decatur, Georgia.

Paulk was embroiled in 2001 in an ongoing scandal involving allegations of numerous incidents of sexual misconduct including adultery and child molestation on the part of Paulk and others on the staff of the Cathedral. Serious accusations continued to be featured in news reports about Paulk's ministry for years and contributed to the replacement of Paulk as Senior Pastor of the church by his nephew Donnie E. Paulk in August 2006. At that point, Paulk's regular TV program, normally broadcast on *Jan and Paul Crouch*'s Trinity Broadcasting Network and on the Internet, disappeared from the broadcast schedules.

In 2007, Donnie Paulk shocked the congregation when he revealed that he had discovered through DNA testing that he was not Earl Paulk's nephew, as he had believed all his life. He was his son. Earl Paulk had engaged in an affair with his brother Don's wife, and Donnie was the result.

Court cases involving Paulk's alleged immorality continued up until his death from cancer in March 2009.

Peter Popoff

Former popular **Word Faith** television evangelist, part of the **Healing Ministries** Movement, who was exposed as a fraud in 1987. Popoff claimed to have an astounding "gift of the **word of**

228

knowledge" whereby he would call "complete strangers" out of the audience at healing crusades and reveal personal details about them and their ailments.

A team of investigators led by *James Randi* discovered that associates of Popoff would actually gather information about those in the audience before the meetings began, note it down in writing, and give it to Popoff's wife. She would then sit in a trailer outside the meeting hall in front of a television monitor showing the audience. And when the meeting began, she would broadcast information to a hidden transmitter in Popoff's ear, identifying for him people in the audience that he could call up for his "performance," and feeding him information about them that he could use to astound them and the audience. Randi appeared on the Johnny Carson *Tonight Show* and played for a live audience a recording his investigators had made of Popoff's wife's voice broadcasting such information to him.

This revelation destroyed Popoff's ministry at the time. Astonishingly, however, Popoff has evidently resurrected his ministry, and now has a website promoting it again, including offers for a number of **Word Faith** books he has written, and descriptions of various dynamic ministry activities. The website home page has a form you can fill out to order "Your Miracle Spring Water and Debt Cancellationing Kit."

The Wikipedia article on Popoff details a litany of his further escapades all the way up to today, including this tidbit:

> In 2009, advertisements appeared in the UK press offering a free cross which contained "blessed water" and "holy sand". The blessed water was supposedly from a source near Chernobyl (the site of a nuclear accident). Animals drinking from this source were purportedly free from any radiation sickness. The cross also bore the inscription 'Jerusalem'. Requests for donations accompanied the cross and follow-up requests for money from Popoff were also sent out.

Frederick K C Price

One of the most popular African-American **Word Faith** televangelists. Price is a protégé of *Kenneth Hagin*, and an alumni of Hagin's Rhema Bible Institute. He is pastor of Crenshaw Christian

Center in Los Angeles, California, which supports his *Ever Increasing Faith* broadcasts and ministry.

More details on Price's ministry and teachings are at the following URLs:

> Frederick K C Price
>
> www.apologeticsindex.org/557-frederick-price
>
> "Is 'The Price is Right?' Or is the Price wrong?"
>
> www.letusreason.org/Wf27.htm
>
> Excerpt:
>
>> He also promotes the myth that Jesus was very rich and incorporates this into his theology of why every believer should be rich. "The whole point is I'm trying to get you to see-to get you out of this malaise of thinking that Jesus and the disciples were poor and then relating that to you thinking that you, as a child of God, have to follow Jesus. The Bible says that He has left us an example that we should follow His steps. That's the reason why I drive a Rolls Royce. I'm following Jesus' steps."
>>
>> ...Price is so proud of what he got in "Jesus' name" that he boasts to his congregation "I've got 25 million dollars in my financial statement, free and clear, I have no debt, I live in a 25 room mansion, I have my own 6 million dollar yacht, I have my own private jet and I have my own helicopter and I have 7 luxury automobiles so I never get bored having to drive the same car more than one time in any given week."

Derek Prince

One of the founders of the controversial so-called "**Shepherding Movement**" of the **Charismatic** renewal of the 1970s, along with *Ern Baxter, Charles Simpson, Bob Mumford,* and *Don Basham.*

A detailed overview of the Shepherding Movement and these five men is available at the following URL:

James Randi

Former professional stage magician ("The Amazing Randi") who has used his knowledge of sleight-of-hand and other magic tricks in recent decades to expose the deceptive and unscrupulous methods of some evangelists, such as *Peter Popoff*. His James Randi Educational Foundation also deals in investigating non-religious claims of paranormal abilities, pseudo-scientific gadgets, etc., such as the "spoon-bending" of Russian Uri Geller.

Bill Randles

Founder and pastor of Believers In Grace Fellowship. Randles is a **Pentecostal** author who writes excellent in-depth critical refutations of what he believes to be serious aberrations promoted by leading teachers in the **Hyper-Charismatic** Movement.

The books by Randles listed below can be ordered on the Believers in Grace website at the following URL.

www.believersingrace.com/store/books.php

- *Making War in the Heavenlies* (re: "spiritual warfare")

- *Weighed and Found Wanting* (re: the "Toronto Blessing")

- *Beware of the New Prophets* (re: "Modern Apostles and Prophets")

- *Mending the Nets* (re: Modern Gnosticism)

Opal Reddin

Pentecostal author whose writings emphasize critical evaluation of the **Spiritual Warfare** movement and the Ecumenical movement within Pentecostal and **Charismatic** circles. Reddin was for many years a professor of the Assemblies of God Central Bible College. A condensation of much of the information in her best-known book *Power Encounter: A Pentecostal Perspective* (Opal L. Reddin, editor, revised edition, © 1999) can be read online on the *Discernment Newsletter* website at the URL below.

www.zyworld.com/Discernment/1999_SeptemberOctober.pdf

Oral Roberts

231

(1918-2009) Pioneer "healing" televangelist. Roberts was the first to broadcast tent healing services on the fledgling television medium in the early 1950s. He popularized the concept of the term **seed faith**, encouraging his audiences to believe that, if they "sowed a seed" of financial contributions to his ministry, they would reap financial and health blessings from God.

He founded Oral Roberts University in Tulsa, Oklahoma, which opened in 1965. The Oral Roberts Evangelistic Association currently produces the daily *Something Good Tonight—Hour of Healing* TV program which is hosted by Roberts' son *Richard Roberts*. Oral Roberts was an active part of the **Healing Ministries** movement and **Word Faith** movement. And he endorsed and participated in activities which promoted the **Toronto Blessing** and the **Holy Laughter** movement.

A 1985 book review of a biography of Roberts, investigating the history of his ministry and evaluating some of his claims, can be seen online at the URL below.

"The Life and Ministry of Oral Roberts"

http://cnview.com/on_line_resources/the_life_and_mini stry_of_oral_roberts.htm

Some interesting quotes from Roberts can be seen at the following URL.

"By Your Words": Quotes from Third Wave Leaders

www.deceptioninthechurch.com/quotes.html#Roberts

Patti Roberts, first wife of Oral Roberts' son Richard, wrote a 1983 book, *Ashes to Gold*, about her experiences in the Roberts' clan before her divorce from Richard. In it she shared her perspective on the "seed faith" doctrine as taught by Oral:

> The seed-faith theology that Oral had developed bothered me a great deal because I saw that, when taken to its natural extremes, it reduced God to a sugar daddy. If you wanted His blessings and His love, you paid Him off. Over and over again we heard Oral say, 'Give out of your need.' I began to question the motivation that kind of giving implied. Were we giving to God out of our love and gratitude to Him or were we bartering with Him? (p.63)

232

The distinction may appear to be too subtle and I know Oral thought I was splitting hairs, but it seemed supremely important to me. If we give to God because we think that by giving we have somehow placed Him in our debt and He is now required to come through for us and meet our needs, we have, I believe, perverted the heart of the gospel. Our only motive for giving should be love. When we encourage people to give in order to have their needs met or so that they will receive "a hundred fold return" I believe we are appealing to their sense of greed or desperation, neither of which seemed admirable to me. It was a wonderful fund-raising tool, but I believe it gave people a very unbalanced view of a very important biblical principle.

At the time I was taking a humanities course from the university and my professor was discussing Martin Luther and the Reformation. When we started looking at the abuses in the Catholic church that Luther had wanted to reform, I began to see parallels in our situation. Luther was incensed by the church's practice of selling indulgences - offering forgiveness of sin and a shorter period of time in purgatory in return for gifts to the church. I had a very difficult time distinguishing between the selling of indulgences and the concept of Seed Faith inflated to the degree to which we had inflated it. Of course, Oral was more subtle. He never promised salvation in exchange for gifts to his ministry, but there were still many people who believed that God was going to look at them in a kindlier way and perhaps that son would get off drugs or they would get their drunken husband into heaven if they gave money to Oral Roberts. (p. 120,121)

Richard Roberts

Son of pioneer healing televangelist *Oral Roberts*. Before his father's death, Richard had taken over as CEO of Oral Roberts University and the Oral Roberts Evangelistic Association. He is the host of the OREA's television program, *Something Good Tonight—Hour of Healing*. He is an active part of the **Healing Ministries** movement and **Word Faith** movement. And he endorses and participates in activities which promote the **Toronto Blessing** and the **Holy Laughter** movement.

233

A 1983 book by Roberts' first wife Patti, *Ashes to Gold*, gave an interesting glimpse into the inner workings of the Roberts empire. A telling quote from that book:

> I know a lot of people were blessed and sincerely ministered to by what we sang on TV, and by what we said - but the overall picture, I'm afraid, seemed to say, "If you follow our formula, you'll be like us," rather than, "If you do what Jesus says, you'll be like Him." It was certainly more exciting to follow us, because to follow us was to identify with success, with glamor, with a theology that made everything good and clean and well-knit together. To identify with Jesus, however, meant to identify with the cross.

Pat Robertson

Founder (1960) of the first U.S. Christian television network, the Christian Broadcasting Network (CBN). Robertson is the host of CBN's "flagship" program, *700 Club*. He is also founder of Regent University in Virginia Beach, VA, and the American Center for Law and Justice, described on his website as "a public interest law firm and education group that defends the First Amendment rights of people of faith. The law firm focuses on pro-family, pro-liberty and pro-life cases nationwide."

Because Robertson often focuses on political or prophetic topics in his broadcasts, many viewers are not aware that his basic theological positions are squarely in the middle of the **Charismatic Word Faith** camp. He also promotes the **Toronto Blessing** and **Holy Laughter** movements.

Useful documentation on his ministry can be seen at the following link. Please note that linking to this site does not indicate a blanket endorsement of the opinions and evaluations of the author of the material there. But the documentation can stand on its own, and the reader can come to his/her own conclusions regarding the significance of the facts as weighed against the teachings of the Bible.

www.rapidnet.com/~jbeard/bdm/exposes/robertson/general.htm

Michael John Rood

234

Self-styled (but non-Jewish) "Messianic Rabbi." Although there is a **Hebrew Roots** emphasis to much of his teaching, he is most notable for offering dogmatic predictions of exactly how Bible prophecy will be fulfilled in immediate contemporary history since at least 1998. From that year to this, he has promoted to his supporters yearly a number of very specific scenarios to be fulfilled within months, none of which has ever yielded any fruit of fulfillment. As each proposed scenario has failed, he has offered excuses for that failure and gone forward to offer an alternative scenario for the upcoming year. And yet each such alternative has also failed.

In his bombastic talks, he has a strong tendency toward mixing wildly speculative material in with solid Biblical teaching in a way that totally muddles just where solid Biblical or historical fact leaves off, and where his own pure conjecture starts. Although he has not claimed the "office of prophet," he has indicated over and over in his writings and speaking that he has been the recipient of many direct divine interventions which he evidently offers as validation of his ministry. And over time he has tended to make bolder and bolder claims about himself and his role in End Times events.

In August 2007, almost all of Rood's associates in the Rood Awakening Ministries, with headquarters in Oregon, joined in rejecting his leadership of the organization, accusing him of "inappropriate behavior," financial irregularities, and heavy-handed leadership. A group of leading Hebrew Roots individuals was called together as a panel to investigate and arbitrate between the two sides of the Rood problem. Those arbitration efforts failed. The panel's findings went against Rood's interests, and he rejected them totally.

Those opposing Rood's leadership had the legal ability to remove him from his role in the ministry, so he moved his base of operations to Michigan, where one of his loyal supporters set him up with a new office and studio space to record his programs. He was soon back in business on the Web. Then in 2010, he alienated all his associates once again and was fired by the board of the new ministry, with accusations made including embezzlement of funds. He then found a few other supporters to start over with again and shifted his operations to North Carolina.

Beyond concern about Michael Rood's false prophecies and related issues these days, and beyond his latest legal troubles, are his turn further and further towards rejecting the integrity of the New Testament. He has for several years appeared around the country and on videos with Nehemia Gordon, a non-Christian, non-Messianic Jew who rejects Jesus.

Sid Roth

Messianic Jewish host of *Messianic Vision*, nationally syndicated radio, TV, and publishing ministry. Roth's radio programs feature interviews with an extremely wide variety of teachers, preachers, prophetic wannabes, promoters of theological novelties such as the **Bible Codes**, and much more. He is particularly influential in four different religious circles: his ministry provides "Messianic" material aimed at "sharing the Gospel with Jews," emphasizes **Hebrew Roots** study topics for non-Jewish Christians, promotes a variety of speculative prophecy teachers in the End Times Prophecy movement, and promotes the manifestations of the more radical fringes of the **Charismatic** movement such as **Holy Laughter** and the **Toronto Blessing**.

Rousas Rushdoony

(1916-2001) Considered the father of the Christian Reconstruction/ **Kingdom Now** movement. Rushdoony is father-in-law of *Gary North*.

Charles Taze Russell

Bible teacher of the 1800s and early 1900s who created the magazine *Zion's Watchtower and Herald of the Coming Kingdom*, the precursor to the *Watchtower* magazine of the Jehovah's Witnesses of today. Russell was author of many articles and books used as part of the doctrinal foundation of the Jehovah's Witnesses. His writings are also accepted by a number of rival groups to the Jehovah's Witnesses, such as the Dawn Bible Students, as their primary doctrinal foundation.

"Judge" Joseph Rutherford

(d. 1942) Head of the Watchtower Bible and Tract Society and dictatorial leader of the Jehovah's Witnesses movement after the death of *Charles Taze Russell* in 1916. Rutherford coined the name "Jehovah's Witnesses" for the movement in the early 1930s.

James Ryle

Vineyard leader, pastor and mentor of *Bill McCartney* (founder of the Promise Keepers movement). Ryle is viewed by some as a "prophet." He claimed to get directly from God the assurance, among other very unusual things, that the Beatles got their musical gift from God.

An extremely enlightening correspondence between Ryle and his ministry and a researcher gathering information regarding this unusual claim, is available at the following URL.

"Promise Keepers and James Ryle"

www.seekgod.ca/ryle.htm

Jerry Savelle

Popular **Word Faith** preacher, teacher, and author. Savelle is founder of Jerry Savelle Ministries International and host of the *Adventures in Faith* weekly TV program. He is a disciple of *Kenneth Copeland*, and is primarily a regurgitator of the standard Word Faith (healing and prosperity) teachings of Copeland and other long-time Word Faith teachers, rather than an innovator in any way in either content or delivery style.

Robert Schuller

Founder and original Senior Pastor of the Crystal Cathedral in Garden Grove, California and televangelist on the *Hour of Power* television program until his retirement. His former ministry is now headed by his oldest daughter. Although Schuller started out as an ordained minister of the Reformed Church, the "Gospel" that he has preached for decades has little in common with either that denomination or most of the rest of Christianity.

Over the years Schuller abandoned almost any reference to such standard Biblical themes as sin, repentance, regeneration, salvation or the central role of Jesus as Lord and Savior, other than in name only. For the central point of his message was the importance of human self-esteem. The teacher who most influenced his own perspective on religion was fellow Reformed minister Norman Vincent Peale, and his Power of Positive Thinking theme. Schuller embellished on Peale's teachings and dubbed his own version "Possiblity Thinking." And he did not just "add" some positive/possibility encouragement and inspirational messages to standard Gospel preaching and writing. He abandoned virtually all

237

Biblical theology to re-create God in the image of his own "success motivation" paradigm.

Although he always used terms that sound biblical, his sermons and writings have given them his own idiosyncratic definitions, which twist their meaning almost beyond recognition. And although for some strange reason he has long been accepted with open arms in many Protestant Christian settings, including in particular the **Charismatic** movement, his theology is so eclectic and ecumenical that was able to just as easily cooperate with Roman Catholics, Muslims, Unitarians, and just about any other group.

John Scotland

Evangelist from Liverpool, England who is a major player in the **Toronto Blessing** and **Holy Laughter** movement. Scotland's main claim to fame is the collection of incredible video clips available on the Internet of some his "drunk in the spirit" pulpit shenanigans from the Toronto Airport Fellowship meetings . In these he behaves no differently from someone literally drunk on alcohol, complete with ignorant, ludicrous manifestations such as crowing like a rooster right in the middle of reading the scriptures. He ... and his apologists ... claim that this behavior is proof that he is powerfully under the influence of the Holy Spirit. Here is a transcript of portions of his performance ...

> "Ok before we take off, clapping, lets get the reading done. Luke, LUKE. (Laughing) Chapter TWOOOOOOO. I tell you what... Lets look at chapter 1. Settle down please, Ladies and Gentlemen! Luke chapter 1 and verse 5. Lets go back to the reading... Luke chapter 1 verse, verse, verse, Chockadodaldoooo. Oh dear, haahah. Luke chapter 1 verse CHOCKADODALDO. For those of you having difficulty with that manifestation like myself... That's a wake up call. Zacharius was in the sanctuary when, ZACHARI. Zacharius was a member of the Dubabupida. Division. service corpse. One day Zacharius was going about his work in the temple Cockadodaldoo. Verse 10. praying, PRAYING!! for I have come to the god has herd your prayer WOW... WOWWWWW. God hears PRAYER! Verse 14 ladies and gentlemen, settle down now, settle down."

"... you know I . WOWHOO. I've been going through different stages of drunkenness. and the stage I'm at, at the moment is Slouching. I've gone through the hick up stage. I've gone through the phase of heckling the preachers. um. I am a sign and a wonder. When a prophet told me there was an anointing for me coming pre-1994, I thought great. But when that anointing came, it came in a package I didn't expect. It came in a package of offence. I've come to the conclusion that my gift is offending people. what can you do? You know I mean. I think Christians are to sensitive anyway you know, always winging. but it is a gift. I don't need to even say anything. um. I SHOT THE SHERIFF. AND I SHOT THE DEPUTY TOO! WOW, the sheriff is legalism. and the deputy is religion.(cheering) Um. that's good isn't it? that's copyrighted now. you can't copy it. heheh. I didn't ask for this. no I didn't. The problem was when I came through the doors November 1994. And the Lord said to me, "What do you want John"? I said I want to get drunk. I just forgot to tell him how long. Now I don't mind being drunk. Its great. But I said to the Lord. I don't like looking drunk, you know your eyes get blood shot. and he said to me. John, You see some of think God doesn't talk like that but he's very, he is a fun God. Lets get the fun back into church. And he said John, you see the rock stars on breakfast TV, they always wear sunglasses. so he said get yourself a pair of sunglasses. I call these glasses glory shades. I'm sure Moses would have worn them if they had them in the old testament. Whoahhh, Now hang in please, hang in. fasten your seat belt. we may have a bit of turbulence tonight. and you might want to run, but hang on in. lets go back to the reading."

Much more can be not only read but seen on video in "The John Scotland Video Collection" at the following URL.

www.cephasministry.com/tongues_video_doc_scotland.ht ml

Demos Shakarian

Pentecostal layman who founded in 1951 the Full Gospel Business Men's Fellowship International (FGBMFI). The FGBMFI was instrumental in introducing the practices and beliefs of the old-time Pentecostals into "respectable" circles, thus paving the way for the rise of the current **Charismatic** movement. To understand the full impact of this, see the *Pentecostal and Charismatic: What's the Difference?* chapter of this *Field Guide*.

Charles Simpson

One of the founders of the controversial so-called "**Shepherding Movement**" of the Charismatic renewal of the 1970s, along with *Bob Mumford*, Derek Prince, *Don Basham*, and *Ern Baxter*.

A detailed overview of the Shepherding Movement and these five men is available at the following URL.

www.seekgod.ca/shepherding.htm

Tovya Singer

Orthodox Jewish rabbi who is the most prominent apologist for Judaism against Christianity. Singer founded a ministry called Outreach Judaism which distributes his recordings and writings on "disproving" the Messianic claims of Jesus. These are widely circulated in both Jewish circles and in some ex-Christian circles.

Chuck Smith

Founder and senior pastor of the Calvary Chapel Church of Costa Mesa, California and teacher on the nationwide radio program *The Word for Today*. Smith was one of the earliest pastoral supporters of the "Jesus Movement" of the late 1960s and early 1970s. His Calvary Chapel Church, started in 1965 with only 25 people, is now the central headquarters church in a Calvary Chapel movement which has hundreds of affiliated churches around the world.

The late *John Wimber*, founder of the **Vineyard** Movement association of churches, was at one time a pastor of a Calvary Chapel affiliate, breaking with Smith's organization in 1977. The Calvary Chapel movement is **Charismatic** in many ways, but rejected some of the more flamboyant of the Charismatic manifestations that were beginning to be promoted by Wimber and others who helped establish the earliest Vineyard churches.

As with many such Charismatic organizations founded by men with strong personalities, the leadership model of the Calvary

Chapel Churches is one of tight control from the top down both on the national level and on the individual congregational level.

David J Smith

Radio evangelist, editor of the *Newswatch* magazine and head of the Church of God Evangelistic Association. Smith was a former member of the Worldwide Church of God under *Herbert W Armstrong* and models his speaking style and ministry closely after Armstrong. He is the self-styled primary spokesman for God on earth today. His broadcasts, sermon tapes, and writings emphasize world news events as fulfillment of Bible prophecy, with particular emphasis on the **British Israel** theory.

Joseph Smith

(1805-1844) Nineteenth Century founder of the Church of Jesus Christ of Latter Day Saints, commonly known as the Mormons.

Elbert Eugene Spriggs

Founder and self-proclaimed super-apostle of the Twelve Tribes Messianic Communities, over which he evidently has total authoritarian control. Below him are other apostles, and then levels of elders and deacons—who are also to be obeyed without question by all in the local communities. As of 2001, there were approximately 2,500 people reported living in 25+ such communities in the Northeastern U.S., Missouri, Colorado, Canada, Australia, Europe (France, Spain, Germany, England), and South America (Brazil, Argentina).

As with many founders/leaders of exclusivist, authoritarian groups, Spriggs has proclaimed that he has restored "true" Biblical faith, which has been missing from the world for 1900 years. One former member described the level of commitment necessary to join the group this way:

> "To enter salvation you must....
>
> Give up all your possessions to The Body (not to charity - like monks, etc.)
> Give up your spouse and children if they don't come with you.
> Give up your mind and all your opinions.
> Obey the elders and shepherds without question.

Give up your parents and relatives and only visit them (with permission) if they do not oppose The Body.
Give up any dreams or aspirations you ever had.
Give up all previous spiritual faith/beliefs/practices.
Publically renounce Christianity, if you were heavily involved in it.
Become a literal slave with no rights, no civil liberties of any kind.. Freedom of movement, Education, Media access, Freedom of religion, Etc. it's all gone."

The most complete description of the group is probably the material at the site of the New England Institute for Religious Research. The site authors note that they had been studying the group since 1994 when they were contacted by a woman attempting to leave the group:

> That encounter began an odyssey for us that has involved literally thousands of hours of research and investigation as we have tried to understand this relatively "new religious movement." We have not taken this lightly and have tried to leave "no stone unturned" in seeking to understand this group. We have visited seven of their communities numerous times (Bellows Falls and Island Pond, Vermont; Boston and Hyannis, Massachusetts; and Providence, Rhode Island; Gorham, Maine; Buffalo, New York), interviewed at least 75 current members, members who left and came back to the group, a variety of other "friends of the Community," close to two dozen ex-members from around the country, distressed relatives of current members, law enforcement officials, lawyers, newspaper reporters and university academics. We studied all the written data we could find including hundreds of news articles dating back to the early '70's in Chattanooga, Tennessee where the group began. We gathered court records, reports from various government agencies, and correspondence to and from the group. We have also collected their own printed materials...Freepapers, InterTribal News, booklets, tracts and other works produced for the public's consumption. Finally, but most significantly, many people gave us hundreds of the "teachings" of their "apostle," without which it would have been difficult to put all that we have found into perspective.

We decided to put our research into writing and on the Web for four reasons. First, there is literally nothing written on Twelve Tribes that is helpful in understanding who they are, how they began, and what they believe. Second, their impact belies the actual size of the group. Third, it has become very evident, upon reviewing all that we have learned, that many lives have been devastated by involvement with Twelve Tribes. Fourth, they are a classic study of how a group begins with the best of intentions but, over time, evolves into something far different than what was originally intended. The "apostle" of the group, Elbert Eugene Spriggs, essentially has a "direct pipeline" to God and no real accountability. This is a very dangerous combination in any situation.

See more details at the URL below.

http://neirr.org//mcconclu.html

Another helpful overview of the history, teachings and practices of the Twelve Tribes group can be seen on the archival location of the Religious Movements site of the University of Virginia at the URL below.

http://web.archive.org/web/20060829151659/http://religiousmovements.lib.virginia.edu/nrms/tribes.html

And a large collection of articles and documentation regarding Spriggs and the Twelve Tribes group can be seen on the Rick Ross Institute site at the URL below.

www.rickross.com/groups/tribes.html

R G Stair

Radio evangelist on the *Overcomer* broadcast, self-styled "God's Last Day Prophet to America." Stair is the dictatorial, authoritarian founder and leader of several Overcomer Communities where followers live in a communal lifestyle. In the past decade he was embroiled in scandal and legal problems involving serious allegations of sexual and other abuse by Stair, which resulted in a significant proportion of the residents of the Overcomer Communities defecting from the organization.

Vinson Synan

Historian who has, more than any other modern author, methodically chronicled the rise of the **Pentecostal and Charismatic** movement in America. He was originally ordained in the Pentecostal Holiness denomination, later served as General Secretary for that group. He has been Dean of the School of Divinity at Regent University (institution founded by televangelist Pat Robertson) since 1994.

Unlike many authors in the Pentecostal tradition, Synan holds an earned PhD, from the University of Georgia. Among his books are *The Century of the Holy Spirit: 100 Years of Pentecostal and Charismatic Renewal, 1901-2001* (Thomas Nelson), *The Old-Time Power* (Centennial Edition), and *Holiness-Pentecostal Tradition* (Eerdmans).

James Tabor

James Tabor, currently the Chair of the Department of Religious Studies at the University of North Carolina, is a former employee of Ambassador College and *Herbert W Armstrong's* Worldwide Church of God, although he severed ties with that organization many years ago. Still, he is a popular figure among some former WCG members, a number of whom assume his background gives him a similar understanding to their own about the Bible. He has particularly gathered support some among such folks for his "Original Bible Project," a new translation of the Bible in progress which purports to be more historically and linguistically accurate than previous translations because it takes into consideration more carefully the Israelite and Judaic background underlying the writings. However, most are unaware that Tabor no longer accepts Jesus Christ as Savior, nor does he accept the New Testament as inspired scripture. He is often featured as an "expert" on various matters of religion and history and prophecy on TV programs such as History Channel specials

Charles Taylor

One of the most prolific "date setters" in End Time Prophecy movement history.

The book *The End of Time* notes:

[Taylor,] One of America's most prominent prophecy teachers, organised a [1988] tour of Israel to coincide with [Edgar] *Whisenant's* date, [which predicted the Rapture to occur that year] priced $11,850 including 'return if necessary'. His publicity material used the possibility of Rapture from the Holy Land as a sales pitch: 'We stay at the Intercontinental Hotel right on the Mount of Olives where you can get the beautiful view of the Eastern Gate and the Temple Mount. And if this is the year of our Lord's return, as we anticipate, you may even ascend to Glory from within a few feet of His ascension."

It is surprising anyone would have paid attention to him by this time—Taylor had set no fewer than ten dates for the Rapture from 1975 through 1988. He then went on to make other predictions for 1989, 1992, and 1994. His death has likely been the only thing holding him back from continuing to set false dates right up to the present.

R. B. Thieme, Jr.

(1918-2009) Popular Bible teacher, founder of Berachah Church in Houston, Texas, referred to by his students as "Colonel Thieme."

The emphasis of Berachah is the dissemination, primarily by a huge collection of tape recordings, of Thieme's unusual teachings. The Berachah website notes that "Thieme teaches from the original languages of Scripture in the light of the historical context in which the Bible was written. He has developed an innovative system of vocabulary, illustrations, and biblical categories designed to communicate the truths of God's Word."

Although the doctrinal statement of Berachah Church would be "orthodox" by the standards of many Protestant denominations, many of Thieme's actual teachings are very controversial, and many if not most of his devoted students believe him to be the only ultimate source for accurate Bible interpretation. These students are referred to by themselves and by Berachah as "tapers," since their primary function seems to be to listen daily to Thieme's recordings. The tapes (and now MP3 files), currently over 11,000 hours of recording according to the Berachah website, are provided free of charge to all who request them, at the rate of 20 every three weeks.

One of his most controversial teachings has been the "Doctrine of Right Pastor." The implication of this doctrine is that each Christian has one and only one pastor who can provide him or her with proper guidance and teaching, and that thus each Christian should seek out that pastor and give him total loyalty and obedience. Given the extreme emphasis on Thieme's own idiosyncratic doctrinal interpretations in the Berachah scheme of things, it seems obvious that his students believe only Thieme himself or those he personally taught can possibly qualify as such a pastor. A number of websites evaluate some of Thieme's teachings, but the definitive analysis and overview of his earliest years is a book titled *Bob Thieme's Teaching on Christian Living* originally written in 1978 by Dr. Joe Wall as a Th.D. dissertation at Dallas Theological Seminary. It can be downloaded in pdf form from the Net at no charge at the URL below.

> http://ebookbrowse.com/thieme-by-joe-wall-pdf-d25792397

Dwight Thompson

Popular **Word Faith** evangelist, founder of Dwight Thompson World Outreach Ministries. Thompson is one of the inner circle on *Paul and Jan Crouch*'s Trinity Broadcasting Network and regularly appears on *Praise the Lord* shows and telethons on TBN. He has an extensive audio recording ministry which distributes his standard **Word Faith** (healing and prosperity) teachings.

Robert Tilton

One of the most obnoxious televangelists in history, with the most ludicrous style of soliciting funds on his show ... which was mostly what he did on that show. Indeed, what he still does—for even though he was exposed as a greedy, unethical, and conscienceless charlatan on national television in 1991, leading to the downfall of his ministry, he has made a startling comeback.

An article from 5/3/2003 in the *Tulsa World* newspaper summarized Tilton's fall.

> www.trinityfi.org/press/tulsaworld02.html

> In 1991, ABC-TV's "PrimeTime Live" program reported that Tilton's Word of Faith World Outreach Center Church, then based in Dallas, was making $80 million a year from followers through its direct mail campaign. At the time, Tilton's television show, "Success-N-Life," was broadcast by 200 stations nationwide and his church claimed 10,000 members.

"PrimeTime Live" suggested Tilton's ministry engaged in mail fraud and showed contributors' letters, many of them requests for help, in a trash Dumpster outside Commercial Bank of Tulsa. A Tulsa recycler said he also found thousands of prayer requests for Tilton's ministry among the waste sent to him by a company that handled Tilton's mail.

The program sparked an investigation by the Texas attorney general and numerous lawsuits. Stations canceled Tilton's television program until it eventually went off the air.

He divorced his first wife, Marte Tilton, in 1993, and married evangelist and former beauty queen Leigh Valentine the following year.

Two years later, his first wife sued for more than $1 million and his marriage to Valentine ended in a bitter public feud. Valentine alleged Tilton, in a drunken rage, verbally abused her, claimed he was the pope and thought rats were eating his brain. She eventually lost her claim to church assets.

Tilton has since married a Florida woman, Maria Rodriguez.

Tilton sold his Dallas church in 1999 for $6.1 million. At the time, headlines dubbed Tilton a "beleaguered TV preacher" and news coverage portrayed a man beset by marital and financial problems. But he was already well into his comeback.

During testimony in his divorce from Valentine, Tilton testified that he was bringing in about $800,000 per month and living aboard a $450,000 yacht in Fort Lauderdale, Fla. Records show the 50-foot yacht, named the Liberty Leigh, was registered to Tilton.

The Tulsa article offered several examples of solicitation letters sent to Tilton's mailing list, including the following two:

A thick mailing includes a large poster of Tilton with one hand raised and his eyes closed tightly, surrounded by 21 squares marking a calendar. The mailing includes 21 stickers that recipients are to peel off and affix each day to

247

the poster. It also includes a red "prayer of agreement miracle cloth" and three forms that recipients can return along with financial donations during each week of the 21-day prayer "campaign."

Tilton is pictured throughout the mailing grimacing in prayer, on his knees praying and clutching a red cloth and praying.

"Take the enclosed poster of me and my hand and put it up on your refrigerator or a mirror . . . somewhere so that you'll see it every day. Then every day for the next 21 days . . . lay your hand on top of mine and agree with me for your miracle," the letter states.

The letter also directs recipients to trace their hand on a "miracle request" form and return it with the red prayer cloth. Tilton promises to take the requests and cloths "to my prayer room or my prayer altar on my daily TV program, Success-N-Life."

The letter ends by requesting "your best financial gift as an expression of appreciation."

"You don't buy God but all throughout the Bible, when people came to God with prayer requests, they always brought a quality offering."

~~~~~

"I must tell you boldly: God wants to make you rich. . . . God wants to make a millionaire out of certain ones who receive this letter. Is it you?"

The letter includes a large slip of paper fashioned into a $1 million bill and a penny glued to the reverse side. The bill includes a checklist of desires, including a new home, new car, a piece of real estate or money for vacation.

"I want you to put a checkmark on the back of the Million Dollar Bill of what you need or desire, and send it back to me, along with a Seed Faith Gift of $200. . . . This ministry has given you spiritual food, so it's time to pay your tithes."

Who would respond to such blatantly phony pitches for money? A woman who worked on a temporary assignment opening letters for Tilton's ministry is quoted in the Tulsa article regarding the letters which accompanied donations to the ministry:

"You cannot help but read them," she said. "All these letters were like, 'Pray for me,' because they were terminal or their son is terminal or there was no money for food . . . desperate situations."

She said nearly all of the letters she opened were from rural Florida or rural Georgia and they often contained cash in odd amounts.

"There would be like $17, and the letter would say, 'I realize I have to give $2 more than I usually give.' "

She described the letter writers as lonely homebound people in rural areas wanting help from God.

Yes, inexplicably, Tilton has been able to make a successful comeback into televangelism. He is using the same type of goofy gimmicks he used over a decade ago to get people to send money ... and sadly they are still doing the job. The Tulsa World article includes the following amazing details of Tilton's current status:

More than 10 years after his ministry collapsed in scandal, Robert Tilton is reaching millions of television viewers with his pitches for money, living comfortably in south Florida and maintaining a connection with Tulsa.

Far from shrinking into obscurity, Tilton is reaping millions from his mailing list and daily shows on Black Entertainment Television. He has formed two companies, bought a 50-foot yacht and purchased a $1.3 million piece of oceanfront property in Miami Beach through his company, records show. _

An update on Tilton's recent activities in 2009 appeared in the *Dallas Morning New*.

www.rickross.com/reference/tv_preachers/tv_preachers7 9.html

Today, Tilton plies his trade on a Web site called streamingfaith.com. On the daily one-hour program called Robert Tilton Live! he promotes his patented Success N Life gospel, which generally postulates that God will reward donors with blessings that far outstrip the amount of the check they send to pastors such as Tilton.

Like any minister, he says he will pray for his donors and ask God to relieve their problems. But he is careful not to promise that their donations will work a miracle such as curing a loved one's illness.

Mr. Tilton, whose Web site says he has authored 25 books, currently is offering a free edition of How to Pay Your Bills Supernaturally.

Tilton still appears on cable's Black Entertainment Network, or BET, at 3 a.m. Mondays with reruns or new editions of Success N Life.

Ole Anthony, an East Dallas preacher who has watchdogged Tilton for years, said he is not surprised the old television warrior climbed aboard the Web.

"It's just another way for him to keep making those outlandish promises," said Anthony, founder of the Trinity Foundation and archenemy of Tilton. "And to replenish his mailing list with fresh names and addresses."

Tilton, who will turn 63 on June 7, also continues to reinvent his personal life in Florida. He and his 49-year-old wife became the proud parents of Elijah and Rebekah in January 2008.

The couple presented the girls on Tilton's Web site in April and let viewers watch them scuttle around the television studio for a few minutes before launching into their "prosperity" sermon.

"Yes, Bob changes diapers," Maria told viewers

Jack Van Impe

Televangelist specializing in End Times Prophecy speculations. Van Impe prides himself on the amount of scripture he has committed to memory—especially from the prophetic sections of the Bible, and promotes himself as "The Walking Bible" because of his ability to quote exact passages without notes during extemporaneous speaking. Van Impe and his wife Rexella co-host his daily television program, *Jack Van Impe Presents*. The show emphasizes almost totally speculation on connections between current world events and trends and Bible prophecy.

Two areas of concern which critics have about Van Impe's ministry:

1. His propensity to strong speculation on specific timing of the Second Coming: he has proposed numerous dates over the past three decades. In the early 1970s, he insisted that the Russians were going to conquer America by 1976. As with most bold prophecy speculators, the failure of that speculation didn't cause him to miss a beat. He came back year after year with fresh speculations. By 1999 he was predicting that Christ would return sometime between 2001 and 2012. He always claims, as do most bold prophecy speculators, that he isn't a "prophet" in the Biblical sense, but that his speculations are based on Bible study and insight from God. Unfortunately, also like most bold prophecy speculators, those who are enamored of his ministry ignore the numerous failures in his speculations and continue to view him as a "prophecy expert" ... even though almost none of the details of any of his speculations have ever panned out.

2. His surprising about-face in the mid-1980s regarding the Roman Catholic Church: in the early years of his ministry, he promoted the standard Baptist perspective that the RCC was identified with the End Time "false religion" which would be aligned with the Beast Power of Revelation and would persecute true Christians. In the mid- 1990s, he began regularly praising Pope John Paul II on his show, quoted enthusiastically from the Catholic *Catechism*, and chastised any Protestants who do not believe that they ought to seek "unity" with Catholics.

> We [Roman Catholics & himself] agree on the great fundamentals of the faith, ...I've been reading the Catholic Catechism, 2,865 points, backed with 5,000 to 6,000 verses of Scripture. This is the Word of God. Of course there are some things where I don't agree. But I find many of these things in our Protestant churches as well. But this thing blessed my heart. This piece of literature, saturated with the precious Word of God. (12/94 tape)

C. Peter Wagner

Key figure in the "Church Growth Movement" and major player in **Charismatic** circles promoting **power evangelism, spiritual warfare, signs and wonders, modern apostles and prophets**, and more. Wagner was formerly Professor of Church Growth at the School of World Mission at Fuller Theological Seminary. He coined the term **Third Wave**. He was at one time a close associate of **Vineyard** founder *John Wimber*, and he and Wimber created the Fuller course on "Signs, Wonders, and Church Growth" which has impacted churches all over the world.

Ron Weinland

Former minister with the Worldwide Church of God under its founder *Herbert W Armstrong*. Weinland incorporated The Church of God–Preparing for the Kingdom of God denomination in 2000, and began attempting to establish a name for himself as a "prophetic voice." In 2005 he declared to his small group of followers that he was one of the Two Witnesses described in the book of Revelation. (In time he announced that his wife was the other one.) In 2006 he announced that the Great Tribulation would start in 2008, and wrote a book about his timeline which he promoted widely on the Web. When that didn't pan out, he wasn't slowed for a moment. By fall 2009 he announced that he was also an Apostle, and then a month later that he was also the final embodiment of the Bible's prediction of an "Elijah to Come."

He has continued to shift his timeline for the End. As of summer 2011 he started insisting Jesus would return in May 2012. This didn't leave much time for a Tribulation (which he seemed to think previously was going to last for 3 ½ years) but as usual this hasn't deterred him. Inexplicably, he still has followers, who sacrifice to support his megalomania.

Edgar Whisenant

Author of the book *88 Reasons Why the Rapture Will Be In 1988*. Although many, many others had set dates for the return of Christ, going clear back to the earliest centuries AD, Whisenant was one of the first to be particularly successful in the 20th century using very widespread media efforts to call attention to his claims. Before it was all over, he had mailed 300,000 copies of his book free of charge to ministers all across America. And another 4.5 million were sold in bookstores. Others have since topped him in publicity, but his name, and particularly the name of his *88 Reasons* book, are still proverbial in prophecy circles.

Ellen G White

(1827-1915) Woman viewed as the only prophet/prophetess since Bible times by the Seventh Day Adventist Church. White authored many documents in the 1800s and early 1900s perceived as directly inspired by God, and providing much of the doctrinal foundation of the SDA denomination. As early as the late 1800s there were questions raised about evident plagiarism in her writings. And by the late 20th century clear documentation was established by researchers showing that a huge proportion of her writings had been plagiarized very directly from earlier writers. The SDA denomination has gone to extreme efforts in the past three decades to cover up or make excuses for this reality. The campaign has been largely successful among the most dedicated Adventists. But among those willing to look into the matter, the truth has greatly disturbed many and led to many leaving the denomination in disillusionment.

David Wilkerson

(1931-2011) Co-author of *The Cross and the Switchblade* (1963), a book about his efforts as a young pastor to reach gang members in New York City with the Gospel. It was made into a movie in 1969 starring Pat Boone as Wilkerson. Up to his death he was pastor of Times Square Church, an 8000-or-so-member church which he planted right on Broadway in New York City in order to be in the center of evangelism opportunities.

At one time he was most well-known for his Teen Challenge outreaches around the world that minister to troubled youths with illegal drug use and other problems. But in recent years Wilkerson had come to be viewed by many primarily as a "prophetic voice" in the modern **Charismatic** movement. This has not been based merely on strong Bible teaching, but on his claims of direct, divine inspiration for specific warnings he had issued about End Times events.

Unfortunately, many if not most of his dogmatic prophetic claims failed to come to pass as predicted. This would include the claims in His 1973 book *The Vision*, in which he shared what he claimed was a direct, divine vision from the Lord of soon-coming calamities on America. Depending on what you think "just ahead" and "very near future" mean, after almost 40 years it is questionable if this was truly a "vision from God" as claimed, or just, as with many such prognosticators, some personal speculation on what the future may bring.

John Wimber

(1934-1997) Founder of the Association of **Vineyard Churches** and author of many popular contemporary praise and worship songs. Wimber was a close associate of *C. Peter Wagner* at Fuller Theological Seminary, with whom he created the Fuller course on "Signs, Wonders and Church Growth" which has impacted churches all over the world.

Ron Wyatt

(1933-1999) Amateur archaeologist whose claims to have discovered, or definitively identified, numerous objects and sites with Biblical significance have been extremely controversial both before and after his death in 1999. These included the remains of the alleged "real" Noah's Ark, the graves of Noah and his wife, the "real" site of the crossing of the Red Sea (with claims to have found debris from the Army of Pharaoh at the bottom of the Red Sea at that spot), the "real" sites of Sodom and Gomorrah, and the Ark of the Covenant—with the blood of Jesus on the Mercy Seat where it allegedly dropped down through a crack in the rock above from the "real" site of the crucifixion. A dedicated Seventh Day Adventist, when he was speaking to SDA audiences, Wyatt explained that he found some of the guidance for these discoveries in the writings of SDA "prophetess" *Ellen G White*. Outside of SDA settings, he seldom mentioned any of this, as it would have no doubt diminished his credibility in many circles. His claims have been investigated closely by a number of researchers who have established them to be inflated at best and outright nonsense at worst.

Chapter 19

Afterword:
Personal from the Author

It was Thanksgiving week, 1978. My husband, George, our seven-year-old daughter, Ramona, and I were visiting friends for the four-day holiday weekend. We all sat around their TV watching an incredible story unfold on the news. Earlier that week, somewhere in a jungle clearing in a small, obscure South American coastal country named Guyana, authorities had come upon a horrifying tragedy. Over 900 bodies of adults and children, many of them American citizens, were found scattered around the grounds of a settlement named Jonestown.

What kind of fiendish terrorist group could have engaged in such a slaughter of innocent people, showing no mercy even to mothers and small children? It wasn't the work of terrorists. Most of the adults had committed suicide, deliberately drinking cups of fruit drink laced with cyanide from a big vat in the center of the compound where they were found. But first, those who were parents had administered the same poisonous brew to their own children. Death by cyanide poisoning is neither instantaneous nor painless. It is difficult enough to fathom how any adults could choose such a grisly death for themselves. But far beyond that—how could so many parents knowingly inflict such suffering on their own children?

As the weekend wore on, more and more incomprehensible details emerged about this mind-numbing situation. The suicides had occurred at the urging and command of the man for whom the settlement was named, Jim Jones. Jones had been, at one time, an honored humanitarian back in the United States, a Christian minister who reached out to the poor and disenfranchised, giving them hope. His "People's Temple" church organization in California attracted individuals of all races, eager to take part in the Temple's efforts to feed the hungry, house the homeless, and help addicts escape their addictions. By 1976, Jones was chairman of the San Francisco Housing Authority. Smiling photographs of him hob-nobbing with such public figures as President Jimmy Carter's wife Rosalynn gave evidence of the respect that he commanded in years past. By 1977 there were rumblings of possible sexual and physical abuse, as well as political and financial corruption, connected with the People's Temple. Some have speculated that this was a significant factor in Jones's decision to leave the country and take a group of his followers to Guyana. They expected to help him establish an experimental community, where the poor could go to get a fresh start, be self-sufficient, and escape what he portrayed as the rampant corruption of American society. Thus came the birth of Jonestown.

By 1978, over 900 people had cast their lot in with his vision, and left their extended families and their homeland to carve out a piece of a South American jungle and make it into a new home. But the Jim Jones of 1978 was not the same benign Jim Jones who had smilingly chatted with Rosalynn Carter. He had become what can only adequately be described as a paranoid megalomaniac, convinced of his own role as a messianic figure, and equally convinced that he and his followers would be unbearably persecuted by "the outside world." He had become a total dictator over the lives of his followers, micro-managing their every thought and move, and demanding total loyalty and obedience. His Christian theological roots were long gone, replaced by his own idiosyncratic belief system, with himself at the center.

Although he had managed to convince hundreds of adults in Jonestown to accept his own warped vision, there were some doubters within the ranks. They had begun leaking to the outside world—and the American authorities—troubling reports of what it was like to live under Jones's regime, rumors of physical cruelty, child abuse, sexual perversity, and more. An investigation was launched, and as Thanksgiving weekend 1978 approached, it became obvious that some intervention by the authorities might be imminent. Jones became aware of the threat that his total control over his followers might be about to end. Some dark recess of his tormented mind could not allow that; he was willing, rather, to die himself and to have them all die with him. A macabre audiotape was found of the events of that horrifying day. Jones can be heard ranting over the loudspeaker system of the community, urging parents to ignore the pitiful sounds of the suffering and dying all around them and do what they know they must do—administer the poison to their own children, and then take it themselves.

As the weekend wore on, and the unending commentary by newscasters and psychology pundits filled the TV screen, at one point I turned to George and said something like, "That's it. I can't go back. This is the same mind-set!" And he grimly agreed.

No, I had never been to Jonestown. In fact, I had never heard of Jim Jones before that day. I wasn't talking about going back to Jonestown. I was talking about going back to an environment that we had been a part of for a decade, one that had some eerie parallels with what I was watching unfold on the national news hour by hour.

Flashback

About 20 years before that dark Thanksgiving weekend, George was a bored young teenager trying to find something to do around the house one day. He rummaged through a stack of old magazines he found in the attic, and chose to flip through a *Capper's Farmer* from the previous December that his mother had kept for the Christmas recipes. In the back of the magazine he found an interesting display ad, with a coupon to clip out. It offered three free booklets and a free magazine subscription to anyone who would send in that coupon. The price was right, and the titles provocative, so George decided to take the advertiser up on the offer. The booklets were titled *1975 in Prophecy, The United States and British Commonwealth in Prophecy,* and *Will Russia Attack America?* The magazine was *The Plain Truth—A Magazine of Understanding.*

Thus began George's short career as a teen prophecy expert. The booklets and magazines that he received purported to lay out a detailed scenario for the events leading up to the Second Coming of Jesus Christ and the end of Man's rule on Earth. After a time of horrible tribulation, wars, famines, and more, Christ would come in person to set up a kingdom on earth that would last a thousand years, with the Christians of all the ages of history resurrected to life again and helping Him rule.

The publications waded with the reader through passages in the biblical books of Daniel, Revelation, and the Gospel of Matthew, and offered commentary to substantiate the scenario they so adamantly insisted was the plain truth. George, a total novice when it came to Bible study, bought it hook, line, and sinker. He began preaching it to his friends and classmates. He didn't seem to notice that the magazines did contain articles on topics other than prophecy—articles on biblical doctrines, Godly living principles, family relationships, and much more. For the prophecy articles were so compelling that it was difficult not to focus on them—"The End" was coming **before** 1975, less than two decades from when he began reading the literature!

The literature George received was published by an institution named Ambassador College in Pasadena, California. The editor of all the literature, and author of much of the material, was listed as Herbert W. Armstrong. It never occurred to George at the time to wonder who this Armstrong was, and why a college was publishing such literature. He just continued to collect the magazines as they came in month by month over the next few years, and eagerly read the articles about prophecy.

A New Convert

I arrived at Michigan State University as a freshman in the fall of 1964. Early the next spring I met George, who was a junior at the time. After a whirlwind courtship of a few weeks, we married. That whirlwind had not included any discussion of our respective views on religion. So I was quite surprised and taken aback when, a few days after we moved into our first apartment as man and wife, he brought home a stack of strange magazines from his parents' house and announced that they were the plain truth. I had no particular religious beliefs of my own, had never read the Bible, and was, for all practical purposes, an agnostic. After skimming some of the articles, I announced to him that it was a pack of fanatic nonsense and that he ought to throw them away. He didn't get around to doing that. Over the next few weeks, while he was away at work each day, I began looking at the magazines a little more closely. At first I did it just for amusement, to while away the boring summer afternoons while waiting for the fall semester at the University to begin. But it wasn't long before some of the claims I saw irritated me and prompted me to want to refute what they were saying.

I got out a Bible for the first time and started to rummage around in it, trying to dispute what I had been reading. A series of articles on Creation v. Evolution particularly irked me, and I went to the University science library and tried to find documentation to refute some of their observations regarding evolution. Weeks went by, and I started writing to the Ambassador College correspondence department to ask for answers to what I thought were airtight arguments against their material. Each time, an answer came back that made sense and made me question my own reasoning.

Every magazine included several offers for more free booklets on specific topics, from Bible prophecy to repentance, salvation, baptism, and more. Then there was the *Bible Correspondence Course* of 50 monthly lessons, also free. I began sending away for every booklet available, and working my way through the *Correspondence Course*. We were married in May 1965. By December 1965, I was totally convinced that the *Plain Truth* did, indeed, contain the plain truth about God and the Bible. George also began studying more than the prophecy articles, and came to the same conclusions. God did exist, the Bible contained His will for Mankind, we were doomed sinners in need of a Savior, we needed to repent and accept Jesus as that Savior and begin living a life pleasing to Him. But mixed in with those beliefs, on an equal level of certainty, was the conviction that we were indeed living in the very Last Days, and that Jesus would return to set up His Kingdom by 1975.

We also began listening to the radio program sponsored by the same Ambassador College. A Radio Log in the back of the *Plain Truth* magazine showed that it aired every day of the week on stations all over the country and around the world. The program was called *The World Tomorrow*, and the authoritative opening words of the announcer on the program always boomed out that you were about to hear the voice of Garner Ted Armstrong, who would be bringing you "The plain truth about today's world news, and the prophecies of the World Tomorrow!" It didn't take us long to figure out that Garner Ted Armstrong, who also wrote for the *Plain Truth* magazine, was the son of editor Herbert W. Armstrong.

What we still didn't realize, at that point in 1965, was that Ambassador College wasn't just a regular college. It was the training center for a church organization called, at the time, the Radio Church of God. (The name was changed to Worldwide Church of God in 1968.) The church organization had been founded in the 1930s by radio evangelist Herbert W. Armstrong. He began the college in the late 1940s, in order to have a place to train young men who believed his teachings to become ministers. Upon graduation, they would help him in building the church organization, planting church congregations across the country, and pastoring the people who would become members as a result of his media evangelism efforts.

Because Armstrong was convinced that a radio program that was overtly religious would turn off many people, he made the format more like a newscast. He also decided it would be better public relations if it was promoted as being presented by a college rather than a church. Although the name Radio Church of God occasionally showed up in the literature, we had no idea this meant that there was actually a real church denomination that had real congregations affiliated with the College. We thought it was more like the Billy Graham Evangelistic Association and the like, a "para-church" ministry that supported the college's efforts to publish religious literature and sponsor evangelistic radio programs.

We were also later to find out that Armstrong and other church leaders were so convinced that the Great Tribulation was scheduled to begin soon, including persecution of true Christians, that they literally wanted to keep the church hidden from the public eye. All congregations around the country met in rented halls such as school auditoriums and motel conference rooms. No advertisement of any kind noted their existence, and no one was allowed to attend the meetings without going through an interview process with an area minister and receiving a specific invitation to attend. Members were even admonished not to tell their own "unbelieving" family members where they attended church services.

Deeper in

By 1967 we were totally immersed in our studies with the literature from Ambassador College, and were sending 10 per cent of our gross income there. This was a *tithe*, as their teachings insisted we were obligated to give to God—through giving to "His Work," which was only being done on earth by Herbert Armstrong and his associates in the ministry. We requested that representatives of the ministry come to visit us and counsel us for baptism, still not realizing that once that happened we would be eligible to attend church services.

And thus in the fall of 1967 we made our first in-person contacts with representatives of Herbert Armstrong. Two men came to visit us in our home. After determining to their satisfaction (over the course of several such meetings) the sincerity of our dedication to the teachings we had been absorbing, we were invited to a "baptism counseling session" at a home over an hour from where we lived. Arriving that evening in January 1968, we found about a dozen other people there, all eagerly awaiting approval from the person in charge (we finally found out that he was the pastor of the area congregation of the Worldwide Church of God) to be baptized by full immersion in water. We all sat in a circle, and one by one he addressed each of us regarding final questions about our readiness to make a commitment to God through this ceremony. When he got to me, he noted that I wore skirts that were too short for appropriate modesty (they were knee-length). I would have to confirm that I would immediately remedy that before I could be approved for baptism. I eagerly apologized and made plans to go shopping for longer skirts. After everyone had been quizzed, and most were getting ready for the baptism ceremony, George went off to a side room with the minister to consult privately. I later found out that he had been secretly continuing to smoke cigarettes, which was forbidden by the teachings of the WCG, and he confessed this to the minister. He was admonished to go back to trying to quit, and when he could honestly report success, only then would he be permitted baptism.

I, however, was all ready. When my turn came, I sat down waist deep in water in a long, portable canvas cattle watering trough in the basement of the home of a WCG deacon, waiting to be tipped backwards by the minister into a position of full immersion. When that was accomplished and I sat up again in the trough, the minister announced that now I could come to weekly Sabbath services the following Saturday. I was startled, as I had no idea such meetings existed anywhere outside Ambassador College. Although he wasn't yet baptized, George was allowed a special dispensation to come with me to attend. (He was baptized in August that year himself.)

And thus began our sojourn of a decade as members of the Only True Church of God on Earth.

Life on the Inside

It didn't take long for us to discover that being a member of the WCG was much more complicated than just getting the literature. The nearest church congregation to our home was in a city over an hour away, but we were expected to be there every Saturday for worship services, Wednesday nights for Bible studies, and George was expected to make another trip weekly for "Spokesman Club" meetings (patterned after Toastmasters International.) And we were relatively close to the activities compared to some. We later met people who would drive 2, 3, 4, or more hours one way to attend the Sabbath services as often as they could. Some families even traveled as far as from northern Ontario to eastern central Michigan at least once a month, if not more. For although Herbert Armstrong's organization had grown by leaps and bounds throughout the 1950s, there were still only a few church congregations in each state, and very few throughout Canada.

People were expected to make whatever sacrifices in time, money, and energy were necessary to be a part in person of such congregations.

Then there were the rules ... rules for everything, rules often not mentioned on the radio program and in the literature offered to the public. Failure to faithfully obey these rules led to very unpleasant consequences, ranging from peer pressure to conform, to public censure from the pulpit at meetings, to potential disfellowshipment. Since this was the Only True Church, being on the outside looking in after being disfellowshipped was viewed as a fate worse than death. Those who had once been truly converted to the only true Way, as taught by the WCG, and who then fell away—apostacized—were obviously on the way to destruction in the Lake of Fire if they died before recanting and re-entering the fold.

Every area of life had rules that were not found clearly in the Bible, but that were established by the reasonings and idiosyncratic biblical interpretations of Herbert Armstrong. Men were not to have hair long enough to touch the collar of their shirts; women were not to have skirts short enough to show their knees when they sat down. Men were not to have beards—or a hairstyle with "bangs." Women were never to wear makeup of any kind. Men were absolutely required to wear a tie to any worship service. Women were not to wear slacks in public at all, except for sporting events or gardening and the like.

Doctors were only to be consulted for setting broken bones or delivering babies—all surgery, prescription drugs, and vaccines were condemned, as well as blood transfusions. Accepting medical intervention was tantamount to an admission that one did not trust God's promises in the Bible to heal. Herbal remedies, other "natural alternative health therapies," and chiropractic treatments, however, were acceptable. As a result of this doctrine, we watched a number of people over the years suffer needlessly from lack of medical treatment for both minor and serious conditions. Women died of treatable breast cancer, children were seriously injured or died from such conditions as appendicitis, and individuals chose to die rather than accept a blood transfusion after serious injuries such as car accidents. Herbert Armstrong's own first wife died in 1967 after an extended bout with an abdominal blockage. Many later admitted that it likely could have been easily treated with surgery, but instead she died a slow, painful death at home without even an aspirin to give slight relief.

By the end of Herbert Armstrong's own life, he had changed his own perspective on medical intervention that he had forced upon the church membership for many decades. In his waning years he had a private nurse in attendance at all times, took numerous prescription medications, and, toward the end, was reportedly receiving regular morphine shots. However, most of this was still kept from the membership, many of whom still avoided doctors and medicine because of the indoctrination they had received from his teachings for so many years.

"Natural foods" were highly recommended, in an era before most grocery stores carried a wide variety of 100% whole-wheat products and other minimally-processed foods, as they do now. This preference was, of course, a good thing from a health point of view. Unfortunately, it couldn't be just left at "wise advice," but had to be promoted to a doctrine, to the point that some ministers became "cupboard police," checking the kitchens of the homes of members for white sugar or white flour. If they found such worldly items, they might well issue a stern warning that God didn't take lightly the actions of those who would ignore that their "bodies are a temple of the Holy Spirit."

Sexual relations within marriage were viewed as a positive blessing—but only if the couple adhered to a narrow set of "approved positions." Birth control was acceptable, but not if it involved surgery or oral contraceptives. Voting and being involved in politics in any way was condemned. Listening to secular music was acceptable, but listening to contemporary religious music was unacceptable, as the songs might include references to doctrines condemned by the church. Individuals were not trusted to make their own evaluation of such matters, but were to defer to the church's ministry.

Divorce was absolutely forbidden (even for a woman forced to flee from a seriously physically abusive spouse). If a person was divorced at the time they requested baptism from the Church, they were never free to remarry again unless the first spouse was dead. In fact, if a person seeking baptism had been married and divorced once decades before, and they and their former spouse had both been remarried and raised children with their new spouses, the same rule still applied. They were viewed as in reality still "bound by God" to that first spouse. They were "living in adultery" with their second spouse, and would have to leave that mate and live a celibate life, or else they were not eligible for baptism. Many, many families were torn apart by this ruling, as new believers were so frightened at the prospect of coming under God's wrath that they were willing to abandon living with husband, wife, or children if necessary to "qualify" for baptism into the Only True Church on Earth.

Attendance at weekly Sabbath meetings and annual Holy Day observances, unless one was seriously ill, was mandatory, but holding a Bible study in one's home for a few friends without a WCG-ordained minister in attendance was forbidden. Sending a full tithe on the gross of one's income to the central headquarters was absolutely mandatory, and contributing generous "free-will offerings" beyond that was strongly encouraged. Regular monthly letters from Herbert Armstrong to the membership of the whole denomination often contained railing accusations that many in the church were not responding liberally enough to his many, many demands for "special offerings" for a variety of projects. These rants often included warnings that slackers who refused to respond generously might find themselves outside the protection of God when the really bad times at The End arrived.

And how was that protection to be provided? Herbert Armstrong did not teach a *Pre-Tribulation Rapture* doctrine, common among many End Times prophecy pundits today, as seen in the overwhelming popularity of the *Left Behind* series of books and movies. That doctrine postulates that, before the rise of the expected Antichrist, all true believers will be "snatched away" (the meaning of *rapture*) up to heaven to be with Jesus and ride out the Tribulation that follows immediately. At that point the Antichrist (also called The Beast, in reference to the vision of John in the book of Revelation) imposes the *Mark of the Beast* on all who worship him, and persecutes to the death any who refuse his mark.

No, Herbert Armstrong did not teach such a "vertical" rapture of the Church. He instead insisted that there would be a "horizontal rapture"—a very physical removal of all true believers ... those in the Worldwide Church of God ... to an earthly "Place of Safety" where they would be miraculously provided for and protected by God during the Great Tribulation. This was to happen, in his time schedule being promoted when we began attending with the WCG in 1968, some time before the spring of 1972.

Nuggets of gold

In spite of the many repressive factors involved in membership in the WCG, there were indeed good aspects to being a part of the organization during those years. Many of the members were truly just seeking with all their hearts to love God and love their spiritual family in the Church, and to be a part of supporting an outreach to the world with what they believed to be the True Gospel. Although some within the pastoral ministry of the Church were harsh and dictatorial, there were many men who truly did have a shepherd's heart and wanted to help those in their care to draw close to God and lead godly lives. Many life-long friendships were forged, friendships that lasted when, years later, the organization began crumbling. And not all activities were gloomy and serious. Lively church socials, picnics, and campouts were held regularly, featuring games, square dancing, sing-alongs, and more for families. Youth activities, including sports teams and teen dances with popular music, were liberally provided in many Church congregations.

And not all teachings of the church were related to esoteric prophecy theories and obscure doctrinal interpretations. Many articles, TV and radio programs, sermons, and Bible studies covered solid biblical doctrinal material and sensible advice for Christian daily living. Although members were expected to agree with the basic doctrinal interpretations of Herbert Armstrong, they were still admonished, encouraged, and helped to do extensive personal Bible study, much more than many denominations expect of their members. Weekly sermons were up to an hour and a half or more long, and were filled with many biblical references. All members were expected to take notes during sermons and turn in their own Bibles to every reference offered.

Church literature, sermons, and Bible studies were full of details of biblical and world history. Members were expected to be familiar with the flow of the story throughout the whole Bible and know about most of the main Bible characters, as well as be at least generally knowledgeable about such matters as the Tabernacle and Temple and their services, the missionary journeys of Paul, and much more. Most knew how to use *Strong's Concordance* to do word and topical studies, and were familiar with a variety of Bible dictionaries, commentaries, and other Bible helps. Thus, although the average member did read the Bible through the filter of the interpretations of Herbert Armstrong, he or she did know a lot more about why they believed what they believed regarding the Bible than the average member of many other denominations.

When Prophecy Fails

Still, the main focus of many average members by 1970 was a jittery expectation that times were about to get steadily worse, world conditions would rapidly deteriorate, and riots and famines and earthquakes would increase. *Plain Truth* articles of that time period predicted that race riots would turn U.S. cities into armed camps, and disease epidemics would decimate populations around the world in the very near future. A large proportion of the membership expected that the Church would be persecuted for teaching Truth.

At a critical juncture, some time between the fall of 1971 and the spring of 1972, a call would go out clarifying just how and when we'd be headed to that Place of Safety. By the mid-1960s, Herbert Armstrong had become convinced that the Place of Safety would end up being the ancient ruins of the city of Petra, in Jordan. If you saw the movie *Indiana Jones and the Last Crusade*, the pink buildings carved out of the rock of the canyon at the end of the movie were part of this archaeological location. This seems an odd place to put 100,000 or so people to hide them, but I found out in later years that Armstrong had not come up with the notion independently. Many prophecy students of the past century have looked at a few obscure passages in the prophetic sections of the Bible and deduced that this site would have some prominent part to play in the End Times.

And then the unthinkable happened. Spring 1972 arrived, and we were all still at home. World conditions, other than the ongoing Vietnam War, and occasional but very limited race riots in the U.S., were not really deteriorating. Herbert Armstrong had no explanation for the failure of what he had so long predicted. In fact, most members were stunned when he wrote to the membership and blamed **them** for overreacting to his teachings over many years about this topic, and jumping to conclusions. He insisted he had always just presented the 1972 date as a possible scenario, and never intended to get everyone's hopes up. This was an outright lie, but back in those days searchable computer archives of church literature were not available, so most could not actually show in print the level of deception of this approach.

Thus, when Armstrong insisted the failure of the date just meant that God was giving him more time to reach more people with his version of the Gospel, most went along with that explanation. When he continued to demand that church members needed to sacrifice more and more to help him "get the job done," many, if not most, dutifully dug deeper in their pockets. (For a psychological explanation for this sort of response by members of religious groups, see the chapter on *When Prophecy Fails.*) We were personally bewildered by it all, but since we still believed most of the Church's doctrines, we realized that it would be futile to look elsewhere for a place of fellowship—we were not aware of any group besides the WCG that believed as we did.

A Breath of fresh air

By the mid-1970s, Herbert Armstrong had embarked on a personal program of spending much of his time out of the country, visiting heads of state around the world to gather good will for the secular activities of Ambassador College. The college's projects included sending students to take part in an archaeological dig in Jerusalem, and sponsoring educational programs in villages in Thailand. Armstrong left the day-to-day administration of the church organization, as well as the publishing and broadcasting efforts, to Garner Ted. Ted had a much less narrow view of many doctrinal areas, and was willing to entertain the notion that perhaps the church needed to examine some of its historical doctrines and consider some changes. He also was willing to work toward some much-needed changes in church policies that would make the organization less secretive, less oppressive, and more open to the public. By the mid-1970s, a "Systematic Theology Project" (STP) was undertaken under his sponsorship by a number of leading ministers, to introduce a more scholarly approach to the teachings of the Church. Up to that point in time, there had been no official written statement of what the Church believed about basic doctrines, and why. Whatever Herbert Armstrong wrote in booklets and articles over the years had become part of a hodge-podge of doctrine, some of it conflicting, some of it based on very poor reasoning and biblical exegesis.

Around the same time, Herbert Armstrong, by then in his 80s, had a heart attack and became gravely ill. He was not expected to recover, or at least not to regain the kind of health and energy necessary to lead the Church any longer. Most expected he would either die or retire to a position of "elder statesman," showing up only for ceremonial functions. Heir apparent Garner Ted Armstrong was expected to take over the full reins of the church. This was viewed by many, at least in the local congregations, as a very good step forward.

Crisis

And then the unthinkable happened. In early 1978, Herbert Armstrong got up from his deathbed, and took back the reins. He was in a rage over the STP, as it was beginning to call into question some of his most cherished doctrines, including the ones related to medical care and to divorce and remarriage. He dismantled the project totally, and began re-instituting his old policies and procedures. In the final shock, he stripped Ted Armstrong of all of his responsibilities in the church, and soon after that kicked him out of the Church entirely. He was both disfellowshipped (denied the right to attend all church activities) and *marked* (publicly branded as someone to be totally shunned by all loyal church members). Any who would dare to ignore this marking, and have contact with Ted, would be viewed as in a position of disloyalty to the Church leadership, and would be disfellowshipped and marked themselves.

We had been so enthusiastic and encouraged over the changes that had been made in the previous two years, and so optimistic about the future of the Church. Now all that was dashed to the ground. Garner Ted Armstrong disappeared from sight, old radio programs made by his dad in the 1950s were resurrected to fill in the *World Tomorrow* radio time, and before long Herbert Armstrong was making his own new TV programs. These were almost embarrassing—the man was obviously feeble and rambling in his talks, but adamant to his supporters that he was being restored to his rightful position as God's Spokesman on Earth.

No one seemed to know—or be willing to talk about—what had really gone on at the Church's headquarters to get to this state of affairs. No clear explanation was made for Ted Armstrong's ouster. As the spring and summer wore on that year, I was amazed to see information offered and assertions made by Herbert Armstrong in letters and Church newspaper articles that I knew for a fact to be either distortions or outright lies. I happened to have a complete collection of all of the letters, newspapers, books, booklets, magazines, and other church publications we had received for many years. So, one day I sat in the middle of my living room floor, piled my collection around me, and got out a box of 3 X 5 index cards. I would read a current article by Herbert Armstrong in which he asserted, "I never said … " and then I would rummage through the pile of literature and nail down the fact that he had, indeed, "said" what he just said he never said. As I did so, I would record the documentation of that on a 3 X 5 card.

I was particularly amazed to find that he was able to lie boldly about things he had written only months or even weeks before. I could not understand how most of those around me in my local congregation, and leaders at the Church headquarters, could seem to be utterly blinded to these blatant contradictions. Most seemed to act as if nothing had ever happened, and that all was well.

Then the rumors started, hinting darkly at what had brought about the current state of affairs in the Church. There had been a "political" battle behind the scenes for power at the top of the church, between Garner Ted Armstrong and a handful of men close to Herbert Armstrong. There were threats and counter-threats to reveal shameful secrets regarding those in leadership. There were charges and counter charges of misuse of funds and other illegal activities.

Wanting to get to the bottom of this whole mess, I subscribed via mail to the local Pasadena, California, daily paper that had regular reports on the ongoing crisis involving Ambassador College and the WCG. I went out weekly to a nearby university library and skimmed that week's editions of the *Los Angeles Times* newspaper, which began running investigative reports on the Armstrong organizations. By summer's end I had a pretty good grasp of what was happening. The organization I had been part of for a decade and had believed to be the One True Church was, instead, a totally carnal human institution. It wasn't guided by the lead of the Holy Spirit, but by human good intentions at best … and politics of greed, corruption, and power grabbing at worst. The money so sacrificially contributed by loyal members wasn't going primarily to relieve the suffering of the poor and preach the Gospel to the world, but was, to a large extent, being invested in a mind-boggling array of luxuries for a few at the top.

Yet I also knew that not everyone wanted it to be thus. Even among the top leadership, I found that there were men who wanted to reform the institutions. So I held out some hope that maybe someone, somewhere, was planning a "coup" that would wrest control from the Bad Guys and take back the Church and the college.

Meanwhile, we found Garner Ted Armstrong. He had gathered a small following of disenfranchised folks like himself, started a church organization he dubbed the *Church of God, International* (CGI), and had begun his own radio program. We got on his mailing list, began receiving weekly tapes of his sermons and regular news reports of his activities, and began supporting his efforts. He made it clear that he wished to renounce many of the same things that had bothered us in the WCG, including the doctrines regarding medical care and the harsh divorce and remarriage position, and planned to start fresh both doctrinally and procedurally. Our fondest hope was that he could somehow gather a big enough following to go back to the WCG and "throw the rascals out," and we could all be together again.

This hope was in vain. It soon became obvious that many, if not most, of the church members refused to entertain the notion that something might be seriously wrong. Even when presented with documentation of financial improprieties and such regarding the Church leadership, they would turn a deaf ear, call it all lies, and avoid anyone who would try to convince them otherwise. Those who may have had some doubts were evidently too afraid to voice them to anyone, lest they find themselves on the way to the Lake of Fire. Part of this may have been due to the fact that Herbert Armstrong once again began darkly implying that it was almost time to "flee" to the Place of Safety.

Jonestown

And thus we reached that horrifying weekend when so many gave so much in loyalty to one man in a jungle in Guyana. It should be obvious by now why we saw parallels with our WCG experience. People in that organization had, indeed, allowed their children to die or suffer needlessly without medical attention out of loyalty to their Leader. Others had died themselves for the same reason. Families had been torn apart at the doctrinal whim of one man. (Armstrong had later changed the divorce doctrine—in time to marry a divorcee' less than half his age when he was 80—and then divorced her himself barely two years later.) People were ready to leave home, family, and country to move to a desolate place, also on the mere word of one man. And they were willing to do this in spite of increasing evidence that he was mentally unstable and deceptive. Over the years I have corresponded with a variety of people who had been loyal WCG members during that time period, who later left the organization. Some have admitted with a shudder that they believe they would have "drunk the Kool-Aid" if Herbert Armstrong had ordered them to back then. Many others, although sure they would have drawn the line at such a drastic step, admitted that they had made a number of foolish choices over the years that caused harm to themselves and their families based on the whims of Armstrong. (It was not uncommon for loyal members to mortgage their homes or otherwise go deep into debt in order to respond to one of Armstrong's many demands for money in times he would characterize as dire "crises" in The Work. Some have never fully recovered financially to this day.)

We never attended services with the WCG again. A few weeks later, we heard that we had been publicly "disfellowshipped and marked" from the pulpit of our former local congregation. The minister had been purposely vague on the "charges" brought against us. The bottom line was that we were disloyal to the leadership of Herbert Armstrong. Although a few more people eventually left also, and began later meeting with us, it was almost two decades before we ever heard from any of our former loving brethren in the WCG. Even our closest friends in the congregation never spoke to us again until the 1990s—when they also finally left the organization.

Onward

So we turned our back on the WCG that weekend in 1978. But we weren't yet ready to turn our back on involvement with an Armstrong. We became enthusiastic participants in Garner Ted Armstrong's new church. And by fall 1980 George was ordained as a minister in the CGI, and pastored a CGI church congregation for the next seven years.

Ted Armstrong did not claim to be heading the Only True Church. He didn't claim he would lead his followers to a Place of Safety. And he didn't impose his every whim on church members. But he did still encourage his supporters to believe that he was especially chosen and gifted by God to be the primary "prophetic voice" in the End Times, warning of the need for repentance before Jesus returned, and preaching a unique version of the Gospel not understood by many. We believed that for a few years. But reality slowly crept in. By 1987 we had become convinced that Ted Armstrong wasn't **all** that different from his father. He didn't micromanage member's lives, but he did intend that the organization itself come under his own authoritarian leadership. We finally realized that George could be removed from his ministerial role at any point in time at the whim of one man, if he disagreed on something important enough to that one man.

CGI ministers served as pastors at no pay or benefits. They had to support their families with full-time secular jobs. We finally realized that we had sacrificed time, energy, emotions, and finances for almost a decade of our lives in service to a local congregation. But the loyalty of the people in that congregation was so strong toward Garner Ted Armstrong that all our service would mean absolutely nothing if we ever got on the wrong side of that one man. A number of controversial policy issues had come up in 1987 that put us on a collision course with the central headquarters of the Church in general, and Garner Ted Armstrong in particular. So we decided to get the inevitable out of the way and get on with our lives.

In March 1988, we made our final break with the movement started by Herbert Armstrong. George resigned from his pastoral ministry, and told the congregation he could no longer whole-heartedly support the leadership of Ted Armstrong. Although there was no formal disfellowshipment policy in the CGI, almost all our former brethren in that organization cut us off totally.

In the ultimate irony, many of those people also left the CGI within just a few years. For one day in 1995, the *Geraldo Rivera Show* broadcast a video tape in which Garner Ted Armstrong was clearly shown stark naked (except for a dancing black dot on the screen) attempting to seduce a therapeutic masseuse in her massage room. He groped her body, tried to get her to touch his private parts, made numerous lewd remarks suitable to only dirty old men, and made it very obvious by his demeanor that this wasn't a one-time incident out of character, but was his true self. He even admitted to her that he was a minister of the Gospel, but was so important to "God's Work" that God would forgive the two of them if she'd only cooperate with him.

Not long after, it was also discovered that Armstrong, married and a grandfather, had been carrying on a five-year affair with a married woman in his local church congregation. And all of this latest scandal brought to light reports of numerous affairs he had conducted clear back before 1972 while he was the chief spokesman for the WCG. Unable to contain the growing scandal, the leadership of the CGI eventually cast Armstrong out of the Church he had founded. (He went on to just start up a new denomination within weeks, dubbing it the Intercontinental Church of God. As is all too common in the Wild World of Religion, he found enough gullible people to support him in his new efforts clear up to his death in 2003, in spite of his incredible record of deception and debauchery.)

When we finally made the break with the Armstrong movement, I realized that I had never dealt with the question of how we had been so easily misled by such men for so long. It was at that point that I decided to embark on a research project that would gather an overview of religious movements, examine the common threads of what attracts people to them, and investigate how some movements have succeeded in using deceptive and abusive methods to attract and keep members. I was particularly interested in those groups that had claimed to be the Only True Church (or the main one doing God's work on earth), claimed that they had "restored first century Christianity," insisted that The End was going to occur in their generation, and warned that only obedience to the leadership of their movement could guarantee safety during the chaos of the End Times. The term "Apocalyptic Groups" is often used to describe such movements.

I discovered records of numerous such groups, going all the way back over a thousand years. But I found that the most interesting and useful portion of this history involved those movements which have grown up in the U.S. in the past 200 years. So I eventually narrowed my studies to that time period. At the same time, however, I expanded the research to investigate many other types of groups beside the apocalyptic ones. For I found that the psychological factors that led to my own acceptance of unusual and unsubstantiated claims by religious leaders are present in many other types of groups.

This book, and the *Field Guide to the Wild World of Religion* website, are the result of over two decades of that research.

Chapter 20

Web Resources and Books for Further Research

Please Note: Inclusion of a website or book in this listing is **not** a blanket endorsement of all of the content of the site or book, particularly the conclusions and opinions of the authors. It is, rather, an indication that the site or book appears to contain generally reliable information and documentation which readers can use to come to their own opinions and conclusions.

Re: *archive.org* web addresses

A number of websites listed in the entries below start out with an URL of http://web.archive.org . These websites are no longer available on the public Web. But the *Internet Archive* website has retained digital copies of the websites from years past, accessible through what they term the "Wayback Machine." So although the extended URLs look odd, with two inclusions of http://, they will indeed take you to the websites cited.

Websites

Apologetics Index

www.apologeticsindex.org/

Self-description from the website:

Apologetics Index / CounterCult.com provides **research resources** on religious cults, sects, new religious movements, alternative religions, apologetics, anti-cult and counter-cult organizations, doctrines, religious practices and world views. These resources reflect a variety of theological and/or sociological perspectives. The site provides information that helps equip Christians to logically present and defend the Christian faith, and that aids non-Christians in their comparison of various religious claims. Issues addressed range from spiritual and cultic abuse to contemporary theological and/or sociological concerns. AI also includes **ex-cult support resources**, up-to-date **religion news**, articles on Christian life and ministry, and a variety of other features.

Believers In Grace Fellowship

www.believersingrace.com/

This is the website of the ministry of Bill Randles, a Pentecostal minister who writes excellent critiques of aspects of the current Charismatic scene which he finds troubling, including the Toronto Blessing Movement, the Modern Prophets and Apostles Movement, the Spiritual Warfare Movement and more.

Cross + Word Christian Resource

www.banner.org.uk

The Cross + Word website is the outreach of Tricia Trillin. Started in 1995 specifically to address what Trillin and her associates believed to be the negative impact of the Toronto Blessing Movement, it now has extensive documentation and commentary on all aspects of the general Charismatic Renewal and Revival Movement.

The Religious Movements Homepage Project

http://web.archive.org/web/20060907005952/http://etext.lib.virginia.edu/relmove/

This website was the brainchild of University of Virginia Professor Jeffrey Hadden (d. 2003). Hadden had taught a course at the University for years on "new religious movements." In 1995, he and some of his students began the creation of a website to supplement the research for the course. It has grown to include over 200 extended profiles of new religious groups, and extensive archives of much more information on the religious landscape of the 21st century. This is an academic website, and the approach is theologically neutral. It focuses on more of an "encyclopedia entry" style of presentation of information, in contrast to most of the other websites in this list. There are extensive weblinks for further research on the groups covered.

Rick Ross's Website

www.rickross.com/

Self-description from the website:

This website was created to offer the public a resource of information concerning controversial and/or potentially unsafe groups, which may have drawn some concern, attention and/or interest. Some groups listed and/or mentioned may have been called "cults." But the mention and/or inclusion of a group or leader within this website does not define that group as a "cult" and/or necessarily denote an individual, organization or group mentioned as either destructive and/or harmful. Instead, visitors to this website must exercise their own judgment after reviewing and considering the information provided.

Here you will find an archive that contains thousands of documents, which includes news stories, related research, reports, court records, book excerpts, personal testimonies and hundreds of links to outside reference resources.

Watchman Fellowship

www.watchman.org/watchman.htm

Self-description from the website:

Watchman Fellowship is an independent Christian research and apologetics ministry focusing on new religious movements, cults, the occult and the New Age. We serve the Christian and secular community as a resource for cult education, counseling, and non-coercive intervention. We accomplish these tasks through our church presentations, our magazine, The Watchman Expositor, personal counseling, this website, and other activities.

Books

The following books, among many other research materials, were consulted for information regarding the movements, groups, and teachers profiled in this *Field Guide*. Those wishing to do more extensive research on any of the topics covered may find this list useful as a starting point. Most of these books include extensive bibliographies of other books related to their specific topic. Many of these books are still available new from book stores and Internet book sellers. And some that are temporarily or even permanently out of print are still available through used book services such as those of Amazon.com . A few of the books on the list are available for free download through the Internet now, and links are provided to those websites where you may download your own copy, or read online. Also, many of these, both new and old, may be available to borrow through your local library via the Inter-library Exchange. Libraries in this network throughout the country regularly swap books from their collections upon specific request. Ask your local librarian for assistance.

Another Wave of Revival

Bartleman, Frank, Whitaker House, Springdale PA, 1962.

This is a revised reprint of a 1925 book that outlined the beginnings of the Pentecostal movement from the positive perspective of a man deeply involved in that movement.

Apocalypse Delayed: The Story of Jehovah's Witnesses

Penton, M. James, University of Toronto Press, Toronto ONT, 1985, 1997.

Author Penton, a retired professor of history and religious studies at the University of Lethbridge, Alberta, Canada, was a fourth generation Jehovah's Witness (JW) before being disfellowshipped in 1980. This volume is a scholarly, comprehensive overview of the movement, from its beginnings in the work of Charles Taze Russell in the 1800s, right up to the date of the 1997 revision of this book. It covers events, personalities, doctrines, organization, policies, and much more, as well as Penton's own commentary, evaluation, and extensive documentation from JW source material.

Armageddon Now! The Premillenarian Response to Russia and Israel Since 1917

Wilson, Dwight, Baker Book House, Gr. Rapids MI, 1977.

This is a fascinating, comprehensive history of prophetic speculation from 1917-1977, as seen in the periodicals published by evangelicals who promoted the pre-millennial view of End Times prophecy during that time period. From the book jacket:

> The author cautions his fellow pre-millenarians that they will lose their credibility if they continue to see in each political crisis a sure fulfillment of biblical prophecy—despite their obvious errors concerning earlier crises. They who pride themselves on interpreting prophecy "literally" end up interpreting it with what the author calls a "loose literalism." He also discusses such disturbing trends in the pre-millennial camp as anti-Semitism (which crops up despite the pre-millennialists' pro-Zionism) and indifference to social involvement.

275

Beware the New Prophets: A Caution Concerning the Modern Prophetic Movement

Randles, Bill, 1999.

Distributed by Believers in Grace Fellowship, 8600 C Ave., Marion IA 52302 (319) 373-3807.

Written by a Pentecostal pastor who cannot be charged with being "prejudiced" against such phenomena as speaking in tongues, this is one of the most effective and balanced overviews available of the Modern Prophets and Apostles Movement within Charismatic circles.

Beware This Cult!: An insider exposes Seventh-day Adventism and their false Prophet, Ellen G. White.

Hunt, Gregory, M.D., 1981.

Chapters 6-18 of this book, sections specifically dealing with Ellen G. White, are available at the URL below. This book particularly deals in detail with the origin of the "health reform" teachings of Ellen G. White.

www.ellenwhite.org/btc

Beyond Mormonism: An Elder's Story

Spencer, James R., Fleming H. Revell, Old Tappan NJ, 1984.

Author Spencer was a convert to Mormonism, and active as an elder, teacher, and more for ten years. He then became disillusioned with the doctrines of the Church, and eventually was disfellowshipped. He later became a pastor in an evangelical church. This volume is a very chatty, informal description of that spiritual journey, and the trauma he and his family experienced around the time of his disfellowshipment.

By His Own Hand Upon Papyrus: A New Look at the Joseph Smith Papyri

Larson, Charles M., Institute for Religious Research, Gr. Rapids MI, 1985, revised 1992.

The complete text of this book is now available for free download at:

www.irr.org/mit/Books/BHOH/bhoh1.html

In 1835, Joseph Smith and the early Latter-day Saints came into possession of some authentic Egyptian mummies, along with some papyrus scrolls that had been with them. Smith claimed to be able to translate the ancient Egyptian writings on the scrolls, and to have discovered that one of them contained the actual writings of the patriarch Abraham done "by his own hand upon papyrus." He proceeded to translate a portion of the writing, creating what is now known in the LDS church as the *Book of Abraham*, a document that establishes some distinctive Mormon doctrines. The scrolls were lost in the 1800s, but resurfaced in the 1967. Larson's book chronicles the history of the documents, and the chaos that resulted in the LDS church when the original papyri used by Smith were shown by modern scholarship to have no connection at all with the claims made for them by Smith. The book includes a full color foldout facsimile of the papyri in question

The Case of D.M. Canright

Douty, Norman, Baker Book House, 1964.

The complete text of this book is now available free download at:

www.ellenwhite.org/canright/case.htm

From the Introduction by the author:

Mr. Canright was in Seventh-day Adventism for 28 years, rose to prominence therein, and then left it (in 1887). He subsequently wrote several books and pamphlets that have proved very damaging to the cause he had formerly espoused. Elder D. A. Delafield, Associate Secretary of the Ellen G. White Publications, told me on July 15, 1962, that Canright has been the most potent adversary Adventism has had during the past eight decades. Ever since Canright left them, the Adventists have been doing all in their power to undermine his testimony against their movement. It is true, he was carried to his grave over forty years ago, but since some of his writings continue to be published, his critics keep active. I have recently been told by some Adventists that their church plans to prepare a 'Life of Canright.' The object, naturally enough, will be to discredit him so thoroughly, that none will ever again venture to quote him as a witness against Adventism.

...Since Canright's death a number of articles have been published in his defense, but they have been rather limited in scope. In view of all the relevant facts, it seems that the time is long overdue for a thoroughgoing account of him to be written, so that everyone may see for himself that his testimony deserves serious consideration

...Having now accumulated a mass of information concerning Canright—such as no other, to my knowledge, possesses—I consider it a sacred duty to share it with the public, especially because it serves to demonstrate the character of the Adventist movement. Before I begin, however, I wish to make a few things plain:

1. I make no use whatever of rumor or hearsay; when I refer to false assertions, I refer either to statements which Adventists have made in conversation with me (or in letters to me), or to materials emanating from them which are in my possession (including photostats).

2. I do not necessarily subscribe to all of Canright's views, but any minor dissent from them involves no reflection on either his sincerity or his ability as a teacher of God's Word.

3. I bear no ill will toward the person of any Adventist. However, this will not prevent me from speaking plainly of those who are manifestly guilty of evading, suppressing or distorting facts. In such cases, I shall only consider my duty to God and to His people.

The Changing World of Mormonism

Tanner, Jerald and Sandra, Moody Press, Chicago IL, 1980.

The complete text of this book is now available free download at:

www.utlm.org/navonlinebooks.htm

This book, written by former dedicated Mormons (Sandra is a great, great granddaughter of Brigham Young) is an exhaustive investigation into the history of Mormonism and the many changes in doctrine within the organization made in recent decades. Many teachings which were formerly touted to be established by direct divine revelation to LDS founder Joseph Smith and later Prophets of the Church have been changed without any explanation how God could have changed His mind. The Tanners provide extensive documentation regarding these matters, including photo-reproductions of actual early Mormon publications. If you would like a hardcopy version, it is still in print also.

Charismatic Chaos

John F. MacArthur, Jr., Zondervan Publishing House, Grand Rapids MI, 1992.

From the back cover:

The charismatic movement of the past quarter-century has made an impact on the church unparalleled in history. But one legacy of the movement is confusion and mushy thinking. In Charismatic Chaos, John F. MacArthur calls for biblical evaluation and analyzes the doctrinal differences between charismatics and non-charismatics in the light of Scripture. "My principal concern," writes John MacArthur, "is to call the church to a firm commitment to the purity and authority of the Scriptures, and thereby to strengthen the unity of the true church." To tough questions that seem to divide, Charismatic Chaos provides tougher answers that strive to unite. This book tackles such questions as - Is experience a valid test of truth? - Does God still give revelation? - Prophets, fanatics, or heretics? - Does God still heal? - What should we think of the Signs and Wonders movement? - Does the Bible promise health and wealth?

Counterfeit Revival: Looking for God in All the Wrong Places

Hanegraaff, Hank,Word Publishing, Dallas TX, 1997.

Publisher's description:

Hank Hanegraaff documents the danger of looking for God in all the wrong places and goes behind the scenes into the wildly popular and bizarre world of contemporary revivalism. Hanegraaff masterfully exposes the stark contrast between these deeds of the flesh and a genuine work of the Spirit by contrasting modern "revivals" with the scriptural examples of God's movement among His people.

Crisis of Conscience: The struggle between loyalty to God and loyalty to one's religion

Franz, Raymond, Commentary Press, Atlanta GA, 1983.

This is an overview of the crisis in the Jehovah's Witness (JW) movement by a former JW headquarters leader. This book is the single most helpful source of information and commentary regarding concerns about the Jehovah's Witnesses and the Watchtower Bible and Tract Society (WBTS). Raymond Franz was a former member of the Governing Body of the JW organization. His uncle, Fred Franz, was the WBTS president and the head of the Governing Body, the single most influential leader in the organization, from 1977-1992. A period of turmoil within the JW organization in the late 1970s and early 1980s led to the expulsion of Raymond Franz and a number of other JW leaders, along with tens of thousands of members. Franz's book chronicles and documents carefully this whole episode. In the process, he gives an extremely vivid view behind the scenes of the organization.

The Daughter of Babylon, The True History of the Worldwide Church of God

Renehan, Bruce

A 130 page book available free in its entirety for download at:

www.herbertwarmstrong.com/babyindex.htm

Renehan was a member of the Worldwide Church of God (WCG) for 23 years. He first became involved with the organization in 1969, and was employed at the Pasadena headquarters of the church in 1970, working for the church for seven years. This book gives a broad overview of the history of the church, with quite a bit of documentation. But its particular emphasis is on the author's research into the WCG's notion of "church history." WCG writers constructed an idiosyncratic view of history which they used to establish the work of Herbert Armstrong as the head of the "Philadelphia Era" of an unbroken sequence of Sabbatarian "church eras" through history that allegedly included the Waldenses and other obscure religious groups of the past 2000 years. Renehan offers extensive historical documentation that brings many facets of this scenario into question.

A Different Gospel

McConnell, D.R., Hendrickson Publishers, Peabody MA, 1988, 1995.

From the cover: "A bold and revealing look at the biblical and historical basis of the Word of Faith movement"

The Disappointed: Millerism and Millenarianism in the Nineteenth Century

Edited by Numbers, Ronald L. and Butler, Jonathan M., Indiana University Press, Bloomington and Indianapolis IN, 1987.

This is a scholarly work, compiling research by a number of historians who have studied the influence of the predictions of William Miller in the development of religious groups and movements in the 1800s.

Doomsday Delusions: What's Wrong with Predictions about the End of the World?

Pate, C. Marvin; Haines, Calvin B. Jr., Intervarsity Press, Downer's Grove IL, 1995.

Publisher's description:

Doomsday prophecy is on the rise. With the year 2000 upon us, we hear more and more predictions of the end - whether from well-meaning Bible believers or from self-appointed cult leaders. What will happen if unwary believers get caught up in a false millennial fever? How can we prepare to face the challenges of end-of-the-world predictions? What can we do to maintain our hope in the return of Christ without succumbing to doomsday delusions? Marvin Pate and Calvin Haines dispel the myths of many popular doomsday prophets, showing how they misinterpret and misapply the Bible. They then examine the social and psychological consequences of the doomsday mentality and offer a constructive view of how the expectation of the Lord's return should affect our lives today.

The Encyclopedia of American Religions: Three Volumes

Melton, J. Gordon, Editor, Triumph Books, Tarrytown NY, 1989.

The 2009 version of this encyclopedia, which is now bound in one massive book, sells on Amazon.com for over $400. But used copies of the paperback version of 1989 listed above are occasionally available through Internet booksellers at a very low price. And used editions between 1989 and 2009 are also available from used booksellers at a reasonable price. Although later editions would have more details on the latest new groups, and more updated statistics and current facts on old groups, the extensive history of the religious families, and the history of hundreds upon hundreds of older groups covered would be similar in all editions.

The description below is regarding the 2002 hardbound edition, and thus the number of religious groups covered is greater than that in the 1989 edition.

Editorial review from Book News, Inc.:

It provides current and detailed information on 1,588 religious groups, ranging from Adventists to Zen Buddhists. The essays provide descriptions of the historical development of the major religious families and traditions in the United States and Canada. Separate religious groups are categorized by major religious family, such as Western Liturgical Family, Pietist-Methodist Family, Pentecostal Family, and Baptist Family. The second section gives factual and descriptive information about each of the 22 religious families. These listings furnish such facts as full names, addresses, contacts, descriptions, membership data, educational institutions, and other information about the individual churches, religious bodies, and spiritual groups. Indexed by religious organizations; publications; location; personal name; educational institution; and subject.

End Time Visions: The Road to Armageddon?

Abanes, Richard, Broadman & Holman Publishers, Nashville TN, 1998.

This is an overview of the history of prophetic speculation.

The Faith Healers

Randi, James, Prometheus Books, Buffalo NY, 1987.

This is an exposé of some of the most flamboyant evangelists of the Healing Ministries Movement of the time, by professional de-bunker and former stage magician, "The Amazing Randi." Some of those covered are still plying their trade.

Fire from Heaven: The rise of Pentecostal spirituality and the reshaping of religion in the twenty-first century

Cox, Harvey, De Capo Press, div. of Perseus Books, Cambridge MA, 1995.

Publisher's description:

It was born a scant ninety-five years ago in a rundown warehouse on Azusa Street in Los Angeles. For days the religious-revival service there went on and on-and within a week the Los Angeles Times was reporting on a "weird babble" coming from the building. Believers were "speaking in tongues," the way they did at the first Pentecost recorded in the Bible-and a pentecostal movement was created that would by the start of the twenty-first century attract over 400 million followers worldwide. Harvey Cox has traveled the globe to visit and worship with pentecostal congregations on four continents, and he has written a dynamic, provocative history of this explosion of spirituality-a movement that represents no less than a tidal change in what religion is and what it means to people. Daniel Mark Epstein, the acclaimed biographer of the evangelist Aimee Semple McPherson, calls Fire from Heaven "a breathtaking story [written] with a novelist's feel for history, a philosopher's clear insight, and a reporter's eye for detail." And the Boston Globe hailed Harvey Cox as "an ideal guide for a pilgrimage through an unfamiliar religious world...able to demystify without desanctifying."

The Gentile Times Reconsidered: Chronology and Christ's Return

Jonsson, Carl Olof, Commentary Press, Atlanta GA, 1983, 1998.

This is a detailed evaluation of the Jehovah's Witness's speculations regarding End Times prophecy.

God Is a Millionaire

Mathison, Richard, Charter Books, Bobbs-Merrill, Indianapolis IN, 1960

This book was issued in hardback under the title *Faiths, Cults and Sects of America*. The cover description notes that it "reveals the strange beliefs, the swindles, the bizarre teachings and frequently erotic rituals into which millions of Americans pour their faith and money."

God Wants You Rich and Other Enticing Doctrines

Bulle, Florence, Bethany House, Minneapolis MN, 1983.

(This book was later expanded and updated in 1989, and released under the title *The Many Faces of Deception*.)

Publisher's description

Provides biblical guidelines for examining controversial movements such as the prosperity gospel, inner healing, and

283

the New Age. Balanced and thought—provoking, it shows the truth on false teachings in the church.

Herbert Armstrong's Tangled Web

Robinson, Dave, John Hadden Publishers, Tulsa OK, 1980.

This is an exposé of the Worldwide Church of God by a former WCG minister.

The description of the late Dave Robinson from the back cover of the *Tangled Web* book:

> He began to listen to Herbert Armstrong on the radio from a Mexican station in 1949 and became a heavy financial contributor soon after. He met HWA [Herbert W. Armstrong] the next year and became a member and supporter of what was then the Radio Church of God. He supported Herbert Armstrong for a full three decades. In 1969 he went to work full-time for the Worldwide Church of God several years after his ordination as a minister in that church. During the next decade, he served in varied capacities for that organization. He came to know most of the top men of the church well, and is eminently qualified to write of the workings of those echelons of the church. Among the responsibilities carried by Dave were those of administrator, counselor, lecturer, security chief, and minister. He was a confidant of many of those men who have either been removed from the church altogether or have been relegated to dishonor within that organization. He writes from firsthand knowledge tempered with deep disappointment and has come to agree completely with Solomon who advised against putting trust in men.

Robinson's book contains the most intimate view of the inner workings of the organization, and the most candid of descriptions of many of the principle players in the saga, of any of the books available on Armstrongism.

A Historical Sketch of the Brethren Movement

Ironside, H.A., Loizeaux Brothers, Neptune NJ, 1985.

This is an historical, scholarly overview of a movement of the 1800s that has had wide influence down to the present through the dissemination of some of its unique teachings.

Holy Laughter & The Toronto Blessing: An Investigative Report (PRO)

Beverley, James A., Zondervan Publishing, Grand Rapids MI, 1995.

Publisher's description:

Professor Beverley is one of Canada's leading scholars of contemporary religion. This provocative study of the Vineyard movement offers a tough but redemptive analysis of the promise and perils of charismatic Christianity. This report is the place to start for careful investigation on Holy Laughter and The Toronto Blessing.

Holy Relics or Revelation—Recent Astounding Archaeological Claims Evaluated

Standish, Russell R. and Colin D., Hartland Publications, Rapidan VA, 1999.

This is a critical examination of the claims of the late amateur archaeologist Ron Wyatt. The authors, like Wyatt was himself, are dedicated members of the Seventh Day Adventist denomination.

Promotional description from the publisher:

For the devout Christian, faith is in the revealed Word. When biblical archeology confirms the Scriptures, it stirs the heart. biblical archaeologists have gathered data with painstaking effort. Their work proves the accuracy of the Bible. Yet mostly within a single decade, Ron Wyatt sought out and claimed the most amazing biblical sites and relics. In this book, the Standish brothers examine the Wyatt claims in-depth, going beyond his videotaped claims. These findings can serve as a benchmark upon which Ron Wyatt's "discoveries" can be more carefully evaluated.

The 300 page paperback book is available for order via the web at
www.hartlandbooks.com//ez-catalog/X311787//HREL1

An e-book version is available, at half the price, also:
www.hartlandbooks.com//ez-catalog/X311787//HREL1-EB

I Was Raised a Jehovah's Witness: The True Story of a Former JW

Hewitt, Joe, Accent Publications, Denver CO, 1979.

This is a very personal account of one man's involvement with the JW movement.

In Search of Christian Freedom

Franz, Raymond, Commentary Press, Atlanta GA, 1991.

This is an overview of Jehovah's Witnesses by a former JW Headquarters leader, a sequel to his *Crisis of Conscience* book. (See the listing for that book above.)

The King James Only Controversy: Can You Trust the Modern Translations?

White, James R., Bethany House Publishers, Minneapolis MN, 1995.

This book provides an overview of the issues raised by those in the *King James Only* movement.

The Last Days Are Here Again

Kyle, Richard, Baker Book House, Gr. Rapids MI, 1998.

Publisher's description:

Rather than simply focusing on specific time periods or movements, Kyle takes a comprehensive look at the history of thought about the end times, offering a fair treatment of various millennial positions by incorporating an intellectual/cultural approach. Kyle also takes a look at secular apocalyptic thought and end-of-the-world ideas espoused by fringe groups such as the Heavens Gate cult. Anyone curious about end-times speculation or interested in prophecy and history will find The Last Days Are Here Again an intriguing resource.

Life of Mrs. E.G. White—Her Claims Refuted

Canright, D.M., 1919.

The complete text of this book is available for free download at:

> http://web.archive.org/web/20041029025200/http:/www.ellenwhite.org/canright/egw16.htm

Norman Douty, in the Introduction to his book *The Case of D. M. Canright*, explains the significance of author Canright this way (see the entry for Douty's book above):

"Mr. Canright was in Seventh-day Adventism for 28 years, rose to prominence therein, and then left it (in 1887). He subsequently wrote several books and pamphlets that have proved very damaging to the cause he had formerly espoused. Elder D. A. Delafield, Associate Secretary of the Ellen G. White Publications, told me on July 15, 1962, that Canright has been the most potent adversary Adventism has had during the past eight decades."

Making War in the Heavenlies: A Different Look

Randles, Bill, 1994.

Distributed by Believers in Grace Fellowship, 8600 C Ave., Marion IA, 52302, (319) 373-3807, 1994.

This is one of the most effective and balanced overviews available of the Spiritual Warfare Movement popular within many Charismatic circles. Author Randles is a Pentecostal pastor who cannot be charged with being "prejudiced" against standard Charismatic phenomena, since he embraces some of them, including speaking in tongues, himself.

The Maze of Mormonism

Martin, Walter, Vision House Publishers, Santa Ana CA, 1962, 1978.

This is an overview of the history and doctrines of Mormonism.

The Mormon Corporate Empire

Heinerman, John and Shupe, Anson, Beacon Press, Boston MA, 1985.

From the back cover:

[The authors] have looked behind the public image of the LDS Church to find a tremendously powerful financial empire with a distinctly authoritarian ideology. The authors document carefully how the Mormon Church has sought to extend its economic, political, and theological influence into nearly every sector of American life, from communications to the CIA, from government to the military. *The Mormon Corporate Empire* is a thorough examination of Mormonism as a corporate entity that influences the lives of all Americans.

The Mormon Papers: Are the Mormon Scriptures Reliable?

Ropp, Harry L., Intervarsity Press, Downer's Grove IL, 1977.

From the back cover:

Harry Ropp discusses the Mormon teachings on God, Christ, salvation and the Bible. But he concentrates on the evidence and the theories for the origin of the Book of Mormon. He cites internal inconsistency and the absence of archaeological evidence to question its credibility. Then he demonstrates the inauthenticity of key Mormon documents by uncovering Joseph Smith's spurious translation from the Egyptian papyri. A final, practical chapter makes the book valuable for those who wish to encourage Mormons to examine the basis for their own faith."

Mormonism 101: Examining the Religion of the Latter-day Saints

McKeever, Bill & Johnson, Eric, Baker Books, Gr. Rapids MI, 2000.

From the back cover:

In this accessible, informative introduction to Mormonism, [the authors] compare the main points of Mormon theology to orthodox Christianity. How do Mormon beliefs about God, man, Scripture, salvation, and revelation differ from those of Christianity? The authors' point-by-point study includes helpful summaries at the end of each major section. ... With a wealth of firsthand experience working with Mormons, the authors provide practical witnessing tips, in dialogue form, at the end of each section.

Mormonism, Mama & Me

Geer, Thelma, Christian Literature Crusade, Fort Washington PA, 1979, 1984.

From the back cover:

Thelma Geer's great-grandfather was the adopted son of Brigham Young and a very well-known Mormon pioneer. John D Lee had 19 wives and 64 children! This is an intensely personal view of Thelma's life, her Mormon heritage, and her conversion to the real Jesus Christ. In addition to her own story and that of her beloved Mama, Thelma also examines several major doctrinal aspects of Mormonism under the searchlight of biblical truth. Her unique approach sets this book apart from many contemporary works dealing with Mormonism. Thelma deals with the real Mormonism—that

Mormonism which traces its roots directly to Joseph Smith and Brigham Young."

Mormonism Unmasked

Roberts, R. Philip with Davis, Tal & Tanner, Sandra, Broadman and Holman, Publishers, 1998.

From the back cover:

Based on years of research and study, this detailed and accurate resource clearly explains the Mormons' basic beliefs, then soundly refutes their subtle heresies while exposing secrets that Mormon authorities don't want you or even many of its own followers to know about. After walking you through the Mormon's confidential evangelistic strategies, *Mormonism Unmasked* then provides specific techniques on witnessing to Mormons, giving you the tools and the confidence you need to effectively and lovingly defend the Christian faith.

Naming the Antichrist: The History of an American Obsession

Fuller, Robert, Oxford University Press, New York NY, 1995.

Publisher's Description

The Antichrist, though mentioned a mere four times in the Bible, and then only obscurely, has exercised a tight hold on popular imagination throughout history. In Naming the Antichrist, Fuller takes us on a fascinating journey through the dark side of the American religious psyche, from the earliest American colonists right up to contemporary fundamentalists such as Pat Robertson and Hal Lindsey.

Fuller begins by offering a brief history of the idea of the Antichrist and its origins in the apocalyptic thought in the Judeo-Christian tradition, and traces the eventual migration of the Antichrist legend across the Atlantic. He shows how the colonists saw Antichrist personified in everyone from native Americans to the Church of England. He looks at the Second Great Awakening in the early nineteenth century, showing how such prominent Americans as Yale president Timothy Dwight saw the work of the Antichrist in phenomena ranging from the French Revolution to Masonry. In the twentieth century, Fuller finds a startling array of hate-mongers, such as the Ku Klux Klan, who drew on apocalyptic imagery in their attacks on Jews, Catholics, blacks, socialists, and others. Finally, he considers contemporary fundamentalist writers such as Hal Lindsey and a host of others who have found Antichrist in the sinister guise of the European Economic Community, feminism, and even supermarket barcodes and fibre optics.

Throughout, Fuller reveals in vivid detail how our unique American obsession with the Antichrist reflects the struggle to understand ourselves--and our enemies--within the mythic context of the battle of absolute good versus absolute evil.

National Sunday Law—Fact or Fiction?

Anderson, D., 1999.

The complete text of this book is available for free download at:

http://web.archive.org/web/20070429233916/http://www.el lenwhite.org/egw22.htm

A 1983 book by SDA Pastor A. Jan Marcussen titled *National Sunday Law* has been zealously spread by dedicated SDA members to their friends, family, neighbors, door to door, and on the Internet since its publication right up to the present. The book insists that there is an immediate threat in the U.S. that individuals will soon be restrained by governmental authorities from worshipping on any day but Sunday, under the eventual threat of the death penalty. What most readers do not realize is that Marcussen is only the most recent in a long line of Adventist teachers who have dogmatically insisted that this threat was about to come to pass in their own lifetime. The earliest to widely disseminate this teaching was Adventist pioneer and alleged prophetess Ellen G. White, clear back in the mid-1800s. Anderson documents the long history of the SDA insistence that this Sunday Law is "imminent."

The New Charismatics: A Concerned Voice Responds to Dangerous New Trends

Moriarty, Michael G., Zondervan Publishing House, Gr. Rapids MI, 1992.

This is a broad overview of Pentecostal/Charismatic history, with emphasis on the more recent developments, such as the Modern Prophets and Apostles, Dominion Theology, and Spiritual Warfare movements.

Pilgrimage Through the Watchtower

Quick, Kevin R., Baker Book House, Gr. Rapids MI, 1989.

The complete text of this book is available on the Internet for free download at:

www.kevinquick.com/kkministries/books/pilgrimage/index.html

This book contains the personal story of one man's experience within the Jehovah's Witness movement.

Rebellion, Racism and Religion: American Militias

Abanes, Richard, Intervarsity Press, Downer's Grove IL, 1996.

Publisher's description:

After the Oklahoma City bombing, Americans became aware of the alarming growth of paramilitary groups over the previous several years. This ominous development has arisen from a volatile mixture of frustration with the government and deep-seated religious beliefs that are primarily apocalyptic. The zeal, unity, plans, and, in many cases, the hatred and paranoia exhibited by those involved with such groups are fueled by the sense that we are near the end of the world. The racist attitudes common among paramilitary organizations are also too often rooted in religious ideas. Understanding the beliefs of militant extremists as we approach the year 2000 - a crucial turning point for many paramilitaries - is critical if social disruption and perhaps even violent confrontations are to be avoided. American Militias seeks to inform the reader exactly what is being taught to, and believed by, hundreds of thousands of extremists. Thorough and balanced, it explains and refutes some of the complex and bizarre conspiracy theories they hold and suggests ways of defusing their sometimes dangerous zealotry.

The Righteous Remnant: The House of David

Fogarty, Robert S., The Kent State University Press, Kent OH, 1981.

This is a scholarly overview of the history of the House of David sect of the late 1800s and early 1900s. Although notorious for a short time for the sex scandal involving the dictatorial founder and many young women in the sect, the biggest lasting claim to fame of the group was its baseball teams. House of David men, all wearing long flowing beards, played exhibition games with secular baseball teams all over the country, much as the Harlem Globetrotters later did with basketball.

Secret Ceremonies: A Mormon Woman's Intimate Diary of Marriage and Beyond

Laake, Deborah, William Morrow and Co., New York NY, 1993.

From the book's flyleaf:

Always lyrical and often unexpectedly funny, *Secret Ceremonies* is a compassionate but brutally honest insider's look at modern Mormon society. It describes the mystery of the rituals, the beauty and rigor of the theology, and the traditions of one of the fastest growing Christian churches. It is also a complex rite-of-passage story, a tale of the war between religious faith and personal integrity. As a book that states the unspeakable—the official and unofficial secret ceremonies that underlie the lives of Mormon wives—it is a triumphant act of self-affirmation.

Laake was born into Mormonism, attended the Latter Day Saints' BrighamYoung University, and married in her teens in the strange secret ceremony of the Mormon Temple. Some of the content of this book is quite sexually explicit and reader discretion is advised.

The Seduction of Christianity: Spiritual Discernment in the Last Days

Hunt, Dave and McMahon, T.A., Harvest House, Eugene OR, 1985.

From the back cover:

The Bible clearly states that a great Apostasy *must* occur before Christ's Second Coming. Today Christians are being deceived by a new world view more subtle and more seductive than anything the world has ever experienced. What are the dangers in the growing acceptance and practice of- positive and possibility thinking, healing of memories, self-help philosophies, holistic medicine?

The seduction of Christianity will not appear as a frontal assault or oppression of our religious beliefs. Instead, it will come as the latest "fashionable philosophies" offering to make us happier, healthier, better educated, even more spiritual. A compelling look at the times we live in. A clear call to every believer to chose between the Original and the counterfeit. Only then can we hope to escape ... THE SEDUCTION OF CHRISTIANITY

The Shaking of Adventism—A documented account of the crisis among Adventists over the doctrine of justification by faith

Paxton, Geoffrey J., Baker Book House, Grand Rapids MI, 1977.

This is an account by a non-Adventist, evaluating the doctrinal shake-ups in the 1960s and 1970s within the SDA Church.

The complete text of this book is available for free download at:

www.presenttruthmag.com/7dayadventist/shaking/

The Sign of the Last Days: When?

Jonsson, Carl Olof and Herbst, Wolfgang, Commentary Press, Atlanta GA, 1987.

This is an overview, examination, and evaluation of Jehovah's Witness speculations on prophecy.

The Social Psychology of Social Movements

Toch, Hans, The Bobbs-Merrill Co., Inc., Indianapolis IN and New York NY, 1965.

This is a classic textbook on the topic.

Soothsayers of the Second Advent

Alnor, William M., Fleming H. Revell Co., Old Tappan NJ, 1989.

From the cover:

A compelling-expose of doomsday-dating, pin-the-tail-on-the-Antichrist, and other nonbiblical games that Christians play.

Televangelism and American Culture

Schultze, Quintin J., Baker Book House, Gr. Rapids MI, 1991.

This is a scholarly overview of the topic.

They Speak With Other Tongues

Sherrill, John L., Fleming H. Revell, Old Tappen NJ, 1964.

This is a positive perspective on the phenomenon of speaking in tongues.

The True Believer

Hoffer, Eric

This classic book was originally issued in 1951. The most recent version, released in 2002, is available in new and used editions from most book-sellers.

The Truth Shall Make You Free

Tuit, John, The Truth Foundation, Freehold Township NJ, 1981.

This is an overview of the turmoil in the Worldwide Church of God in the late 1970s and early 80s. Author Tuit began reading the church's *Plain Truth* magazine in 1957, and began financially contributing to what was then called the Radio Church of God in the early1960s. He became a baptized member of the Worldwide Church of God in 1975. In 1978, WCG founder Herbert Armstrong disfellowshipped his own son, Garner Ted Armstrong. Tuit became so totally disillusioned with the leadership during the ensuing turmoil within the organization that he cooperated with a handful of other members to organize a suit against the WCG that resulted in the imposition by the state of California of a Receivership in January 1979. Although he does touch upon a variety of details about the history, doctrine, and practices of the WCG, his book adds little to the collection of this information available from many other sources. However, the book is the most effective chronicle available of the events leading up to and during the Receivership because Tuit had first-hand knowledge of much that went on behind the scenes.

The Visions of E.G. White Not of God

Snook and Brinkerhoff, 1866.

This is an early pamphlet investigating and refuting the claims of the SDAs for Ellen G. White's visions.

The complete text of this booklet is available for free download at:

Weighed and Found Wanting: The Toronto Experience Examined in the Light of the Bible

Randles, Bill, 1999.

Distributed by Believers in Grace Fellowship, 8600 C Ave., Marion IA, 52302, (319) 373-3807.

The complete text of this booklet is available for free download at:

www.picknowl.com.au/homepages/rlister/charis/randles/ran dle.htm

This is one of the most effective and balanced overviews of the Toronto Blessing Movement available. Author Randles is a Pentecostal pastor who cannot be charged with being "prejudiced" against such Charismatic phenomena as speaking in tongues since he embraces some of them himself,

What's Going On in There? —
  The Verbatim Text of the Mormon Temple Rituals
  Annotated and Explained by a Former Temple Worker

Sackett, Chuck, Sword of the Shepherd Ministries, Thousand Oaks CA, 1982.

In 1990, the Latter Day Saints leadership quietly revised certain portions of the historical secret Mormon temple rituals. Included with this book is a "News Update" explaining and evaluating the impact of those changes—and the secrecy around the fact that they were even made.

When Prophecy Fails: A Social and Psychological Study of a Modern Group that Predicted the Destruction of the World

Festinger, Leon; Riecken, Henry W.; Schachter, Stanley, Harper & Row, Publishers, New York NY, 1956.

Author Festinger, a social psychologist, coined the term "cognitive dissonance," and introduced it to the general public in this work. The book is considered a classic in the field of Social Psychology. Festinger and his social-psych team were interested in testing a theory they had about how people in religious groups that dogmatically predict a date for "the end of the world" respond when the prediction fails. They happened to stumble on a small group just forming around a woman who claimed to be receiving messages from extra-terrestrials. She declared that a great series of natural disasters would occur on earth on December 21 of the current year, and that only those who heeded the messages of her unearthly contacts would be rescued. The book first surveys the history of End Times prophecy teachers and groups from the first century to the 20th. Then it describes how the authors were able to infiltrate this growing cult with research assistants and obtain reports of the reactions of the members before and after the date of the predicted cataclysm. For more details on the book, see the **When Prophecy Fails** chapter of this **Field Guide**.

When Time Shall Be No More: Prophecy Belief in Modern American Culture

Boyer, Paul, The Belknap Press of Harvard University Press, Cambridge MA, 1992.

This is a scholarly overview of apocalyptic religious groups of the past two centuries.

From the Preface by the author:

"… one cannot fully understand the American public's response to a wide range of international and domestic issues without bearing in mind that millions of men and women view world events and trends, at least in part, through the refracting lens of prophetic belief."

Where Does It Say That?

Witte, Bob, Gospel Truths, Gr. Rapids MI, no copyright date listed.

This book, including most of the photo-reprints, is available for free download at:

http://web.archive.org/web/20071221084119/http://www.irr.org/mit/WDIST/Where-Does-It-Say-That-Main.html

From the back cover:

In the pages of this volume, the reader will find a wealth of information taken almost exclusively from primary Mormon historical sources. There are almost 200 actual photo-reprints, dozens of additional sources cited as well as special helps to the person trying to examine the claims of Mormonism.… when Mormons see some of these "unbelievable" statements made by their leaders, they will often dismiss them by saying,

'That is obviously out of context or misquoted!' In most cases they have never even seen the original source material themselves and what they really mean is, 'I cannot believe that my founding prophets and apostles could have meant what they said!' Thus the whole purpose for the existence of this volume is to make actual photo-copies of these original documents available to everyone. You now have at your fingertips, selected pages from several thousand dollars worth of rare books, pamphlets, diaries and manuscripts as well as companion quotations from many current Mormon sources.

The White Lie

Rea, Walter, M&R Publications, 1982.

The Introduction and Chapters 1-6 and 11-12 of this book are available for free download at:

www.ellenwhite.org/egw17.htm

This book, by a former life-long Seventh Day Adventist and long-time SDA pastor, is the classic that broke open to the public the mounting evidence of SDA prophetess Ellen G. White's (EGW) career of plagiarism. The book chronicles Rea's painful discoveries that shook his faith in EGW, his fruitless attempts to get the denomination's leadership to honestly address the mounting crisis of the reality of her deceptions, and his eventual ouster from the organization. It also provides extensive documentation of some of the plagiarism he and others discovered—including photo-reproductions of pages from some of the actual EGW publications and the books from which she was plagiarizing.

White-Washed: Uncovering the Myths of Ellen G. White

Cleveland, Sydney, available directly from the author, 172 Suncrest Dr., Greenwood IN, 46143, Phone 317-885-8122, email scleveland@prodigy.net, 2000.

This is one of the most detailed recent compilations of the mounting evidence regarding Ellen G. White's plagiarism and other deceptions. Like *The White Lie* of twenty years earlier, it was written by a former life-long Seventh Day Adventist and long-time SDA pastor. It is loaded with hard-hitting documentation including photographs.

www.ingramcontent.com/pod-product-compliance
Lightning Source LLC
Chambersburg PA
CBHW071321310526
45789CB00015B/75